AMERICAN GOVERNMENT

The Essentials

SEVENTH EDITION

James Q. Wilson

University of California, Los Angeles

John J. DiIulio, Jr.

Princeton University

HOUGHTON MIFFLIN COMPANY   Boston   New York

Sponsoring Editor: Melissa Mashburn
Editorial Assistant: Vikram Mukhija
Senior Project Editor: Janet Young
Editorial Assistant: Carrie Wagner
Senior Production/Design Coordinator: Carol Merrigan
Manufacturing Manager: Florence Cadran
Marketing Manager: Sandra McGuire

Cover design: Judy Arisman, Arisman Design
Photo credits appear on page A73.
Cover photograph: *Lincoln Memorial, Washington, D.C.,* FPG International.

Printed in the U.S.A.

Library of Congress Catalog Card Number: 97-72563

ISBN: 0-395-85764-3

456789-QH-01 00 99

James Q. Wilson
is an emeritus professor of management and public policy at the University of California, Los Angeles. From 1961 to 1987, he was a professor of government at Harvard University. Raised in California, he received a B.A. degree from the University of Redlands and a Ph.D. from the University of Chicago. Wilson is the author or coauthor of fourteen books, including *Moral Judgment* (1997), *The Moral Sense* (1993), *Bureaucracy* (1989), *Crime and Human Nature* (1985, with Richard J. Herrnstein), *Thinking about Crime* (1983), and *Political Organizations* (1974).

Wilson has served in a number of advisory posts in the federal government. He was chairman of the White House Task Force on Crime in 1967, chairman of the National Advisory Council on Drug Abuse Prevention in 1972–1973, a member of the Attorney General's Task Force on Violent Crime in 1981, and a member of the President's Foreign Intelligence Advisory Board in 1986–1990.

In 1977 the American Political Science Association conferred on him the Charles E. Merriam Award for advancing the art of government through the application of social science knowledge and in 1990 the James Madison Award for distinguished scholarship. In 1991–1992 he was President of the Association.

He is a Fellow of the American Academy of Arts and Sciences and a member of the American Philosophical Society. When not writing, teaching, or advising, he goes scuba diving. He says that it clears the brain.

John J. DiIulio, Jr.
is a professor of politics and public affairs at Princeton University, teaching in both the Princeton Politics Department and the Woodrow Wilson School of Public and International Affairs. He is also Douglas Dillon Senior Fellow in Public Management at the Brookings Institution, and director of the Partnership for Research on Religion and At-Risk Youth. Raised in Philadelphia, he received a B.A. from the University of Pennsylvania and a Ph.D. from Harvard University. He is the author, coauthor, or editor of nine books, including *Making Health Reform Work* (with Richard P. Nathan); *Improving Government Performance* (with Donald F. Kettl and Gerald J. Garvey); *Deregulating the Public Service; Governing Prisons;* and *Courts, Corrections, and the Constitution.*

DiIulio has served on the National Commission on the State and Local Public Service and advised officials at the National Performance Review, the Office of Management and Budget, the General Accounting Office, the Office of National Drug Control Policy, the U.S. Justice Department, and other federal agencies.

In 1995 the Association of Public Policy Analysis and Management conferred on him the David N. Kershaw Award for outstanding research achievements by a scholar under age 40, and in 1987 he received the American Political Science Association's Leonard D. White Award in public administration. In 1991–1994 he chaired the latter association's standing committee on professional ethics. He spends all his free time with family and old friends from Philadelphia.

Preface

The Seventh Edition of *American Government: The Essentials* has been substantially revised to reflect major changes that have occurred in national politics. The Republicans won control of Congress in 1994 and retained it in 1996, the procedures by which the House of Representatives operates were substantially altered, an important federal program (Aid to Families with Dependent Children) was converted into a block grant to the states, and both a Democratic president and a Republican Congress agreed on a budget plan that (if their predictions turn out to be correct) will produce a balanced budget by the year 2002.

Important as these changes were, the overall tone and thrust of the book required little alteration. The essential processes of American politics remain unchanged, still governed, as always, by the Constitution, slow judicial modifications in its meaning, and popular attitudes toward politics and policies that have not altered much in several decades.

As before, we stress the history of our institutions and comparisons with other democratic nations. In some ways, the rest of the world is becoming a bit more like the United States. More nations are democratic today than ever before, and several of those that have always been that way are creating (as did Canada) new constitutions. Market economics now has a wider appeal in Europe and Latin America than once was the case. The former Soviet Union is struggling to find its democratic sea legs and something resembling an open economy. The global economy has brought every nation closer together and made a quiver in one place resonate loudly in many.

We extensively revised Chapters 11 and 16 on civil rights. In the Seventh Edition we have also added a new feature called "Who Governs? To What Ends?" that examines key legislation and asks who is responsible, focusing on the interplay of policy elites versus the influence of public opinion. The themes introduced in the Sixth Edition—more attention to critical thinking, an emphasis on the differences between direct and representative democracy, attention to crime and criminal justice, and recognition of the growing importance of immigrants—have proved valuable and are retained in the Seventh.

Many of the unique features in previous editions have been retained here, including two in particular. The boxes headed "Politically Speaking" that give the origin of certain common political terms (such as *litmus test, lame duck, logrolling, boycott,* and *muckraker*) have proved to be useful ways of making unfamiliar words accessible and interesting. Another series of boxes headed "What Would You Do?" presents to the student material very much like presidential decision memorandums (albeit ones for a variety of political actors). Should we send troops? rule a state statute unconstitutional? take money from a political action committee? These boxes can be the basis of classroom debates or term papers.

The lists of "Political Trivia" and "Laws of Politics" remain; students (like the authors of this text) seem to have an unflagging appetite for such minutiae and folk wisdom.

Finally, the Summary, Suggested Readings, and lists of Key Terms at the end of each chapter continue to serve as easy references and help students review for examinations.

Supplements

The outstanding ancillary program that has always supported *American Government* has been improved and enlarged.

For the Instructor: The **Instructor's Guide** revised by MaryAnne Borrelli of Connecticut College helps instructors using the Seventh Edition to plan their course, lectures, and discussion sections. Professor Borrelli has thoroughly integrated the *Instructor's Guide* with the textbook so that instructors will be able to capitalize upon the richness of *American Government*. Elements new to the edition are summarized, and the resources and references sections as well as the Video and Film Guide have been completely updated.

The **Test Item File** revised by J. Edwin Benton of the University of South Florida contains over 4,000 questions. Each chapter has multiple-choice, true/false, and essay questions—averaging 180 items per chapter—designed to aid in your class testing of *American Government,* Seventh Edition. The file is available in print or in electronic form for Windows and for the Macintosh.

The **Transparency Package** contains fifty full-color transparencies from the illustration program of *American Government,* Seventh Edition.

For the Student: The **Student Handbook** has been thoroughly updated by J. Edwin Benton of the University of South Florida to help students using *American Government,* Seventh Edition, master the facts and principles introduced in the text. For each textbook chapter, the handbook includes focus points, a study outline, key terms, notes about possible misconceptions, a data check, examination practice, and special application projects, as well as answers to all chapter exercises (excluding the essay questions). It is ideal for class preparation, reviewing class reading, and especially preparing for examinations.

New! **Guide to the Internet** with an introduction by James Q. Wilson, is a brief, useful guide to surfing and browsing the Internet. It introduces students to using the Internet for political research and lists various web sites along with addresses and descriptions of each site.

New! **Wilson/DiIulio American Government Web Site** <http://www.hmco.com/college> will allow students and instructors access to text-specific materials. The web site includes chapter outlines and summaries, links to web sites mentioned in the text, and other additional resources.

For the Instructor and the Student: *New!* The **Houghton Mifflin American Government Web Site** located at <http://www.hmco.com/college> contains a complete array of resources to accompany our American government titles, including an extensive **Documents Collection** with accompanying discussion questions and web exercises, various instructor's resources, web-based research activities, an annotated collection of links to innovative and useful web sites, and a downloadable, updated version of the award-winning **Crosstabs,** a computerized software program allowing students to cross-tabulate survey data on the 1996 presidential election and the 1994–95 voting records of members of Congress in order to analyze voter attitudes and behavior.

Acknowledgments

A number of scholars reviewed the Sixth Edition and made many useful suggestions for the Seventh. They include Sam Van Leer, Jr., University of California, Berkeley; Walter A. Rosenbaum, University of Florida; Richard Himelfarb, Hofstra University; Eugene R. Goss, Long Beach City College; James Penning, Calvin College; Jack Riley, Coastal Carolina University; Nat Cipollina, City University of New York, Baruch College; and Stephen S. Smith, Winthrop University.

Other scholars read, at the authors' request, particular chapters and made useful suggestions: Aaron Friedberg of Princeton University, Don Kettl of the University of Wisconsin, Tom Mann of the Brookings Institution, and Richard Nathan of the State University of New York at Albany.

We also owe thanks to Meena Bose, Fred Dews, Carey R. Macdonald, Tara Adams Ragone, and Cynthia D. Terrels.

J.Q.W. and J.J.D.

The Power of the Federal Courts   459
Checks on Judicial Power   463

PART FOUR

Liberties and Rights
471

15 Civil
Liberties   473
Politics, Culture, and Civil Liberties   474
Interpreting and Applying the First
     Amendment   478
What Is Speech?   481
Who Is a Person?   484
Church and State   485
Crime and Due Process   490

16 Civil
Rights   499
The Black Predicament   500
The Campaign in the Courts   502
The Campaign in Congress   509
Women and Equal Rights   516
Women and the Economy   520
Affirmative Action   522
Gays and the Supreme Court   527

PART FIVE

Politics and Public Policy
531

17 Politics and
Public Policy   533
How the American System Affects Policy
     Making   534
How the American System Has Changed   536
Restraints on Growth   538
Relaxing the Restraints   539
Should the System Be Changed?   543

Appendix

The Declaration of Independence   A1
The Constitution of the United States   A4
The *Federalist* No. 10   A21
The *Federalist* No. 51   A26
Presidents and Congresses, 1789–1997   A30

Glossary   **A33**

References   **A47**

Index   **A57**

Photograph Credits   **A73**

AMERICAN GOVERNMENT

The Essentials

PART ONE

The American System

"In framing a government which is to be administered by men over men, the great difficulty lies in this: You must first enable the government to control the governed; and in the next plave oblige it to control itself."

— FEDERALIST NO. 51

1

The Study of American Government

★ **Formal authority**

★ **Legitimacy of government**

★ **Forms of democracy**

★ **Democratic centralism**

★ **Participatory democracy**

★ **Representative democracy**

★ **Majoritarian politics**

★ **Theories as to who rules**

★ **Political power**

There are two questions about politics: Who governs? To what ends?

We want to know the answer to the first question because we believe that those who rule—their personalities and beliefs, their virtues and vices—will affect what they do to and for us. Many people think they already know the answer to the question, and they are prepared to talk and vote on that basis. That is their right, and the opinions they express may be correct. But they may also be wrong. Indeed, many of these opinions *must* be wrong because they are in conflict. When asked, "Who governs?" some people will say "the unions" and some will say "big business"; others will say "the politicians" or "the people" or "the special interests." Still others will say "Wall Street," "the military," "crackpot liberals," "the media," "the bureaucrats," or "white males." Not all these answers can be correct—at least not all of the time.

The answer to the second question is important because it tells us how government affects our lives. We want to know not only who governs, but what difference it makes who governs. In our day-to-day lives, we may not think government makes much difference at all. In one sense that is right, because our most pressing personal concerns—work, play, love, family, health—are essentially private matters on which government touches but slightly. But in a larger and longer perspective, government makes a substantial difference. Consider: in 1935, 96 percent of all American families paid no federal income tax, and for the 4 percent or so who did pay, the average rate was only about 4 percent of their incomes. Today almost all families pay federal income taxes, and the average rate is 20 percent of their incomes. Through laws that have been enacted since the 1930s, the federal government has taken charge of an enormous amount of the nation's income, with results that are still being debated. Or consider: in 1960, in many parts of the country, blacks could ride only in the backs of buses, had to use washrooms and drinking fountains that were labeled "colored," and could not be served in most public restaurants.

Such restrictions have been almost eliminated, in large part because of decisions by the federal government.

It is important to bear in mind that we wish to answer two different questions, and not two versions of the same question. You cannot always predict what goals government will establish knowing only who governs, nor can you always tell who governs by knowing what activities government undertakes. Most people holding national political office are middle-class, middle-aged, white Protestant males, but we cannot then conclude that the government will only adopt policies that are to the narrow advantage of the middle class, or the middle-aged, or whites, or Protestants, or men. If we thought that, we would be at a loss to explain why the rich are taxed more heavily than the poor, why a War on Poverty was declared, why constitutional amendments giving rights to blacks and women passed Congress by large majorities, or why Catholics and Jews have been appointed to so many important governmental posts.

This book is chiefly devoted to answering the question, Who governs? It is written in the belief that this question cannot be answered without looking at how government makes—or fails to make—decisions about a large variety of concrete issues. Thus, in this book we shall inspect government policies to see what individuals, groups, and institutions seem to exert the greatest power in the continuous struggle to define the purposes of government. We shall see that power and purpose are inextricably intertwined.

What Is Political Power?

By **power** we mean the ability of one person to get another person to act in accordance with the first person's intentions. Sometimes an exercise of power is obvious, as when the president tells the air force that it can or cannot build the B-1 bomber. More often, power is exercised in subtle ways that may not be evident even to the participants, as when the president's economic advisers persuade him to impose or lift wage and price controls. The advisers may not think they are using power—after all, they are the president's subordinates—but if the presi-

dent acts in accord with their intentions as a result of their arguments, they have used power.

Power is found in all human relationships, but we shall be concerned here only with power as it is used to affect who will hold government office and how government will behave. This fails to take into account many important things. If a corporation closes a factory in a small town where it was the major employer, it is using power in ways that affect deeply the lives of people. When a university refuses to admit a student or a medical society refuses to license a would-be physician, it is also using power. But to explain how all these things happen would be tantamount to explaining how society as a whole, and in all its particulars, operates. We limit our view here to government, and chiefly to the American federal government. However, we shall repeatedly pay special attention to how things once thought to be "private" matters become "public"—that is, how they manage to become objects of governmental action. Indeed, one of the most striking transformations of American politics has been the extent to which, in recent decades, almost every aspect of human life has found its way onto the governmental agenda. In the 1950s the federal government would have displayed no interest in a factory closing its doors, a university refusing an applicant, or a profession not accrediting a member. Now government actions can and do affect all these things.

People who exercise political power may or may not have the authority to do so. By **authority** we mean the right to use power. The exercise of rightful power—that is, of authority—is ordinarily easier than the exercise of power that is not supported by any persuasive claim of right. We accept decisions, often without question, if they are made by people who we believe have the right to make them; we may bow to naked power because we cannot resist it, but by our recalcitrance or our resentment we put the users of naked power to greater trouble than the wielders of authority. In this book, we will on occasion speak of "formal authority." By this we mean that the right to exercise power is vested in a governmental office. A president, a senator, and a federal judge have formal authority to take certain actions.

What makes power rightful varies from time to time and from country to country. In the United

Dramatic changes have occurred in what people believe it is legitimate for the government to do. We now submit to searches before boarding an aircraft, unthinkable before hijackings made such government regulations seem necessary.

States we usually say that a person has political authority if his or her right to act in a certain way is conferred by a law or by a state or national constitution. But what makes a law or constitution a source of right? That is the question of **legitimacy**. In the United States the Constitution today is widely, if not unanimously, accepted as a source of legitimate authority, but that was not always the case.

Much of American political history has been a struggle over what constitutes legitimate authority. The Constitutional Convention in 1787 was an effort to see whether a new, more powerful federal government could be made legitimate; the succeeding administrations of George Washington, John Adams, and Thomas Jefferson were in large measure preoccupied with disputes over the kinds of decisions that were legitimate for the federal government to make. The Civil War was a bloody struggle over the legitimacy of the federal union; the New Deal of Franklin Roosevelt was hotly debated by those who disagreed over whether it was legitimate for the federal government to intervene deeply in the economy.

In the United States today no government at any level would be considered legitimate if it were not in some sense democratic. That was not always the prevailing view, however; at one time people disagreed over whether democracy itself was a good idea. In 1787 Alexander Hamilton worried that the new government he helped create might be too democratic, while George Mason, who refused to sign the Constitution, worried that it was not democratic enough. Today virtually everyone believes that "democratic government" is the only proper kind. Most people probably believe that our existing government is democratic; and a few believe that other institutions of public life—schools, universities, corporations, trade unions, churches—should be run on democratic principles if they are to be legitimate. We shall not discuss the question of whether democracy is the best way of governing all institutions. Rather we shall consider the different meanings that have been attached to the word *democratic* and which, if any, best describes the government of the United States.

What Is Democracy?

Democracy is a word used to describe at least three different political systems. In one system the government is said to be democratic if its decisions will

Before Boris Yeltsin came to power in Russia, the old Soviet Union was run on the principle of what the communists called "democratic centralism."

serve the "true interests" of the people, whether or not those people directly affect the making of those decisions. It is by using this definition of democracy that various authoritarian regimes—China, Cuba, and certain European, Asian, and Latin American dictatorships—have been able to claim that they were "democratic." Presidents of the now-defunct Soviet Union, for example, used to claim that they operated on the principle of **democratic centralism,** whereby the true interests of the masses were discovered through discussion within the Communist party and then decisions were made under central leadership to serve those interests. The collapse of the Soviet Union occurred in part because many average Russians doubted that the Communist party knew or would act in support of the people's true interests.

Second, the term *democracy* is used to describe those regimes that come as close as possible to Aristotle's definition—the "rule of the many."[1] A government is democratic if all, or most, of its citizens participate directly in either holding office or making policy. This is often called **direct** or **participatory democracy.** In Aristotle's time—Greece in the fourth century B.C.—such a government was possible. The Greek city-state, or *polis,* was quite small, and within it citizenship was extended to all free adult male property holders. (Slaves, women, minors, and those without property were excluded from participation in government.) In more recent times the New England town meeting approximates the Aristotelian ideal. In such a meeting the adult citizens of a community gather once or twice a year to vote directly on all major issues and expenditures of the town. As towns have become larger and issues more complicated, many town governments have abandoned the pure town meeting in favor of either the representative town meeting (in which a large number of elected representatives, perhaps two or three hundred, meet to vote on town affairs) or representative government (in which a small number of elected city councillors make decisions).

The third definition of democracy is the principle of governance of most nations that are called democratic. It was most concisely stated by the economist Joseph Schumpeter: "The democratic method is that institutional arrangement for arriving at political decisions in which individuals [that is, leaders] acquire the power to decide by means of a competitive struggle for the people's vote."[2] Sometimes this method is called, approvingly, **representative democracy;** at other times it is referred to, disapprovingly, as the elitist theory of democracy. It is justified by one or both of two arguments: First, it is impractical, owing to limits of time, information, energy, interest, and expertise, for the people to decide on public policy, but it is not impractical to expect them to make reasonable choices among competing leadership groups. Second, some people (including, as we shall see in the next chapter, many of the Framers of the Constitution) believe that direct democracy is likely to lead to bad decisions, because people often decide large issues on the basis of fleeting passions and in response to popular demagogues. This fear of direct democracy persists today, as can be seen from the statements of those who do not like what the voters have decided. For example, politicians who favored Proposition 13, the referendum measure that in 1978 sharply cut property taxes in California, spoke approvingly of the "will of the people." Politicians who disliked Proposition 13 spoke disdainfully of "mass hysteria."

Direct Versus Representative Democracy: Which Is Best?

Whenever the word *democracy* is used alone in this book, it will have the meaning Schumpeter gave it. As we shall see in the next chapter, the men who wrote the Constitution did not use the word *democracy* in that document. They wrote instead of a "republican form of government," but by that they meant what we call "representative democracy." Whenever we refer to that form of democracy involving the direct participation of all or most citizens, we shall use the term *direct* or *participatory democracy.*

For representative government to work, there must, of course, be an opportunity for genuine leadership competition. This requires in turn that individuals and parties be able to run for office, that communication (through speeches or the press, and in meetings) be free, and that the voters perceive that a meaningful choice exists. Many questions still remain to be answered. For instance: How many offices should be elective and how many appointive? How many candidates or parties can exist before the choices become hopelessly confused? Where will the money come from to finance electoral campaigns? There is more than one answer to such questions. In some European democracies, for example, very few offices—often just those in the national or local legislature—are elective, and much of the money for campaigning for these offices comes from the government. In the United States many offices—executive and judicial as well as legislative—are elective, and most of the money the candidates use for campaigning comes from industry, labor unions, and private individuals.

Some people have argued that the virtues of direct or participatory democracy can and should be reclaimed even in a modern, complex society. This can be done either by allowing individual neighbor-

In ancient Athens citizens participated directly in politics by meeting in the Agora.

hoods in big cities to govern themselves (community control) or by requiring those affected by some government program to participate in its formulation (citizen participation). In many states a measure of direct democracy exists when voters can decide on referendum issues—that is, policy choices that appear on the ballot. The proponents of direct democracy defend it as the only way to ensure that the "will of the people" prevails.

How Is Power Distributed in a Democracy?

Representative democracy is any system of government in which leaders are authorized to make decisions by winning a competitive struggle for the popular vote. It is obvious then that very different sets of hands can control political power, depending on what kinds of people can become leaders, how the struggle for votes is carried on, how much freedom to act is given to those who win the struggle, and what other sorts of influence (besides the desire for popular approval) affect the leaders' actions.

In some cases the leaders will be so sharply constrained by what most people want that the actions of officeholders will follow the preferences of citizens very closely. We shall call such cases examples of *majoritarian politics.* In this case elected officials are the delegates of the people, acting as the people (or a majority of them) would act were the matter put to a popular vote. The issues handled in a majoritarian fashion can only be those that are sufficiently important to command the attention of most citizens, sufficiently clear to elicit an informed opinion from citizens, and sufficiently feasible to address so that what citizens want done can in fact be done.

Direct or participatory democracy can still be found in the New England town meeting.

When circumstances do not permit majoritarian decision making, then some group of officials will have to act without knowing (and perhaps without caring) exactly what people want. Indeed, even on issues that do evoke a clear opinion from a majority of citizens, the shaping of the details of a policy will reflect the views of those people who are sufficiently motivated to go to the trouble of becoming active participants in policy-making. These active participants usually will be a small, and probably an unrepresentative, minority. Thus the actual distribution of political power, even in a democracy, will depend importantly on the composition of the political elites who are actually involved in the struggles over policy. By **elite,** we mean an identifiable group of persons who possess a disproportionate share of some valued resource—in this case, political power.

Four Theories of Who Governs

At least four theories purport to describe and explain the actions of political elites. One theory is associated with the writings of Karl Marx. To **Marxists**—or at least to some of them, since not all Marxists agree—government, whatever its outward form, is merely a reflection of underlying economic forces, primarily the pattern of ownership of the means of production. All societies, they claim, are divided into classes on the basis of the relationships of people to the economy-capitalists (the bourgeoisie), workers, farmers, intellectuals. In modern society two major classes contend for power—capitalists and workers. Whichever class dominates the economy also controls the government, which is nothing more than a piece of machinery designed to express and give legal effect to underlying class interests. In the United States the government "is but a committee for managing the common affairs of the whole bourgeoisie."[3] To a traditional Marxist it would be pointless to study the government since, as it is controlled by the dominant social class, it would have no independent power. There are many variations, some quite subtle, on this fundamental argument, and some newer Marxists find it more interesting to study how the government actually operates than did Marx himself, for whom government was a mere "epiphenomenon." But even neo-Marxists believe that the answer to the questions of

Thinking

Do We Want Push-Button Democracy?

The choice between representative and direct democracy is a profound one. Today many Americans are dissatisfied with representative government, which, they argue, acts too slowly, serves only special interests, and is unresponsive to majority opinion. During the 1992 presidential campaign, independent candidate Ross Perot promised to bring televised town hall–style meetings to the nation. Viewers would listen to experts debate an issue and then "vote" via toll-free telephone services capable of processing tens of thousands of calls per minute. Although he came in third in the 1992 election behind Bill Clinton and George Bush, Perot received 19.2 million votes, or 19 percent of all votes cast.

This type of "push-button" democracy is rapidly becoming technologically feasible, but is it desirable? Is government by electronic plebiscite preferable to government by deliberative institutions? Do you believe that most citizens have the time, information, interest, and expertise to make reasonable choices among competing policy positions? Or do you suspect that even highly educated people can be manipulated by demagogic leaders who play on their fears and prejudices?

How you respond to such questions ought not to depend on how you feel about any particular public figure,

whether you like watching television, or how much you enjoy playing with computers. Rather, your answer ought to depend primarily on what you believe about the arguments for and against representative government versus direct democracy. For example, it is true that representative democracy often proceeds slowly and prevents sweeping changes in policy. But it is also true that a government capable of doing great good quickly can also do great harm quickly.

Representative democracy is often plagued by special interests, but it is by no means clear that direct democracy would solve rather than exacerbate this problem. For example, in California in 1990 about $125 million was spent to influence voters on initiatives (laws and amendments proposed by citizens with a required number of signatures on a petition and then decided by popular vote). That is more than was spent in 1990 by all special interests to lobby California legislators on all legislation (over one thousand bills).

Majority opinion figures in the enactment of many government policies, but few Americans would want the protection of their civil rights or civil liberties—the right to a fair trial; the freedoms of speech, press, and religion; or the right to vote itself—to hinge on a majority vote.

When people vote on referenda, the "special interests" are *us*.

As we will discuss in Chapter 2, the Framers of the United States Constitution believed strongly that government should mediate, not mirror, popular views, and that elected officials should represent, not register, majority sentiments. They favored representative democracy as a way of minimizing the chances that power would be abused either by a tyrannical popular majority or by self-serving office holders.

who really governs, and to what ends, is to be found in the pattern of economic interests, especially those represented by the large corporation.

A second theory, closely related to the first, argues that a nongovernmental elite makes most of the major decisions but that this elite is not com-

posed exclusively, or even primarily, of corporate leaders. C. Wright Mills, an American sociologist, expresses this view in his book *The Power Elite.*[4] To him, the most important policies are set by a loose coalition of three groups—corporate leaders, top military officers, and a handful of key political lead-

Karl Marx (left) (1818–1883), a German philosopher and radical political leader, was the founder of modern socialist thought. A brilliant, complex, and vituperative writer, Marx was best known for his *Communist Manifesto.* His major work was *Das Kapital,* a four-volume analysis of nineteenth-century capitalism.

Max Weber (right) (1864–1920), a German scholar, was a founder of sociology. Trained in law and history, he produced a major analysis of the evolution of modern society, which stressed the role of bureaucracy.

ers. Different people have different versions of the "power elite" theory. Some would add to the triumvirate listed by Mills the leaders of the major communications media; others would add major labor leaders or the heads of various special-interest groups. The essential argument is the same, however: government is dominated by a few top leaders, most of whom are outside the government and enjoy great advantages in wealth, status, or organizational position. They act in concert, and the policies they make serve the interests of the elite. Some people have such leaders in mind when they use the term *the Establishment,* though when that expression was first coined it referred to the influence exercised by Wall Street lawyers who alternated between governmental and private employment.[5]

A third theory directs attention to the appointed officials—the **bureaucrats**—who operate government agencies from day to day. Max Weber, a German historian and sociologist who wrote in the early years of this century, criticized the Marxist position because it assigned exclusive significance to economic power. Weber thought Marx had neglected the dominant social and political fact of modern times—that all institutions, governmental and nongovernmental, have fallen under the control of large bureaucracies whose expertise and specialized competence are essential to the management of contemporary affairs. Capitalists or workers may

come to power, but the government agencies they create will be dominated by those who operate them on a daily basis. This dominance would have advantages, Weber thought, because decisions would be made more rationally; but it would also have disadvantages, because the political power of the bureaucrats would become "overtowering."[6]

A fourth answer has no single intellectual parent but can be described loosely as the **pluralist** view. Political resources, such as money, prestige, expertise, organizational position, and access to the mass media, are so widely scattered in our society and in the hands of such a variety of persons that no single elite has anything like a monopoly on them. Furthermore there are so many governmental institutions in which power may be exercised—city, state, and federal governments and, within these, the offices of mayors, managers, legislators, governors, presidents, judges, bureaucrats—that no single group, even if it had many political resources, could dominate most, or even much, of the political process. Policies are the outcome of a complex pattern of political haggling, innumerable compromises, and shifting alliances.[7] Pluralists do not argue that political resources are distributed equally—that would be tantamount to saying that all decisions are made on a majoritarian basis. They believe that political resources are sufficiently divided among such different kinds of elites (businesspeople, politicians,

What the Majority Wants: Of Government and Baseball

The choice between representative and direct democracy is central to governance. According to public opinion surveys, a majority of Americans would

- sentence all rapists to death

- oppose extending civil rights laws to homosexuals

- not allow anyone accused of a violent crime to get out on bail while awaiting trial

- spend less on foreign aid

- oppose military intervention if Arab forces invaded Israel

- spend more government money on medical care, protecting the environment, big cities, and transportation

- spend either the same amount or less government money on welfare, unemployment insurance, and programs that benefit minority citizens

- oppose the construction of nuclear power plants

- oppose giving financial aid to Russia

- have rejected the Marshall Plan (the financial support America gave to rebuild Europe after World War II)

- favor term limits for members of Congress

- favor amending the Constitution to require a balanced budget

Most Americans are in the majority on some issues but not on others. (Are you in the majority on some, all, or none of the issues listed above?) Thus, for most Americans, simply knowing what the majority wants is not a way to resolve the tension between direct and representative democracy.

As it is in government, so it is in major-league baseball. Most baseball fans like getting a chance to vote on which players merit selection to the All-Star teams. In 1992 at the All-Star break, Edgar Martinez of the Seattle Mariners was hitting .319 (third in the American League), with forty-six runs batted in, and fourteen home runs; he was a standout fielder. Wade Boggs of the New York Yankees was hitting .268 (sixty-fourth in the American League), with just twenty-five runs batted in, and only six home runs; he was having an average year fielding. But Boggs received 1.2 million votes versus Martinez's 500,000. Boggs played third base on the All-Star team; Martinez watched the game on TV. Direct democracy in baseball appeals to the fans, but does it produce the best All-Star teams?

SOURCE: Adapted from Christopher J. Georges, "Perot or Con," *The Washington Monthly* (June 1993): 38–43, and *The Gallup Monthly Poll* (April 1993): 31–34.

union leaders, journalists, bureaucrats, professors, environmentalists, lawyers, and whomever) that all, or almost all, relevant interests have a chance to affect the outcome of decisions. Not only are the elites divided, they are responsive to their followers' interests, and thus they provide representation to almost all citizens affected by a policy.

Contemplating these contending theories may lead some people to the cynical conclusion that, whichever theory is correct, politics is a self-seeking enterprise in which everybody is out for personal gain. Though there is surely plenty of self-interest among political elites (at least as much as there is among college students!), it does not necessarily follow that the resulting policies will be wholly self-serving. For one thing, a policy may be good or bad independently of the motives of the person who decided it, just as a product sold on the market may be useful or useless regardless of the profit-seeking or wage-seeking motives of those who produced it. For another thing, the self-interest of individuals is often an incomplete guide to their actions. People must frequently choose between two courses of action,

neither of which has an obvious "payoff" to them. We caution against the cynical explanation of politics that Americans seem especially prone to adopt. Alexis de Tocqueville, the French author of a perceptive account of American life and politics in the early nineteenth century, noticed this trait among us.

> *Americans . . . are fond of explaining almost all the actions of their lives by the principle of self-interest rightly understood. . . . In this respect I think they frequently fail to do themselves justice; for in the United States as well as elsewhere people are sometimes seen to give way to those disinterested and spontaneous impulses that are natural to man; but the Americans seldom admit that they yield to emotions of this kind; they are more anxious to do honor to their philosophy than to themselves.*[8]

The belief that people will usually act on the basis of their self-interest, narrowly defined, is a theory to be tested, not an assumption to be made. Two examples of how such an assumption can prove misleading will suffice for now. In the 1960s leaders of the AFL-CIO in Washington were among the most influential forces lobbying Congress for the passage of certain civil rights bills. Yet at the time they did this, the leaders did not stand to benefit either personally (they were almost all white) or organizationally (rank-and-file labor union members were not enthusiastic about such measures).[9] Another example: In the late 1970s, many employees of the Civil Aeronautics Board worked hard to have their agency abolished, even though this meant that they would lose their jobs. To understand why they took these positions, it is not enough to know their incomes or their jobs; one must also know something about their attitudes, their allies, and the temper of the times. In short, political preferences cannot invariably be predicted simply by knowing economic or organizational position.

Direct Democracy and the Computerized Presidency

Shortly after being elected to office, President Clinton starred in a television program that was billed as a "nationwide electronic town meeting" on jobs and the economy. The White House communications staff also employed a former disc jockey to develop "BC TV" (Bill Clinton TV), an interactive cable television station that would provide twenty-four-hour coverage of the presidency. Subscribers to major on-line computer services such as CompuServe can now punch in the command "GO WHITEHOUSE" to hook into the "White House forum," send or receive messages and information on dozens of subjects, or gain instant access to presidential speeches and photographs. During the Reagan years (1980–1988), the White House operators received five thousand calls on a busy day. But in the first months of the Clinton presidency, about forty thousand calls a day lit up the White House switchboard.

Political Change

The question of who governs will be answered differently at different times. Circumstances change, as does our knowledge about politics. As we shall see in

Part Three, the presidency and Congress in the second half of the nineteenth century were organized rather differently from how they are today. Throughout this book we shall make frequent reference to the historical evolution of institutions and policies. We shall do this partly because what government does today is powerfully influenced by what it did yesterday, and partly because the evolution of our institutions and policies has not stopped but is continuing. If we get some sense of how the past has shaped the government, we may better understand what we see today and are likely to see tomorrow.

When we view American government from the perspective of the past, we will find it hard to accept as generally true any simple, mechanistic theory of politics. Economic interests, powerful elites, entrenched bureaucrats, and competing pressure groups have all played a part in shaping our policies, but the great shifts in the direction of that policy respond to changing *beliefs* about what government is supposed to do.

In the 1920s it was widely assumed that the federal government would play a small role in our lives. From the 1930s through the 1970s it was generally believed that the federal government would try to solve whatever social or economic problem existed. From 1981 through 1988 the administration of Ronald Reagan sought to reverse that assumption and to cut back on the taxes Washington levied, the money it spent, and the regulations it imposed. It is clear that no simple theory of politics is likely to explain both the growth of federal power after 1932 and the effort to cut back on that power starting in 1981. Every student of politics sooner or later learns that the hardest things to explain are usually the most important ones.

Take the case of foreign affairs. During certain periods in our history we have taken an active interest in the outside world—at the time the nation was founded, when France and England seemed to have it in their power to determine whether or not America would survive as a nation; in the 1840s, when we sought to expand the nation into areas where Mexico and Canada had claims; in the late 1890s, when many leaders believed we had an obligation to acquire an overseas empire in the Caribbean and the Pacific; and in the period from the 1940s to the 1960s, when we

Direct political action can be peaceful or violent, as when abortion-rights advocates march (top) or opponents bomb an abortion clinic (bottom).

Thinking   *Raising Taxes*

From the birth of the nation to the present, few issues have excited more debate than taxation. The signers of the Declaration of Independence charged the king of Great Britain with "imposing taxes on us without our consent." Today, many Americans would make the same charge against their own elected representatives.

Americans seem especially unhappy with their federal tax burden: 80 percent rate the value they get from taxes paid to Washington as only fair or poor, and nearly three-quarters favor having all citizens vote on all proposals to raise federal taxes. But when asked which federal programs should be cut, solid majorities say no to cuts in Social Security, Medicare, Medicaid, environmental spending, unemployment insurance, student loans, and more.

How different do you suppose the distribution of federal tax burdens and benefits would be if average Americans had to approve or reject all major tax and spending proposals? When it comes to specific proposals for raising (or lowering) federal, state, or local taxes on income, property, sales, or "sins" (for example, taxes on cigarettes and liquor), how might one find out "who governs" and "to what ends"?

For starters, consider the federal income tax. For most of American history, there was no federal income tax. The Sixteenth Amendment to the Constitution, ratified in 1913, authorized Congress "to lay and collect taxes on incomes." As you might guess, not everyone was for it. Over the last eight decades, the federal income tax system has changed repeatedly in response to new economic ideas and competing political pressures. Today the federal government taxes income at five different rates that vary according to citizens' income level and marital status (see table below).

For example, let's say you graduate from college and land a job that pays you a taxable income of $31,000 a year. Under present federal tax laws, if you remained single you would owe Uncle Sam 15 percent on the first $23,350 of your taxable income ($3,502) and 28 percent on the next $7,650 of your taxable income ($2,142), for a total of $5,644. (That's not counting either the $2,371 you will have automatically deducted from your pay-

check for Social Security and Medicare or any of the state and local income, property, or other taxes you would be required to pay.) Should you ever be so prosperous as to make over $256,500 a year, you would pay about forty cents of every extra dollar you earned to the Internal Revenue Service.

The present federal income tax system is "progressive," meaning that rates rise with income. Some argue that the system should be more steeply progressive (it once was); others insist that the top federal tax rate should be lower than 39.6 percent (it once was); and still others favor a "flat tax," under which all citizens would pay at the same rate (such as 20 percent) on all taxable income above a certain minimum.

What do you think? In your view, who should make decisions about taxation, and what would constitute a fair income tax system? Jot down your preliminary answers to the questions posed above, think up and answer related questions of your own, and then return to review and critique what you wrote after you have finished reading this book.

Federal Income Tax Rates

Taxable Income, by Filing Status

Rates	Married filing jointly	Head of household	Single	Married filing separately
15%	0–$39,000	0–$31,250	0–$23,350	0–$19,500
28	$39,000–$94,250	$31,250–$80,750	$23,350–$56,550	$19,500–$47,125
31	$94,250–$143,600	$80,750–$130,800	$56,550–$117,950	$47,125–$71,800
36	$143,600–$256,500	$130,800–$256,500	$117,950–$256,500	$71,800–$128,250
39.6	over $256,500	over $256,500	over $256,500	over $128,250

SOURCES: *The American Enterprise*, March/April 1995, pp. 101, 103; *The Public Perspective*, April/May 1995, p. 5; *The American Enterprise*, July/August 1996, p. 19; *Consumer Reports Books: Guide to Income Tax 1996* (Consumers Union, 1995), p. 35.

openly accepted the role of the world's police officer. At other times America has looked inward, spurning opportunities for expansion and virtually ignoring events that in other periods would have been a cause for war, or at least mobilization.

\Deep-seated beliefs, major economic developments, and widely shared (or competing) opinions about what constitutes the dominant political problem of the time shape the nature of day-to-day political conflict.\What this means is that, in any broad historical or comparative perspective, politics is not just about "who gets what," though that is part of the story. It is about how people, or elites claiming to speak for people, define the public interest. Lest one think that such definitions are mere window dressing, signifying nothing of importance, bear in mind that on occasion men and women have been prepared to fight and die for one definition or another. Suppose you, the reader, had been alive in 1861. Do you think you would have viewed slavery as a matter of gains and losses, costs and benefits, winners and losers? Some people did. Or do you think you would have been willing to fight to abolish or preserve it? Many others did just that. The differences in these ways of thinking about such an issue are at least as important as how institutions are organized or elections conducted.

Finding Out Who Governs

Ideally political scientists ought to be able to give clear answers, amply supported by evidence, to the questions, How is political power distributed? and To what purposes will it be used under various circumstances? In reality they can (at best) give partial, contingent, and controversial answers. The reason is to be found in the nature of our subject. Unlike economists, who assume that people have more or less stable preferences and can compare ways of satisfying those preferences by looking at the relative prices of various goods and services, political scientists are interested in how preferences are formed, especially for those kinds of services, such as national defense or pollution control, that cannot be evaluated chiefly in terms of monetary costs.

Understanding preferences is vital to understanding power. Who did what in government is not hard to find out, but who wielded power—that is, who made a difference in the outcome and for what reason—is much harder to discover. *Power* is a word that conjures up images of deals, bribes, power plays, and arm-twisting. In fact most power exists because of shared understanding, common friendships, communal or organizational loyalties, and different degrees of prestige. These are hard to identify and almost impossible to quantify.

Nor can the distribution of political power be inferred simply by knowing what laws are on the books or what administrative actions have been taken. The enactment of a consumer-protection law does not mean that consumers are powerful any more than the absence of such a law means that corporations are powerful. The passage of such a law could reflect an aroused public opinion, the lobbying of a small group claiming to speak for consumers, the ambitions of a senator, or the intrigues of one business firm seeking to gain a competitive advantage over another. A close analysis of what the law entails and how it was passed and administered is necessary before much of anything can be said.

This book will avoid sweeping claims that we have an "imperial" presidency (or an impotent one), an "obstructionist" Congress (or an innovative one), or "captured" regulatory agencies. Such labels do an injustice to the different roles that presidents, members of Congress, and administrators play in different kinds of issues and in different historical periods.

The view taken in this book is that judgments about institutions and interests can be made only after one has seen how they behave on a variety of important issues or potential issues, such as economic policy, the regulation of business, social welfare, civil rights and liberties, and foreign and military affairs. The policies adopted or blocked, the groups heeded or ignored, the values embraced or rejected—these constitute the raw material out of which one can fashion an answer to the central questions we have asked: Who rules? and To what ends?

The way in which our institutions of government handle social welfare, for example, differs from the way other democratic nations handle it, and it differs as well from the way our own institutions once treated it. The description of our institutions in Part Three will therefore include not only an account of how they work today but also a brief historical background on their workings and a comparison with similar institutions in other countries. There is a tendency to assume that how we do things today is the only way they could possibly be done. In fact there are other ways to operate a government based on some measure of popular rule. History, tradition, and belief weigh heavily on all that we do.

In any event the place to begin a search for how power is distributed in national politics and what purposes that power serves is with the founding of the federal government in 1787: the Constitutional Convention and the events leading up to it. Though the decisions of that time were not made by philosophers or professors, the practical men who made them had a philosophic and professorial cast of mind, and thus they left behind a fairly explicit account of what values they sought to protect and what arrangements they thought ought to be made for the allocation of political power.

SUMMARY

There are two major questions about politics: Who governs? To what ends? This book will focus mainly on answering the first.

Four answers have traditionally been given to the question of who governs.

- The *Marxist*—those who control the economic system will control the political one.
- The *elitist*—a few top leaders, not all of them drawn from business, make the key decisions without reference to popular desires.
- The *bureaucratic*—appointed civil servants run things.
- The *pluralist*—competition among affected interests shapes public policy.

To choose among these theories or to devise new ones requires more than describing governmental institutions and processes. In addition one must examine the kinds of issues that do (or do not) get taken up by the political system and how that system resolves them.

The distinction between different types of democracies is important. The Framers of the Constitution intended that America be a representative democracy in which the power to make decisions is determined by means of a free and competitive struggle for the citizens' votes.

KEY TERMS

power   *p. 4*

authority   *p. 4*

legitimacy   *p. 5*

democracy   *p. 5*

democratic centralism   *p. 6*

direct or participatory democracy   *p. 6*

representative democracy   *p. 6*

elite   *p. 8*

Marxists   *p. 8*

bureaucrats   *p. 10*

pluralist   *p. 10*

SUGGESTED READINGS

Banfield, Edward C. *Political Influence.* New York: Free Press, 1961. A method of analyzing politics—in this case, in the city of Chicago—comparable to the approach adopted in this book.

Crick, Bernard. *The American Science of Politics.* London: Routledge & Kegan Paul, 1959. A critical review of the methods of studying government and politics.

Marx, Karl, and Friedrich Engels. "The Manifesto of the Communist Party." In *The Marx-Engels Reader,* edited by Robert C. Tucker. 2d ed. New York: Norton, 1978, 469–500. The classic statement of the Marxist view of history and politics. Should be read in conjunction with Engels, "Socialism: Utopian and Scientific," in the same collection, 683–717.

Mills, C. Wright. *The Power Elite.* New York: Oxford University Press, 1956. An argument that self-serving elites dominate American politics.

Schumpeter, Joseph A. *Capitalism, Socialism, and Democracy.* 3d ed. New York: Harper, 1950, Chs. 20–23. A lucid statement of the theory of representative democracy and how it differs from participatory democracy.

Truman, David B. *The Government Process.* 2d ed. New York: Knopf, 1971. A pluralist interpretation of American politics.

Weber, Max. *From Max Weber: Essays in Sociology.* Translated and edited by H. H. Gerth and C. Wright Mills. London: Routledge & Kegan Paul, 1948, Ch. 8. A theory of bureaucracy and its power.

2

The Constitution

★ **Revolution fought for liberty**

★ **Colonists' views on government**

★ **Problems with the Confederation**

★ **Innovative state constitutions**

★ **Shays's Rebellion**

★ **Framing the Constitution**

★ *Federalist* **papers**

★ **Checks on popular rule**

★ **Protecting liberty**

★ **Need for Bill of Rights**

★ **Position on slaves and women**

★ **Motives of the Framers**

★ **Constitutional reform**

The goal of the American Revolution was liberty. It was not the first revolution with that object; it may not have been the last; but it was perhaps the clearest case of a people altering the political order violently, simply in order to protect their liberties. Subsequent revolutions had more complicated, or utterly different, objectives. The French Revolution in 1789 sought not only liberty, but "equality and fraternity." The Russian Revolution (1917) and the Chinese Revolution (culminating in 1949) chiefly sought equality and were little concerned with liberty as we understand it.

The Problem of Liberty

What the American colonists sought to protect when they signed the Declaration of Independence in 1776 were the traditional liberties to which they thought they were entitled as British subjects. These liberties included the right to bring their legal cases before truly independent judges rather than ones subordinate to the king; to be free of the burden of having British troops quartered in their homes; to engage in trade without burdensome restrictions; and, of course, to pay no taxes voted by a British Parliament in which they had no direct representation. During the ten years or more of agitation and argument leading up to the War of Independence, most colonists believed that their liberties could be protected while they remained a part of the British Empire.

Slowly but surely opinion shifted. By the time war broke out in 1775, a large number of colonists (though perhaps not a majority) had reached the conclusion that the colonies would have to become independent of Great Britain if their liberties were to be assured. The colonists had many reasons for regarding independence as the only solution, but one is especially important: they no longer had confidence in the English constitution. This constitution was not a single written document but rather a collection of laws, charters, and traditional understandings that proclaimed the liberties of British subjects. Yet these liberties, in the eyes of the colonists, were regularly

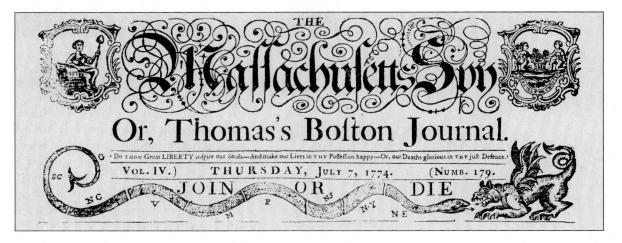

Even before the Revolutionary War, many felt that some form of union would be necessary if the rebellious colonies were to survive. In 1774 the *Massachusetts Spy* portrayed the colonies as segments of a snake that must "Join or Die."

violated despite their constitutional protection. Clearly, then, the English constitution was an inadequate check on the abuses of political power. The revolutionary leaders sought an explanation of the insufficiency of the constitution and found it in human nature.

The Colonial Mind

"A lust for domination is more or less natural to all parties," one colonist wrote.[1] Men will seek power, many colonists believed, because they are ambitious, greedy, and easily corrupted. John Adams denounced the "luxury, effeminacy, and venality" of English politics; Patrick Henry spoke scathingly of the "corrupt House of Commons"; and Alexander Hamilton described England as "an old, wrinkled, withered, worn-out hag."[2] This was in part flamboyant rhetoric designed to whip up enthusiasm for the conflict, but it was also deeply revealing of the colonial mind. Their belief that English politicians—and by implication, most politicians—tended to be corrupt was the colonists' explanation of why the English constitution was not an adequate guarantee of the liberty of the citizens. This opinion was to persist and, as we shall see, profoundly affect the way the Americans went about designing their own governments.

The liberties the colonists fought to protect were, they thought, widely understood. They were

based not on the generosity of the king or the language of statutes but on a "higher law" embodying "natural rights" that were ordained by God, discoverable in nature and history, and essential to human progress. These rights, John Dickinson wrote, "are born with us; exist with us; and cannot be taken away from us by any human power."[3] There was general agreement that the essential rights included life, liberty, and property long before Thomas Jefferson wrote them into the Declaration of Independence. (Jefferson changed "property" to "the pursuit of happiness," but almost everybody else went on talking about property.)

This emphasis on property did not mean that the American Revolution was thought up by the rich and wellborn to protect their interests or that there was a struggle between property owners and the propertyless. In late eighteenth-century America most people (except the black slaves) had property of some kind. The overwhelming majority of citizens were self-employed—as farmers or artisans—and rather few people benefited financially by gaining independence from England. Taxes were higher during and after the war than before, trade was disrupted by the conflict, and debts mounted perilously as various expedients were invented to pay for the struggle. There were, of course, war profiteers and those who tried to manipulate the currency to their own advantage, but most Americans at the time of the war saw the con-

WILLIAM WALCUTT, *PULLING DOWN THE STATUE OF GEORGE III AT BOWLING GREEN*, 1857

The American colonists' desire to assert their liberties led in time to a deep hostility to British government, as when these New Yorkers toppled a statue of King George III, melted it down, and used the metal to make bullets.

flict clearly in terms of political rather than economic issues. It was a war of ideology.

Everyone recognizes the glowing language with which Jefferson set out the case for independence in the second paragraph of the Declaration:

> *We hold these truths to be self-evident, that all men are created equal, that they are endowed by their Creator with certain unalienable Rights, that among these are Life, Liberty, and the pursuit of Happiness.—That to secure these rights, Governments are instituted among Men, deriving their just powers from the consent of the governed—that whenever any Form of Government becomes destructive of these ends, it is the Right of the People to alter or to abolish it, and to institute new Government, having its foundation on such principles, and organizing its powers in such form, as to them shall seem most likely to effect their Safety and Happiness.*

What almost no one recalls, but what are an essential part of the Declaration, are the next twenty-seven paragraphs, in which Jefferson listed, item by item, the specific complaints the colonists had against George III and his ministers. None of these items spoke of social or economic conditions in the colonies; all spoke instead of specific violations of political liberties. The Declaration was in essence a lawyer's brief prefaced by a stirring philosophical claim that the rights being violated were **unalienable**—that is, based on nature and Providence, and not on the whims or preferences of people. Jefferson, in his original draft, added a twenty-eighth complaint—that the king had allowed the slave trade to continue *and* was inciting slaves to revolt against their masters. Congress, faced with so contradictory a charge, decided to include a muted reference to slave insurrections and omit all reference to the slave trade.

The Real Revolution

The Revolution was more than the War of Independence. It began before the war, continued after it, and involved more than driving out the British army by force of arms. The *real* Revolution, as John Adams afterward explained in a letter to a friend, was the *"radical change in the principles, opinions, and sentiments, and affections of the people."*[4] This radical change had to do with a new vision of what could make political authority legitimate and personal liberties secure. Government by royal pre-

NORTH AMERICA IN 1787

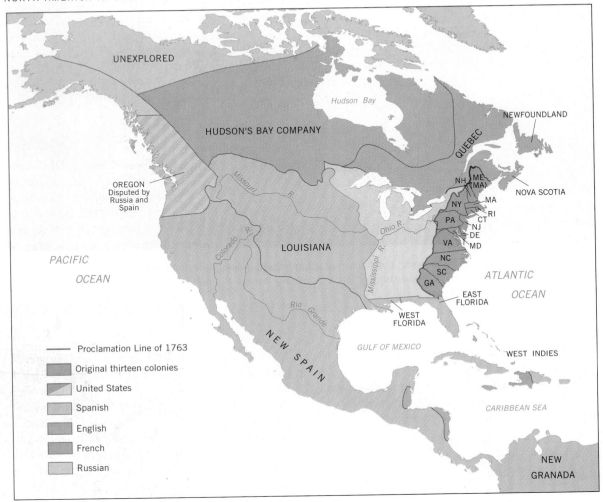

- —— Proclamation Line of 1763
- Original thirteen colonies
- United States
- Spanish
- English
- French
- Russian

rogative was rejected; instead legitimate government would require the consent of the governed. Political power could not be exercised on the basis of tradition but only as a result of a direct grant of power contained in a written constitution. Human liberty existed before government was organized, and government must respect that liberty. The legislative branch of government, in which the people were directly represented, should be superior to the executive branch.

These were indeed revolutionary ideas. No government at the time had been organized on the basis of these principles. And to the colonists such no-

tions were not empty words but rules to be put into immediate practice. In 1776 eight states adopted written constitutions. Within a few years every former colony had adopted one except Connecticut and Rhode Island, two states that continued to rely on their colonial charters. Most state constitutions had detailed bills of rights defining personal liberties, and most placed the highest political power in the hands of elected representatives.

Written constitutions, representatives, and bills of rights are so familiar to us now that we forget how bold and unprecedented those innovations were in 1776. Indeed, many Americans did not think they would succeed: such arrangements would be either so strong that they would threaten liberty or so weak that they would permit chaos.

The eleven years that elapsed between the Declaration of Independence and the signing of the Constitution in 1787 were years of turmoil, uncertainty, and fear. George Washington had to wage a bitter, protracted war without anything resembling a strong national government to support him. The supply and financing of his army were based on a series of hasty improvisations, most badly administered and few adequately supported by the fiercely independent states. When peace came, many parts of the nation were a shambles. At least a quarter of New York City was in ruins, and many other communities were nearly devastated. Though the British lost the war, they still were powerful on the North American continent, with an army available in Canada (where many Americans loyal to Britain had fled) and a large navy at sea. Spain claimed the Mississippi River Valley and occupied what are now Florida and California. Men who had left their farms to fight came back to discover themselves in debt with no money and heavy taxes. The paper money printed to finance the war was now virtually worthless.

Weaknesses of the Confederation

The thirteen states had formed only a faint semblance of a national government with which to bring order to the nation. The **Articles of Confederation,** which went into effect in 1781, created little more than a "league of friendship" that could not levy taxes or regulate commerce. Each state retained

ARTICLES

Of Confederation and perpetual Union between the States of *New-Hampshire, Massachusetts-Bay, Rhode-Island* and *Providence Plantations, Connecticut, New-York, New-Jersey, Pennsylvania, Delaware, Maryland, Virginia, North-Carolina, South-Carolina* and *Georgia.*

ARTICLE I. THE stile of this confederacy shall be " The United " States of America."

> Stile of the Confederacy

ART. II. Each state retains its sovereignty, freedom and independence, and every power, jurisdiction and right, which is not by this confederation expressly delegated to the United States, in Congress assembled.

> Sovereignty and Independence of the respective States.

ART. III. The said states hereby severally enter into a firm league of friendship with each other, for their common defence, the security of their liberties, and their mutual and general welfare, binding themselves to assist each other, against all force offered to, or attacks made upon them, or any of them, on account of religion, sovereignty, trade, or any other pretence whatever.

> Design of the Confederation, as it regards common security.

ART. IV. The better to secure and perpetuate mutual friendship and intercourse among the people of the different states in this union, the free inhabitants of each of these states, paupers, vagabonds, and fugitives from justice excepted, shall be entitled to all privileges and immunities of free citizens in the several states ; and the people of each state shall have free ingress and regress to and from any other state, and shall enjoy therein all the privileges of trade and commerce, subject to the same duties, impositions and restrictions as the inhabitants thereof respectively, provided that such restriction shall not extend so far as to prevent the removal of property imported into any state, to any other state of which the owner is an inhabitant ; provided also that no imposition, duties or restriction shall be laid by any state, on the property of the united states, or either of them.

> Social and mutual intercourse among the States.

John Hancock was proud to have signed the Declaration of Independence, but thought so little of the presidency under the Articles of Confederation that he never bothered to accept the job.

The Articles of Confederation had made it plain that the United States was not to have a true national government but was to be governed by a compact among sovereign and independent states.

Independence Hall in Philadelphia, where the Declaration of Independence and the Constitution were signed.

its sovereignty and independence, each state (regardless of size) had one vote in Congress, nine (of thirteen) votes were required to pass any measure, and the delegates who cast these votes were picked and paid for by the state legislatures. Congress did have the power to make peace, and thus it was able to ratify the treaty with England in 1783. It could coin money, but there was precious little to coin; it could appoint the key army officers, but the army was small and dependent for support on independent state militias; it was allowed to run the post office, then, as now, a thankless task that nobody else wanted. John Hancock, who in 1785 was elected to the meaningless office of "president" under the Articles, never showed up to take the job. Several states claimed the unsettled lands in the West, and they occasionally pressed those claims with guns. Pennsylvania and Virginia went to war near

Pittsburgh, and Vermont threatened to become part of Canada. There was no national judicial system to settle these or other claims among the states. To amend the Articles of Confederation, all thirteen states had to agree.

Many of the leaders of the Revolution, such as George Washington and Alexander Hamilton, believed that a stronger national government was essential. They lamented the disruption of commerce and travel caused by the quarrelsome states and deeply feared the possibility of foreign military intervention, with England or France playing one state off against another. A small group of men, conferring at Washington's home at Mount Vernon in 1785, decided to call a meeting to discuss trade regulation. That meeting, held at Annapolis, Maryland, in September 1786, was not well attended (no delegates arrived from New England), and so another meeting, this one in Philadelphia, was called for the following spring—in May 1787—to consider ways of remedying the defects of the Confederation.

The Constitutional Convention

The delegates assembled at Philadelphia for what was advertised (and authorized by Congress) as a meeting to revise the Articles; they adjourned four months later having written a wholly new constitution. When they met, they were keenly aware of the problems of the confederacy but far from agreeing as to what should be done about those problems. The protection of life, liberty, and property was their objective in 1787 as it had been in 1776, but they had no accepted political theory that would tell them what kind of national government, if any, would serve that goal.

The Lessons of Experience

They had read ancient and modern political history, only to learn that nothing seemed to work. James Madison spent a good part of 1786 studying books sent to him by Thomas Jefferson, then in Paris, in hopes of finding some model for a workable American republic. He took careful notes on various confederacies in ancient Greece and on the more modern confederacy of the United Netherlands. He reviewed the history of Switzerland and Poland and the ups and downs of the Roman republic. He concluded that there was no model; as he later put it in one of the *Federalist* papers, history consists only of beacon lights "which give warning of the course to be shunned, without pointing out that which ought to be pursued."[5] The problem seemed to be that confederacies were too weak to govern and tended to collapse from internal dissension, while all stronger forms of government were so powerful as to trample the liberties of the citizens.

State Constitutions   Madison and the others did not need to consult history, or even the defects of the Articles of Confederation, for illustrations of the problem. These could be found in the government of the American states at the time. Pennsylvania and Massachusetts exemplified two aspects of the problem. The Pennsylvania constitution, adopted in 1776, created the most radically democratic of the new state regimes. All power was given to a one-house (unicameral) legislature, the Assembly, the members of which were elected annually for one-year terms. No legislator could serve more than four years. There was no governor or president, only an Executive Council that had few powers. Thomas Paine, whose pamphlets had helped precipitate the break with England, thought the Pennsylvania constitution was the best in America, and in France philosophers hailed it as the very embodiment of the principle of rule by the people. Though popular in France, it was a good deal less popular in Philadelphia. The Assembly disfranchised the Quakers, persecuted conscientious objectors to the war, ignored the requirement of trial by juries, and manipulated the judiciary.[6] To Madison and his friends the Pennsylvania constitution demonstrated how a government, though democratic, could be tyrannical as a result of concentrating all powers into one set of hands.

The Massachusetts constitution, adopted in 1780, was a good deal less democratic. There was a clear separation of powers among the various branches of government, the directly elected governor could veto acts of the legislature, and judges served for life. Both voters and elected officials had to be property owners; the governor, in fact, had to own at least £1,000 worth of property. The principal officeholders had to swear that they were Christians.

The presiding officer at the Constitutional Convention was George Washington (1732–1799). He participated just once in the debates, but the effect of his presence was great. He was a national military hero, and it was generally expected that he would be the nation's first president.

Shays's Rebellion   But if the government of Pennsylvania was thought to be too strong, that of Massachusetts seemed too weak, despite its "conservative" features. In January 1787 a group of ex-Revolutionary War soldiers and officers, plagued by debts and high taxes and fearful of losing their property to creditors and tax collectors, forcibly prevented the courts in western Massachusetts from sitting. This became known as **Shays's Rebellion,** after one of the officers, Daniel Shays. The governor of Massachusetts asked the Continental Congress to send troops to suppress the rebellion, but it could not raise the money or the manpower. Then he turned to his own state militia, but discovered he did not have one. In desperation private funds were collected to hire a volunteer army, which marched on Springfield and, with the firing of a few shots, dispersed the rebels, who fled into neighboring states.

Shays's Rebellion, occurring between the aborted Annapolis and the coming Philadelphia conventions, had a powerful effect on opinion. Delegates who might have been reluctant to attend the Philadelphia meeting, especially those from New England, were galvanized by the fear that state governments were about to collapse from internal dissension. George

Shays's Rebellion in western Massachusetts in 1786–1787 stirred deep fears of anarchy in America. The ruckus was put down by a hastily assembled militia, and the rebels were eventually pardoned.

Washington wrote a friend despairingly: "For God's sake..., if they [the rebels] have *real* grievances, redress them; if they have not, employ the force of government against them at once."[7] Thomas Jefferson, living in Paris, took a more detached view: "A little rebellion now and then is a good thing," he wrote. "The tree of liberty must be refreshed from time to time with the blood of patriots and tyrants."[8] Though Jefferson's detachment might be explained by the fact that he was in Paris and not in Springfield, there were others, like Governor George Clinton of New York, who shared the view that no strong central government was required. (Whether Clinton would have agreed about the virtues of spilled blood, especially his, is another matter.)

The Framers

The Philadelphia convention attracted fifty-five delegates, only about thirty of whom participated regularly in the proceedings. One state, Rhode Island, refused to send anyone. The convention met during a miserably hot Philadelphia summer, with the delegates pledged to keep their deliberations secret. The talkative and party-loving Benjamin Franklin was often accompanied by other delegates to make sure that neither wine nor his delight in telling stories would lead him to divulge delicate secrets.

Those who attended were for the most part young (Hamilton was thirty; Madison, thirty-six) but experienced. Eight delegates had signed the Declaration of Independence, seven had been governors, thirty-four were lawyers and reasonably well-to-do, a few were wealthy. They were not "intellectuals," but men of practical affairs. Thirty-nine had served in the ineffectual Congress of the Confederation; a third were veterans of the Continental army.

Some names made famous by the Revolution were conspicuously absent. Thomas Jefferson and John Adams were serving as ministers abroad; Samuel Adams was ill; Patrick Henry was chosen to attend but refused, commenting that he "smelled a rat in Philadelphia, tending toward monarchy."

The convention produced not a revision of the Articles of Confederation, as it had been authorized to do, but instead a wholly new written constitution creating a true national government unlike any that had existed before. That document is today the world's oldest written national constitution. Those who wrote it were neither saints nor schemers, and the deliberations were not always lofty or philosophical—much hard bargaining, not a little confusion, and the accidents of personality and time helped shape the final product. The delegates were split on many issues—what powers should be given to a central government, how the states should be represented, what was to be done about slavery, the role of the people—each of which was resolved by a compromise. The speeches of the delegates (known to us from the detailed notes kept by Madison) did not explicitly draw on political philosophy or quote from the writings of philosophers. Everybody present was quite familiar with the traditional arguments and, on the whole, well read in history. But though the leading political philosophers were only rarely mentioned, the debate was profoundly influenced by philosophical beliefs, some formed by the revolutionary experience and others by the eleven-year attempt at self-government.

From the debates leading up to the Revolution, the delegates had drawn a commitment to liberty, which, despite the abuses sometimes committed in its name, they continued to share. Their defense of liberty as a natural right was derived from the writings of the English philosopher John Locke and based on his view that such rights are discoverable by reason. In a "state of nature," Locke argued, all men cherish and seek to protect their life, liberty, and property. But in a state of nature—that is, a society without a government—the strong can use their liberty to deprive the weak of theirs. The in-

Patrick Henry

James Madison

Thomas Jefferson

Edmund Randolph

John Locke

William Paterson

The Federalist Papers

*I*n 1787, to help win ratification of the new Constitution in the New York state convention, Alexander Hamilton decided to publish a series of articles defending and explaining the document in the New York City newspapers. He recruited John Jay and James Madison to help him, and the three of them, under the pen name "Publius," wrote eighty-five articles that appeared from late 1787 through 1788. The identity of the authors was kept secret at the time, but we now know that Hamilton wrote fifty-one of them, Madison twenty-six, and Jay five, and Hamilton and Madison jointly authored three. The two most famous articles—Numbers 10 and 51—were by Madison alone (and are reprinted here in the Appendix).

The *Federalist* papers probably played only a small role in securing ratification. Like most legislative battles, this one was not decisively influenced by philosophical writings. But these essays have had a lasting value as an authoritative and profound explanation of the Constitution. Though written for political purposes, the *Federalist* has become the single most important piece of American political philosophy ever produced. Ironically Hamilton and Madison were later to become political enemies; even at the Philadelphia convention they had different views of the kind of government that should be created. But in 1787–1788 they were united in the belief that the new constitution was the best that could have been obtained under the circumstances.

James Madison

Alexander Hamilton

John Jay

stinct for self-preservation leads people to want a government that will prevent this exploitation. But if the government is not itself to deprive its subjects of their liberty, it must be limited. The chief limitation on it, he said, should derive from the fact that it is created, and governs, by the consent of the governed. People will not agree to be ruled by a government that threatens their liberty; therefore the government to which they freely choose to submit themselves will be a limited government designed to protect liberty.

The Pennsylvania experience as well as the history of British government led the Framers to doubt whether popular consent alone would be a sufficient guarantor of liberty. A popular government may prove too weak (as in Massachusetts) to prevent one faction from abusing another, or a popular majority can be tyrannical (as in Pennsylvania). In fact the tyranny of the majority can be an even graver threat than rule by the few. In the former case there may be no defenses for the individual—one lone person cannot count on the succor of public opinion or the possibility of popular revolt.

The problem, then, was a delicate one: how to devise a government strong enough to preserve order but not so strong that it would threaten liberty. The answer, the delegates believed, was not "democracy" as it was then understood. To many conservatives in the late eighteenth century, democracy meant mob rule—it meant, in short, Shays's Rebellion (or if they had been candid about it, the Boston Tea Party). On the other hand, *aristocracy*—the rule of the few—was no solution, since the few were likely to be self-seeking. Madison, writing later in the *Federalist* papers, put the problem this way:

> *If men were angels, no government would be necessary. If angels were to govern men, neither external nor internal controls on government would be necessary. In framing a government which is to be administered by men over men, the great difficulty lies in this: you must first enable the government to control the governed; and in the next place oblige it to control itself.*[9]

Striking this balance could not be done, Madison believed, simply by writing a constitution that set limits on what government could do. The example

of British rule over the colonies proved that laws and customs were inadequate checks on political power. As he expressed it, "A mere demarcation on parchment of the constitutional limits [of government] is not a sufficient guard against those encroachments which lead to a tyrannical concentration of all the powers of government in the same hands."[10]

The Challenge

The resolution of political issues, great and small, often depends crucially on how the central question is phrased. The delegates came to Philadelphia in general agreement that there were defects in the Articles of Confederation that ought to be remedied. Had they, after convening, decided to make their business that of listing these defects and debating alternative remedies for them, the document that emerged would in all likelihood have been very different from what in fact was adopted. But immediately after the convention had organized itself and chosen Washington to be its presiding officer, the Virginia delegation, led by Governor Edmund Randolph but relying heavily on the draftsmanship of James Madison, presented to the convention a comprehensive plan for a wholly new national government. The plan quickly became the major item of business of the meeting; it, and little else, was debated for the next two weeks.

The Virginia Plan

When the convention decided to make the Virginia Plan its agenda, it had fundamentally altered the nature of its task. The business at hand was not to be the Articles and their defects, but rather how one should go about designing a true national government. The Virginia Plan called for a strong national union organized into three governmental branches—the legislative, executive, and judicial. The legislature was to be composed of two houses, the first elected directly by the people and the second chosen by the first house from among the people nominated by state legislatures. The executive was to be chosen by the national legislature, as were members of a national judiciary. The executive and some members of the judiciary

CRITICAL Thinking

How to Read the Federalist *Papers 10 and 51*

James Madison is rightly regarded as the single most important mind behind the Constitution, and his ideas are worth knowing first-hand. The Appendix to this book contains reprints of Madison's *Federalist* papers 10 and 51. After you have finished this chapter, turn to the Appendix and try to read them. On your first reading of the papers you may find Madison's language difficult to understand and his ideas overly complex. The following pointers will help you decipher his meaning.

In *Federalist* No. 10, Madison begins by stating that "a well constructed Union" can "break and control the violence of faction." He goes on to define a "faction" as any group of citizens who attempt to advance their ideas or economic interests at the expense of other citizens or in ways that conflict with "the permanent and aggregate interests of the community" or "public good." Thus, what Madison terms "factions" are what we today call "special interests."

One way to defeat factions, according to Madison, is to remove whatever causes them to arise in the first place. This can be attempted in two ways. First, government can deprive people of the liberty they need to organize: "Liberty is to faction what air is to fire." But that is surely a cure "worse than the disease." Second, measures can be taken to make all citizens share the same ideas, feelings, and economic interests. However, as Madison

observes, some people are smarter or more hard working than others, and this "diversity in the faculties" of citizens is bound to result in different economic interests as some people acquire more property than others. Consequently, protecting property rights, not equalizing property ownership, "is the first object of government." Even if everyone shared the same basic economic interests they would still find reasons "to vex and oppress each other" rather than cooperate "for their common good." Religious differences, loyalties to different leaders, even "frivolous and fanciful distinctions" (not liking how other people dress or their taste in music) can be fertile soil for factions. In Madison's view people are factious by nature; the "causes of faction" are "sown" into their very being.

Madison thus proposes a second and, he thinks, more practical and desirable way of defeating faction. The way to cure "the mischiefs of faction" is not by removing its causes but by "controlling its effects." Factions will always exist, so the trick is to establish a form of government that is likely to serve the public good through the even-handed "regulation of these various and interfering interests." Wise and public-spirited leaders can "adjust these clashing interests and render them all subservient to the public good," but, he cautions, "Enlightened statesmen will not always be at the helm." (Madison implies that

"enlightened statesmen"—such as himself, Washington, and Jefferson—were at the "helm" of government in 1787.)

Madison's proposed cure for the evils of factions is in fact nothing other than a republican form of government. Use the following questions to guide your own analysis of Madison's ideas. Why does Madison think the problem of a "minority" faction is easy to handle? Conversely, why is he so troubled by the potential of a majority faction? How does he distinguish direct democracy from republican government? What is he getting at when he terms elected representatives "proper guardians of the public weal," and why does he think that "extensive republics" are more likely to produce such representatives than small ones?

When you are finished with *Federalist* No. 10, try your hand at *Federalist* No. 51. You will find that the ideas in the former paper anticipate many of those in the latter. And you will find many points on which you may or may not agree with Madison. For example, do you agree with his assumption that people—even your best friends or college roommates—are factious by nature? Likewise, do you agree with his view that government is "the greatest of all reflections on human nature"?

By attempting to meet the mind of James Madison, you can sharpen your own mind and deepen your understanding of American government.

---

were to constitute a "council of revision" that could veto acts of the legislature; that veto, in turn, could be overridden by the legislature. There were other interesting details, but the key features of the Virginia Plan were two: (1) a national legislature would have

supreme powers on all matters on which the separate states were not competent to act, as well as the power to veto any and all state laws, and (2) at least one house of the legislature would be elected directly by the people.

The New Jersey Plan

As the debate went on, the representatives of New Jersey and other small states became increasingly worried that the convention was going to write a constitution in which the states would be represented in both houses of Congress on the basis of population. If this happened, the smaller states feared they would always be outvoted by the larger ones, and so, with William Paterson of New Jersey as their spokesman, they introduced a new plan. The New Jersey Plan proposed to amend, not replace, the old Articles of Confederation. It enhanced the power of the national government (though not as much as the Virginia Plan), but it did so in a way that left the states' representation in Congress unchanged from the Articles—each state would have one vote. Thus not only would the interests of the small states be protected, but Congress itself would remain to a substantial degree the creature of state governments.

If the New Jersey resolutions had been presented first and taken up as the major item of business, it is quite possible that they would have become the framework for the document that finally emerged. But they were not. Offered after the convention had been discussing the Virginia Plan for two weeks, the resolutions encountered a reception very different from what they would have received if introduced earlier. The debate had the delegates already thinking in terms of a national government that was more independent of the states, and thus it had accustomed them to proposals that, under other circumstances, might have seemed quite radical. On June 19 the first decisive vote of the convention was taken: seven states preferred the Virginia Plan, three states the New Jersey Plan, and one state was split.

With the tide running in favor of a strong national government, the supporters of the small states had to shift their strategy. They now began to focus their efforts on ensuring that the small states could not be outvoted by the larger ones in Congress. One way was to have the members of the lower house elected by the state legislatures rather than the people, with each state getting the same number of seats rather than seats proportional to its population.

The debate was long and feelings ran high, so much so that Benjamin Franklin, at eighty-one the oldest delegate present, suggested that each day's meeting begin with a prayer. It turned out that the convention could not even agree on this: Hamilton is supposed to have objected that the convention did not need "foreign aid," and others pointed out that the group had no funds with which to hire a minister. And so the argument continued.

The Compromise

Finally a committee was appointed to meet during the Fourth of July holidays to work out a compromise, and the convention adjourned to await its report. Little is known of what went on in that committee's session, though some were later to say that Franklin played a key role in hammering out the plan that finally emerged. That compromise, the most important reached at the convention, and later called the **Great Compromise** (or sometimes the Connecticut Compromise), was submitted to the full convention on July 5 and debated for another week and a half. The debate might have gone on even longer, but suddenly the hot weather moderated, and Monday, July 16, dawned cool and fresh after a month of misery. On that day the plan was adopted: five states were in favor, four opposed, and two not voting.* Thus, by the narrowest of margins, the structure of the national legislature was set, as follows:

- A House of Representatives consisting initially of sixty-five members apportioned among the states roughly on the basis of population and elected by the people

- A Senate consisting of two senators from each state to be chosen by the state legislatures

The Great Compromise reconciled the interests of small and large states by allowing the former to predominate in the Senate and the latter in the House. This reconciliation was necessary to ensure that there would be support for a strong national government from small as well as large states. It represented major concessions on the part of several groups. Madison, for one, was deeply opposed to the idea of having the states equally represented in the

---

* The states in favor were Connecticut, Delaware, Maryland, New Jersey, and North Carolina. Those opposed were Georgia, Pennsylvania, South Carolina, and Virginia. Massachusetts was split down the middle; the New York delegates had left the convention. New Hampshire and Rhode Island were absent.

Senate. He saw in that a way for the states to hamstring the national government and much preferred some measure of proportional representation in both houses. Delegates from other states worried that representation on the basis of population in the House of Representatives would enable the large states to dominate legislative affairs. Although the margin by which the compromise was accepted was razor-thin (five states in favor, four opposed), it held firm. In time most of the delegates from the dissenting states accepted it.

After the Great Compromise many more issues had to be resolved, but by now a spirit of accommodation had developed. When one delegate proposed having the Congress choose the president, another, James Wilson, proposed that he be elected directly by the people. When neither side of that argument prevailed, a committee invented a plan for an "Electoral College" that would choose the president. When some delegates wanted the president chosen for a life term, others proposed a seven-year term, and still others wanted the term limited to three years without eligibility for reelection. The convention settled on a four-year term with no bar to reelection. Some states wanted the Supreme Court picked by the Senate; others wanted it chosen by the president. They finally agreed to let the justices be nominated by the president and then confirmed by the Senate.

Finally, on July 26, the proposals that were already accepted, together with a bundle of unresolved issues, were handed over to a "Committee of Detail" of five delegates. This committee included Madison and Gouverneur Morris, who was to be the chief draftsman of the document that finally emerged. The committee hardly contented itself with mere "details," however. It inserted some new proposals and made changes in old ones, drawing for inspiration on existing state constitutions and the members' beliefs as to what the other delegates might accept. On August 6 the report—the first complete draft of the Constitution—was submitted to the convention. There it was debated, item by item, revised, amended, and finally, on September 17, approved by all twelve states in attendance. (Not all *delegates* approved, however; three, including Edmund Randolph, who first submitted the Virginia Plan, refused to sign.)

The Constitution and Democracy

A debate continues to rage over whether the Constitution created, or was even intended to create, a democratic government. The answer is complex. The Framers did not intend to create a "pure democracy"—one in which the people rule directly. For one thing the size of the country and the distances between settlements would have made that physically impossible. But more important, the Framers worried that a government in which all citizens directly participate, as in the New England town meeting, would be a government excessively subject to temporary popular passions and one in which minority rights would be insecure. They intended instead to create a **republic,** by which they meant a government in which a system of representation operates. In designing that system the Framers chose, not without argument, to have the members of the House of Representatives elected directly by the people. Some delegates did not want to go even that far. Elbridge Gerry of Massachusetts, who refused to sign the Constitution, argued that though "the people do not want [that is, lack] virtue," they are often the "dupes of pretended patriots." Roger Sherman of Connecticut agreed. But George Mason of Virginia and James Wilson of Pennsylvania carried the day when they argued that "no government could long subsist without the confidence of the people," and this required "drawing the most numerous branch of the legislature directly from the people." Popular elections for the House were approved: six states were in favor, two opposed.

But though popular rule was to be one element of the new government, it was not to be the only one. State legislatures, not the people, would choose the senators; electors, not the people directly, would choose the president. As we have seen, without these arrangements, there would have been no Constitution at all, for the small states adamantly opposed any proposal that would have given undue power to the large ones. And direct popular election of the president would clearly have made the populous states the dominant ones. In short the Framers wished to observe the principle of majority rule, but they felt that, on the most important questions, two kinds of majorities were essential—a majority of the voters and a majority of the states.

The power of the Supreme Court to declare an act of Congress unconstitutional—**judicial review**—is also a way of limiting the power of popular majorities. It is not clear whether the Framers intended that there be judicial review, but there is little doubt that in the Framers' minds the fundamental law, the Constitution, had to be safeguarded against popular passions. They made the process for amending the Constitution easier than it had been under the Articles but still relatively difficult.

An amendment can be proposed either by a two-thirds vote of both houses of Congress *or* by a national convention called by Congress at the request of two-thirds of the states.* Once proposed, an amendment must be ratified by three-fourths of the states, either through their legislatures or through special ratifying conventions in each state. Twenty-seven amendments have survived this process, all of them proposed by Congress and all but one (the Twenty-first) ratified by state legislatures rather than state conventions.

In short the answer to the question of whether the Constitution brought into being a democratic government is yes, if by *democracy* one means a system of representative government based on popular consent. The degree of that consent has changed since 1787, and the institutions embodying that consent can take different forms. One form, rejected in 1787, gives all political authority to one set of representatives, directly elected by the people. (That is the case, for example, in most parliamentary regimes, such as Great Britain, and in some city governments in the United States.) The other form of democracy is one in which different sets of officials, chosen directly or indirectly by different groups of people, share political power. (That is the case with the United States and a few other nations where the separation of powers is intended to operate.)

Key Principles

The American version of representative democracy was based on two major principles, the separation of powers and federalism. In America political power was to be shared by three separate branches of government; in parliamentary democracies that power was concentrated in a single, supreme legislature. In America political authority was divided between a national government and several state governments—**federalism**—whereas in most European systems authority was centralized in the national government. Neither of these principles was especially controversial at Philadelphia. The delegates began their work in broad agreement that separated powers and some measure of federalism were necessary, and both the Virginia and New Jersey plans contained a version of each. How much federalism should be written into the Constitution was quite controversial, however.*

Government and Human Nature

The desirability of separating powers and leaving the states equipped with a broad array of rights and responsibilities was not controversial at the Philadelphia convention because the Framers' experiences with British rule and state government under the Articles had shaped their view of human nature.

These experiences had taught most of the Framers that people would seek their own advantage in and out of politics; this pursuit of self-interest, unchecked, would lead some people to exploit others. Human nature was good enough to make it possible to have a decent government that was based on popular consent, but it was not good enough to make it inevitable. One solution to this problem would be to improve human nature. Ancient political philosophers such as Aristotle believed that the

---

* There have been many attempts to get a new constitutional convention. In the 1960s thirty-three states, one short of the required number, requested a convention to consider the reapportionment of state legislatures. In the 1980s efforts were made to call a convention to consider amendments to ban abortions and to require a balanced federal budget.

* To the delegates a truly "federal" system was one, like the New Jersey Plan, that allowed for very strong states and a weak national government. When the New Jersey Plan lost, the delegates who defeated it began using the word *federal* to describe their plan even though it called for a stronger national government. Thus men who began as "Federalists" at the convention ultimately became known as "Antifederalists" during the struggle over ratification.

Checks and Balances

*T*he Constitution creates a system of *separate* institutions that *share* powers. Because the three branches of government share powers, each can (partially) check the powers of the others. This is the system of **checks and balances.** The major checks possessed by each branch are listed below.

CONGRESS

1. Can check the president in these ways:
   a. By refusing to pass a bill the president wants
   b. By passing a law over the president's veto
   c. By using the impeachment powers to remove the president from office
   d. By refusing to approve a presidential appointment (Senate only)
   e. By refusing to ratify a treaty the president has signed (Senate only)
2. Can check the federal courts in these ways:
   a. By changing the number and jurisdiction of the lower courts
   b. By using the impeachment powers to remove a judge from office
   c. By refusing to approve a person nominated to be a judge (Senate only)

THE PRESIDENT

1. Can check Congress by vetoing a bill it has passed
2. Can check the federal courts by nominating judges

THE COURTS

1. Can check Congress by declaring a law unconstitutional
2. Can check the president by declaring actions by him or his subordinates to be unconstitutional or not authorized by law

In addition to these checks specifically provided for in the Constitution, each branch has informal ways of checking the others. For example, the president can try to withhold information from Congress (on the grounds of "executive privilege"), and Congress can try to get information by mounting an investigation.

The exact meaning of the various checks is explained in Chapter 11 on Congress, Chapter 12 on the presidency, and Chapter 14 on the courts.

first task of any government was to cultivate virtue among the governed.

Many Americans were of the same mind. To them, Americans would first have to become good people before they could have a good government. Samuel Adams, a leader of the Boston Tea Party, said that the new nation must become a "Christian Sparta." Others spoke of the need to cultivate frugality, industry, temperance, and simplicity.

But to James Madison and the other architects of the Constitution, the deliberate cultivation of virtue would require a government too strong and thus too dangerous to liberty, at least at the national level. Self-interest, freely pursued within reasonable limits, was a more practical and durable solution to the problem of government than any effort to improve the virtue of the citizenry. He wanted, he said, to make republican government possible "even in the absence of political virtue."

Madison argued that the very self-interest that leads people toward factionalism and tyranny might, if properly harnessed by appropriate constitutional arrangements, provide a source of unity and a guarantee of liberty. This harnessing was to be accomplished by dividing the offices of the new government among many people and giving to the holder of each office the "necessary means and personal motives to resist encroachments of the others." In this way "ambition must be made to counteract ambition" so that "the private interest of every individual may be a sentinel over the public rights."[11] If men were angels, all this would be unnecessary. But Madison and the other delegates pragmatically insisted on taking human nature pretty much as it was, and therefore they adopted "this policy of supplying, by opposite and rival interests, the defect of better motives."[12] The **separation of powers** (see box) would work, not in spite of the imperfections of human nature, but because of them.

So also with federalism. By dividing power between the states and the national government, one level of government can serve as a check on the other. This should provide a "double security" to the rights of the people: "The different governments will control each other, at the same time that each will be controlled by itself."[13] This was especially likely to happen in America, Madison thought, because it was a large country filled with diverse interests—

rich and poor, Protestant and Catholic, northerner and southerner, farmer and merchant, creditor and debtor. Each of these interests would constitute a **faction** that would seek its own advantage. One faction might come to dominate government, or a part of government, in one place, and a different and rival faction might dominate it in another. The pulling and hauling among these factions would prevent any single government—say, that of New York—from dominating all of government. The division of powers among several governments would give to virtually every faction an opportunity to gain some—but not full—power.

The Constitution and Liberty

A more difficult question is whether the Constitution created a system of government that would respect personal liberties. And that in fact is the question that was debated in the states when the document was presented for ratification. The proponents of the Constitution called themselves the **Federalists** (though they might more accurately have been called "nationalists"). The opponents came to be known as the **Antifederalists** (though they might more accurately have been called "states' rights"). To be put into effect, the Constitution had to be approved at ratifying conventions in at least nine states. This was perhaps the most democratic feature of the Constitution: it had to be accepted, not by the existing Congress (still limping along under the Articles of Confederation), nor by the state legislatures, but by special conventions elected by the people.

Though democratic, the process established by the Framers for ratifying the Constitution was technically illegal. The Articles of Confederation, which still governed, could be amended only with the approval of all thirteen state legislatures. The Framers wanted to bypass these legislatures because they feared that, for reasons of ideology or out of a desire to retain their powers, the legislators would oppose the Constitution. The Framers wanted ratification with less than the consent of all thirteen states because they knew that such unanimity could not be attained. And indeed the conventions in North Carolina and Rhode Island did initially reject the Constitution.

RATIFICATION OF THE FEDERAL CONSTITUTION BY STATE CONVENTIONS, 1787–1790

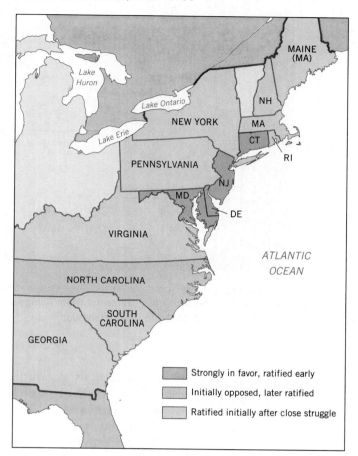

Strongly in favor, ratified early

Initially opposed, later ratified

Ratified initially after close struggle

The Antifederalist View

The great issue before the state conventions was liberty, not democracy. The opponents of the new Constitution, the Antifederalists, had a variety of objections but were in general united by the belief that liberty could be secure only in a small republic in which the rulers were physically close to—and closely checked by—the ruled. Their central objection was stated by a group of Antifederalists at the ratifying convention in an essay published just after they had lost: "a very extensive territory cannot be governed on the principles of freedom, otherwise than by a confederation of republics."[14]

These dissenters argued that a strong national government would be distant from the people and

By steadily moving westward, Americans both searched for economic opportunity and sought to protect their freedom from government. Here George Caleb Bingham depicts Daniel Boone escorting settlers through the Cumberland Gap.

would use its powers to annihilate or absorb the functions that properly belonged to the states. Congress would tax heavily, the Supreme Court would overrule state courts, and the president would come to head a large standing army. (Since all these things have occurred, we cannot dismiss the Antifederalists as cranky obstructionists who opposed without justification the plans of the Framers.) These critics argued that the nation needed, at best, a loose confederation of states, with most of the powers of government kept firmly in the hands of state legislatures and state courts.

But if a stronger national government was to be created, the Antifederalists argued, it should be hedged about with many more restrictions than those in the constitution then under consideration. They proposed several such limitations, including narrowing the jurisdiction of the Supreme Court, checking the president's power by creating a council that would review his actions, leaving military affairs in the hands of the state militias, increasing the size of the House of Representatives so that it would reflect a greater variety of popular interests, and reducing or eliminating the power of Congress to levy

taxes. And some of them insisted that a *bill of rights* be added to the Constitution.

James Madison gave his answer to these criticisms in *Federalist* papers 10 and 51 (reprinted in the Appendix). It was a bold answer, for it flew squarely in the face of widespread popular sentiment and much philosophical writing. Following the great French political philosopher Montesquieu, many Americans believed that liberty was safe only in small societies governed either by direct democracy or by large legislatures with small districts and frequent turnover among members.

Madison argued quite the opposite—that liberty is safest in *large* (or as he put it, "extended") republics. In a small community, he said, there will be relatively few differences in opinion or interest; people will tend to see the world in much the same way. If anyone dissents or pursues an individual interest, he or she will be confronted by a massive majority and will have few, if any, allies. But in a large republic there will be many opinions and interests; as a result it will be hard for a tyrannical majority to form or organize, and anyone with an unpopular view will find it easier to acquire allies. If Madison's argument seems strange or abstract, ask yourself the following question: If I have an unpopular opinion, an exotic lifestyle, or an unconventional interest, will I find greater security living in a small town or a big city?

By favoring a large republic, Madison was not trying to stifle democracy. Rather he was attempting to show how democratic government really works, and what can make it work better. To rule, different interests must come together and form a **coalition**—that is, an alliance. In *Federalist* No. 51, he was arguing that the coalitions that formed in a large republic would be more moderate than those that formed in a small one because the bigger the republic, the greater the variety of interests, and thus the more a coalition of the majority would have to accommodate a diversity of interests and opinions if it hoped to succeed. He concluded that in a nation the size of the United States, with its enormous variety of interests, "a coalition of a majority of the whole society could seldom take place on any other principles than those of justice and the general good." Whether he was right in that prediction is a matter to which we shall return repeatedly.

The implication of Madison's arguments was daring, for he was suggesting that the national government should be at some distance from the people and insulated from their momentary passions, because the people did not always want to do the right thing. Liberty was threatened as much (or even more) by public passions and popularly based factions as by strong governments. Now the Antifederalists themselves had no very lofty view of human nature, as is evidenced by the deep suspicion with which they viewed "power-seeking" officeholders. What Madison did was take this view to its logical conclusion, arguing that if people could be corrupted by office, they could also be corrupted by factional self-interest. Thus the government had to be designed to prevent both the politicians and the people from using it for ill-considered or unjust purposes.

To argue in 1787 against the virtues of small democracies was like arguing against motherhood, but the argument prevailed, probably because many citizens were convinced that a reasonably strong national government was essential if the nation were to stand united against foreign enemies, facilitate commerce among the states, guard against domestic insurrections, and keep one faction from oppressing another. The political realities of the moment and the recent bitter experiences with the Articles probably counted for more in ratifying the Constitution than did Madison's arguments. His cause was helped by the fact that, for all their legitimate concerns and their uncanny instinct for what the future might bring, the Antifederalists could offer no agreed-upon alternative to the new Constitution. In politics, then as now, you cannot beat something with nothing.

But this does not explain why the Framers failed to add a bill of rights to the Constitution. If they were so preoccupied with liberty, why didn't they take this most obvious step toward protecting liberty, especially since the Antifederalists were demanding it? Some historians have suggested that this omission was evidence that liberty was not as important to the Framers as they claimed. In fact, when one delegate suggested that a bill of rights be drawn up, the state delegations at the convention unanimously voted the idea down. There were several reasons for this.

First, the Constitution, as written, *did* contain a number of specific guarantees of individual liberty, including the right of trial by jury in criminal cases and the privilege of the writ of habeas corpus. The liberties guaranteed in the Constitution (before the Bill of Rights was added) are listed below.

- **Writ of habeas corpus*** may not be suspended (except during invasion or rebellion).

- No **bill of attainder** may be passed by Congress or the states.

- No **ex post facto law** may be passed by Congress or the states.

- Right of trial by jury in criminal cases is guaranteed.

- The citizens of each state are entitled to the privileges and immunities of the citizens of every other state.

- No religious test or qualification for holding federal office is imposed.

- No law impairing the obligation of contracts may be passed by the states.

* For a definition of this and the following terms used in connection with certain rights, see the Glossary.

The Bill of Rights

The First Ten Amendments to the Constitution Grouped by Topic and Purpose

PROTECTIONS AFFORDED CITIZENS TO PARTICIPATE IN THE POLITICAL PROCESS

Amendment 1: Freedom of religion, speech, press, and assembly; the right to petition the government.

PROTECTIONS AGAINST ARBITRARY POLICE AND COURT ACTION

Amendment 4: No unreasonable searches or seizures.

Amendment 5: Grand jury indictment required to prosecute a person for a serious crime.

No "double jeopardy" (being tried twice for the same offense).

Forcing a person to testify against himself or herself prohibited.

No loss of life, liberty, or property without due process.

Amendment 6: Right to speedy, public, impartial trial with defense counsel and right to cross-examine witnesses.

Amendment 7: Jury trials in civil suits where value exceeds $20.

Amendment 8: No excessive bail or fines, no cruel and unusual punishments.

PROTECTIONS OF STATES' RIGHTS AND UNNAMED RIGHTS OF PEOPLE

Amendment 9: Unlisted rights are not necessarily denied.

Amendment 10: Powers not delegated to the United States or denied to states are reserved to the states.

OTHER AMENDMENTS

Amendment 2: Right to bear arms.

Amendment 3: Troops may not be quartered in homes in peacetime.

Second, most states in 1787 had bills of rights. When Elbridge Gerry proposed to the convention that a federal bill of rights be drafted, Roger Sherman rose to observe that it was unnecessary because the state bills of rights were sufficient.[15]

But third, and perhaps most important, the Framers thought they were creating a government with specific, limited powers. It could do, they thought, only what the Constitution gave it the power to do, and nowhere in that document was there permission to infringe on freedom of speech or of the press or to impose cruel and unusual punishments. Some delegates probably feared that if any serious effort were made to list the rights that were guaranteed, later officials might assume that they had the power to do anything not explicitly forbidden.

Need for a Bill of Rights

Whatever their reasons, the Framers made at least a tactical and perhaps a fundamental mistake. It quickly became clear that without at least the promise of a **bill of rights**, the Constitution would not be ratified. Though the small states, pleased by their equal representation in the Senate, quickly ratified (in Delaware, New Jersey, and Georgia, the vote in the conventions was unanimous), the battle in the large states was intense and the outcome uncertain. In Pennsylvania Federalist supporters dragged boycotting Antifederalists to the legislature in order to ensure that a quorum was present so that a convention could be called. There were rumors of other rough tactics.

In Massachusetts the Constitution was approved by a narrow majority, but only after key leaders promised to obtain a bill of rights. In Virginia James Madison fought against the fiery Patrick Henry, whose climactic speech against ratification was dramatically punctuated by a noisy thunderstorm outside. The Federalists won by ten votes. In New York Alexander Hamilton argued the case for six long weeks against the determined opposition of most of the state's key political leaders; he carried the day, but only by three votes, and then only after New York City threatened to secede from the state if it did not ratify. By June 21, 1788, the ninth state—New Hampshire—had ratified and the Constitution was law.

Despite the bitterness of the ratification struggle, the new government that took office in 1789–1790, headed by President Washington, was greeted enthusiastically. By the spring of 1790 all thirteen states had ratified. There remained, however, the task of fulfilling the promise of a bill of rights. To that end James Madison introduced into the first session of the First Congress a set of proposals, many based on the existing Virginia bill of rights. Twelve were approved by Congress; ten of these were ratified by the states and went into effect in 1791. These amendments did not limit the power of state governments over citizens, only the power of the federal government. Later the Fourteenth Amendment, as interpreted by the Supreme Court, extended many of the guarantees of the Bill of Rights to cover state governmental action.

The Constitution and Slavery

Though black slaves amounted to one-third of the population of the five southern states, nowhere in the Constitution can one find the words *slave* or *slavery*. There are three provisions bearing on the matter, all designed to placate the slave-owning states. The apportionment of seats in the House of Representatives was to be made by counting all free persons and three-fifths of all "other persons." This meant giving a few extra seats in the House to those states that had a lot of "other persons"—that is, slaves. Congress was forbidden from prohibiting the "importation" of "persons" (that is, slaves) before the year 1808. And if any "person held to service or labour" (that is, any slave) were to escape from a slave-owning state and get to a free state, that person would not become free but would have to be returned to his or her master.

To some the failure of the Constitution to address the question of slavery was a great betrayal of the promise of the Declaration of Independence that "all men are created equal."[16] For the Constitution to be silent on the subject of slavery, and thereby to allow that odious practice to continue, was to convert, by implication, the wording of the Declaration to "all white men are created equal."

The Constitution was silent on slavery, and so buying and selling black slaves continued for many years.

It is easy to accuse the signers of the Declaration and the Constitution of hypocrisy. They knew of slavery, many of them owned slaves, and yet they were silent. Indeed, British opponents of the independence movement took special delight in taunting the colonists about their complaints of being "enslaved" to the British Empire while ignoring the slavery in their very midst. Increasingly, revolutionary leaders during this period spoke to this issue. Thomas Jefferson had tried to get a clause opposing the slave trade put into the Declaration of Independence. James Otis of Boston had attacked slavery and argued that black as well as white men should be free. As revolutionary fervor mounted, so did northern criticisms of slavery. The Massachusetts legislature and then the Continental Congress voted to end the slave trade; Delaware prohibited the importation of slaves; Pennsylvania voted to tax it out of existence; and Connecticut and Rhode Island decided that all slaves brought into those states would automatically become free.

Slavery continued unabated in the South, defended by some whites because they thought it right, by others because they found it useful. But even in the South there were opponents, though rarely conspicuous ones. George Mason, a large Virginia slaveholder and a delegate to the convention, warned

prophetically that "by an inevitable chain of causes and effects, providence punishes national sins [slavery] by national calamities."[17]

The blunt fact, however, was that any effort to use the Constitution to end slavery would have meant the end of the Constitution. The southern states would never have signed a document that seriously interfered with slavery. Without the southern states there would have been a continuation of the Articles of Confederation, which would have left each state entirely sovereign and thus entirely free of any prospective challenge to slavery.

Thus the Framers compromised with slavery; political scientist Theodore Lowi calls this their Greatest Compromise.[18] Slavery is dealt with in three places in the Constitution, though never by name. In determining the representation each state was to have in the House, "three-fifths of all other persons" (that is, of slaves) are to be added to "the whole number of free persons."[19] The South originally wanted slaves to count fully even though, of course, none would be elected to the House; they settled for counting 60 percent of them. The convention also agreed not to allow the new government by law or even constitutional amendment to prohibit the importation of slaves until the year 1808.[20] The South thus had twenty years in which it could acquire more slaves from abroad; after that, Congress was free (but not required) to end the importation. Finally, the Constitution guaranteed that if a slave were to escape his or her master and flee to a nonslave state, the slave would be returned by that state to "the party to whom . . . service or labour may be due."[21]

The unresolved issue of slavery was to prove the most explosive question of all. Allowing slavery to continue was a fateful decision, one that led to the worst social and political catastrophe in the nation's history—the Civil War. The Framers chose to sidestep the issue in order to create a union that, they hoped, would eventually be strong enough to deal with the problem when it could no longer be postponed. The legacy of that choice continues to this day.

The Motives of the Framers

The Framers were not saints or demigods. They were men with political opinions who also had economic interests and human failings. It would be a mistake to conclude that everything they did in 1787 was motivated by a disinterested commitment to the public good. But it would be an equally great mistake to think that what they did was nothing but an effort to line their pockets by producing a government that would serve their own narrow interests. As in almost all human endeavors, the Framers acted out of a mixture of motives. What is truly astonishing is that economic interests played only a modest role in their deliberations.

Economic Interests at the Convention

Some of the Framers were wealthy; some were not. Some owned slaves; some had none. Some were creditors (having loaned money to the Continental Congress or to private parties); some were deeply in debt. For nearly a century scholars have argued over just how important these personal interests were in shaping the provisions of the Constitution.

In 1913 Charles Beard, a historian, published a book—*An Economic Interpretation of the Constitution*—arguing that the better-off urban and commercial classes, especially those members who held the IOUs issued by the government to pay for the Revolutionary War, favored the new Constitution because they stood to benefit from it.[22] But in the 1950s that view was challenged by historians who, after looking carefully at what the Framers owned or owed, concluded that one could not explain the Constitution exclusively or even largely in terms of the economic interests of those who wrote it.[23] Some of the richest delegates, such as Elbridge Gerry of Massachusetts and George Mason of Virginia, refused to sign the document, while many of its key backers—James Madison and James Wilson, for example—were men of modest means or heavy debts.

In the 1980s a new group of scholars, primarily economists applying more advanced statistical techniques, found evidence that some economic considerations influenced how the Framers voted on some issues during the Philadelphia convention. Interestingly, however, the economic position of the *states*

Elbridge Gerry (left, 1744–1814) was a wealthy Massachusetts merchant and politician who participated in the convention but refused to sign the new constitution.

James Wilson (right, 1742–1798) of Pennsylvania, a brilliant lawyer and terrible businessman, was the principal champion of the popular election of the House. Near the end of his life he was jailed repeatedly for debts incurred as a result of his business speculations.

from which they came had a greater effect on their votes than did their *own* monetary condition.[24]

We have already seen how delegates from small states fought to reduce the power of large states and how those from slaveowning states made certain that the Constitution would contain no provision that would threaten slavery.

But contrary to what Beard asserted, the individual interests of the Framers themselves did not dominate the convention except in a few cases where a constitutional provision would have affected them directly. As you might expect, all slaveowning delegates, even those who did not live in states where slavery was commonplace (and several northern delegates owned slaves), tended to vote for provisions that would have kept the national government's power over slavery as weak as possible. However, the effects of other personal business interests were surprisingly weak. Some delegates owned a lot of public debt that they had purchased for low prices. A strong national government of the sort envisaged by the Constitution was more likely than the weak Continental Congress to pay off this debt at face value, thus making the delegates who owned it much richer. Despite this, the ownership of public debt had no significant effect on how the Framers voted in Philadelphia. For example, five men who among them owned one-third of all the public securities held by all the delegates voted against the Constitution. Nor did the big land speculators vote their interests. Some, such as George Washington and Robert Morris, favored the Constitution, while others, such as George Mason and William Blount, opposed it.[25]

In sum, the Framers tended to represent their states' interests on important matters. Since they were picked by the states to do so, this is exactly what one would expect. If they had not met in secret, perhaps they would have voted even more often as their constituents wanted. But except with respect to slavery, they usually did not vote their own economic interests. They were reasonably but not wholly disinterested delegates who were probably influenced as much by personal beliefs as by economics.

Economic Interests and Ratification

At the popularly elected state ratifying conventions, economic factors played a larger role. Delegates who were merchants, who lived in cities, who owned large amounts of western land, who held government IOUs, and who did not own slaves were more likely to vote to ratify the new Constitution than were delegates who were farmers, who did not own public debt, and who did own slaves.[26] There were plenty of exceptions, however. Small farmers dominated the conventions in some states where the vote to ratify was unanimous.

Though interests made a difference, they were not simply elite interests. In most states the great majority of adult white males could vote for delegates to the ratifying conventions. This means that women and blacks were excluded from the debates, but by the standards of the time—standards that did not change for over a century—the ratification process was remarkably democratic.

The Constitution and Equality

Ideas counted for as much as interests. At stake were two views of the public good. One, espoused by the Federalists, was that a reasonable balance of liberty, order, and progress required a strong national government. The other, defended by the Antifederalists, was that liberty would not be secure in the hands of a powerful, distant government; freedom required decentralization.

Today that debate has a new focus. The defect of the Constitution, to some contemporary critics, is not that the government it created is too strong but that it is too weak. In particular the national government is too weak to resist the pressures of special interests that reflect and perpetuate social inequality.

This criticism reveals how our understanding of the relationship between liberty and equality has changed since the Founding. To Jefferson and Madison citizens naturally differed in their talents and qualities. What had to be guarded against was the use of governmental power to create *un*natural and undesirable inequalities. This might happen, for example, if political power was concentrated in the hands of a few people (who could use that power to give themselves special privileges) or if it was used in ways that allowed some private parties to acquire exclusive charters and monopolies. To prevent the inequality that might result from having too strong a government, its powers must be kept strictly limited.

Today some people think of inequality quite dif-

Critical Thinking

Were Women Left Out of the Constitution?

In one sense, yes: Women were nowhere mentioned in the Constitution when it was written in 1787. Moreover, Article 1, which set forth the provisions for electing members of the House of Representatives, granted the vote to those people who were allowed to vote for members of the lower house of the legislature in the states in which they resided. In no state at the time could women participate in those elections. In no state could they vote in any elections or hold any offices. Furthermore, wherever the Constitution uses a pronoun, it uses the masculine form—*he* or *him*.

In another sense, no: Wherever the Constitution or the Bill of Rights defines a right that people are to have, it either grants that right to "persons" or "citizens," not to "men," or it makes no mention at all of people or gender. For example:

- "The *citizens* of each State shall be entitled to all privileges and immunities of citizens of the several States."
  [Art. I, sec. 9]

- "No *person* shall be convicted of treason unless on the testimony of two witnesses to the same overt act, or on confession in open court." [Art. III, sec. 3]

- "No bill of attainder or ex post facto law shall be passed." [Art. I sec. 9]

- "The right of the *people* to be secure in their persons, houses, papers, and effects, against unreasonable searches and seizures, shall not be violated."
  [Amend. IV]

- "No *person* shall be held to answer for a capital, or otherwise infamous crime, unless on presentment or indictment of a grand jury. . . . nor shall any *person* be subject for the same offense to be twice put in jeopardy of life or limb; . . . nor be deprived of life, liberty, or property, without due process of law."
  [Amend. V]

- "In all criminal prosecutions the *accused* shall enjoy the right to a speedy and public trial, by an impartial jury." [Amend. VI]

Moreover, when the qualifications for elective office are stated, the word *person,* not *man,* is used.

- "No *person* shall be a Representative who shall not have attained to the age of twenty-five years." [Art. 1, sec. 2]

- "No *person* shall be a Senator who shall not have attained to the age of thirty years." [Art. 1, sec. 3]

- "No *person* except a natural born citizen, . . . shall be eligible to the office of President; neither shall any *person* be eligible to that office who shall not have attained to the age of thirty-five years." [Art. 2, sec. 1]

In places the Constitution and the Bill of Rights used the pronoun *he,* but always in the context of referring back to a *person* or *citizen.* At the time, and until quite recently, the male pronoun was often used in legal documents to refer generically to both men and women.

Thus, though the Constitution did not give women the right to vote until the Nineteenth Amendment was ratified in 1920, it did use language that extended fundamental rights, and access to office, to women and men equally.

Of course what the Constitution permitted did not necessarily occur. State and local laws denied to women rights that in principle they ought to have enjoyed. Except for a brief period in New Jersey, no women voted in statewide elections until, in 1869, they were given the right to cast ballots in territorial elections in Wyoming.

When women were first elected to Congress, there was no need to change the Constitution; nothing in it restricted office-holding to men.

When women were given the right to vote by constitutional amendment, it was not necessary to amend any existing language in the Constitution, because nothing in the Constitution itself denied women the right to vote; the amendment simply added a new right:

- "The right of citizens of the United States to vote shall not be denied or abridged by the United States or any state on account of sex." [Amend. XIX]

SOURCE: Adapted from Robert Goldwin, "Why Blacks, Women and Jews Are Not Mentioned in the Constitution," *Commentary* (May 1987): 28–33.

---

ferently. To them it is the natural social order—the marketplace and the acquisitive talents of people operating in that marketplace—that leads to undesirable inequalities, especially in economic power.

The government should be powerful enough to restrain these natural tendencies and produce, by law, a greater degree of equality than society allows when left alone.

Ways of Amending the Constitution

*U*nder Article V there are two ways to *propose* **amendments** to the Constitution and two ways to *ratify* them.

TO PROPOSE AN AMENDMENT

1. Two-thirds of both houses of Congress vote to propose an amendment, *or*

2. Two-thirds of the state legislatures ask Congress to call a national convention to propose amendments.

TO RATIFY AN AMENDMENT

1. Three-fourths of the state legislatures approve it, *or*

2. Ratifying conventions in three-fourths of the states approve it.

SOME KEY FACTS

- Only the first method of proposing an amendment has been used.

- The second method of ratification has been used only once, to ratify the Twenty-first Amendment (repealing Prohibition).

- Congress may limit the time within which a proposed amendment must be ratified. The usual limitation has been seven years.

- Thousands of proposals have been made, but only thirty-three have obtained the necessary two-thirds vote in Congress.

- Twenty-seven amendments have been ratified.

- The first ten amendments, ratified on December 15, 1791, are known as the Bill of Rights.

To the Framers liberty and (political) equality were not in conflict; to some people today these two principles are deeply in conflict. To the Framers the task was to keep government so limited as to prevent it from creating the worst inequality—political privilege. To some modern observers the task is to make government strong enough to reduce what they believe is the worst inequality—differences in wealth.

Constitutional Reform—Modern Views

Almost from the day it was ratified, the Constitution has been the object of debate over ways in which it might be improved. These debates have rarely involved the average citizen, who tends to revere the document even if he or she cannot recall all its details. Because of this deep and broad popular support, scholars and politicians have been wary of attacking the Constitution or suggesting many wholesale changes. But such attacks have occurred. During the 1980s—the decade in which we celebrated the bicentennial of its adoption—we heard a variety of suggestions for improving the Constitution, ranging from particular amendments to wholesale revisions. In general there are today, as in the eighteenth century, two kinds of critics: those who think the federal government is too weak and those who think it is too strong.

Reducing the Separation of Powers

To the first kind of critic the chief difficulty with the Constitution is the separation of powers. By making every decision the uncertain outcome of the pulling and hauling between the president and Congress, the Constitution precludes the emergence—except perhaps in times of crisis—of the kind of effective national leadership the country needs. In this view our nation today faces a number of challenges that require prompt, decisive, and comprehensive action. Our problem is gridlock. Our position of international leadership, the dangerous and unprecedented proliferation of nuclear weapons among the nations of the globe, and the need to find ways of stimulating economic growth while reducing our deficit and conserving our environment—all these situations require that the president be able to formulate and carry out policies free of some of the pressures and delays from interest groups and members of Congress tied to local interests.

Not only would this increase in presidential authority make for better policies, these critics argue, it would also help the voters hold the president and his party accountable for their actions. As matters now stand, nobody in government can be held responsible for policies: Everybody takes the credit for successes and nobody takes the blame for failures.

The Twenty-seventh Amendment: A Rip Van Winkle Ratification

The Twenty-sixth Amendment to the Constitution gave citizens of the United States who are eighteen years of age or older the right to vote. It cleared Congress on March 23, 1971, and was ratified by the states on June 30, 1971. Since 1971 five other proposed constitutional amendments have come to a vote in one or both chambers of Congress:

- *Equal Rights Amendment* Cleared Congress in 1972; ratification deadline extended by Congress in 1978; deadline expired in 1982 after thirty-five states (of thirty-eight needed) had approved it.

- *Voting representation in Congress for the District of Columbia* Cleared Congress in 1978; ratification deadline expired in 1985 after sixteen states (of thirty-eight needed) had approved it.

- *Prohibition of busing for school desegregation* House rejected in 1979.

- *Balanced Budget Amendment* Passed Senate in 1982, but rejected in House.

- *Denial of a constitutional right to abortion* Senate rejected in 1983.

Most amendments proposed in recent times have been sent to the states with a seven-year deadline for ratification; however there is no constitutional requirement that Congress impose such deadlines. A dozen amendments sent to the states in 1789 had no deadline; ten of them became the Bill of Rights (see box on page 38). The other two were a proposal to change the apportionment of the House and a proposal to keep congressional pay increases from taking effect until after an election has intervened. The former proposal was never ratified. The latter, after a 203-year ratification process, became the Twenty-seventh Amendment in 1992.

The Twenty-seventh Amendment states: "No law varying the compensation for the services of Senators and Representatives, shall take effect, until an election of Representatives shall have intervened." Between 1789 and 1992 forty states (of thirty-eight needed) ratified the amendment. The amendment was certified by the United States Archivist on May 18, 1992, and printed in the *Federal Register* the day after. On May 18, 1992, the Senate passed two resolutions recognizing the amendment by a vote of 99–0. On May 19, 1992, the House passed a resolution recognizing it by a vote of 414–3. And on May 20, 1992, both chambers of Congress passed resolutions endorsing the amendment.

But Congress did not need to pass any resolutions in order to make the amendment official. Because there is no limit on the amount of time it can take to ratify an amendment (unless Congress specifically imposes a deadline), the Twenty-seventh Amendment automatically became law once the requisite thirty-eight states had ratified it. Still, some members of Congress recommended holding hearings on the 203-year-old amendment's constitutionality, but because of the political furor over congressional pay increases, they did not do so. Despite its Rip Van Winkle–like ratification, the Twenty-seventh Amendment is now as much a part of the Constitution as the Bill of Rights.

Typically the president, who tends to be the major source of new programs, cannot get his policies adopted by Congress without long delays and much bargaining, the result of which often is some watered-down compromise that neither the president nor Congress really likes but that each must settle for if anything is to be done at all.

Finally, critics of the separation of powers complain that the government agencies responsible for implementing a program are exposed to undue interference from legislators and special interests. In this view the president is supposed to be in charge of the bureaucracy but in fact must share this authority with countless members of Congress and congressional committees.

Not all critics of the separation of powers agree with all these points, nor do they all agree on what should be done about the problems. But they all have in common a fear that the separation of powers makes the president too weak and insufficiently accountable. Their proposals for reducing the separation of powers include the following:

- Allow the president to appoint members of Congress to serve in the cabinet (the Constitution forbids members of Congress from holding any federal appointive office while in Congress).

- Allow the president to dissolve Congress and call for a special election (elections now can be held only on the schedule determined by the calendar).

- Allow Congress to require a president who has lost its confidence to face the country in a special election before his term would normally end.

- Require the presidential and congressional candidates to run as a team in each congressional district; thus a presidential candidate who carries a given district could be sure that the congressional candidate of his party would also win in that district.

- Have the president serve a single six-year term instead of being eligible for up to two four-year terms; this would presumably free the president to lead without having to worry about reelection.

- Lengthen the terms of members of the House of Representatives from two to four years so that the entire House would stand for reelection at the same time as the president.[27]

Some of these proposals are offered by critics out of a desire to make the American system of government work more like the British parliamentary system, in which, as we shall see in Chapters 11 and 12, the prime minister is the undisputed leader of the majority in the British parliament. The parliamentary system is the major alternative in the world today to the American separation-of-powers system.

Both the diagnosis and the remedies proposed by these critics of the separation of powers have been challenged. Many defenders of our present constitutional system believe that nations, such as Great Britain, with a different, more unified political system have done no better than the United States in dealing with the problems of economic growth, national security, and environmental protection. Moreover, they argue, close congressional scrutiny of presidential proposals has improved these policies more often than it has weakened them. Finally, congressional "interference" in the work of government agencies is a good way of ensuring that the average citizen can fight back against the bureaucracy; without that so-called interference, citizens and interest groups might be helpless before big and powerful agencies.

Each of the specific proposals, defenders of the present constitutional system argue, would either make matters worse or have, at best, uncertain effects. Adding a few members of Congress to the president's cabinet would not provide much help in getting his program through Congress; there are 535 senators and representatives, and probably only about half a dozen would be in the cabinet. Giving either the president or Congress power to call a special election in between the regular elections (every two or four years) would cause needless confusion and great expense; the country would live under the threat of being in a perpetual political campaign with even weaker political parties. Linking the fate of the president and congressional candidates, by having them run as a team in each district, would reduce the stabilizing and moderating effect of having them separately elected. A Republican presidential candidate who wins in the new system would have a Republican majority in the House; a Democratic candidate winner would have a Democratic majority. We might as a result expect dramatic changes in policy as the political pendulum swings back and forth. Giving presidents a single six-year term would indeed free them from the need to worry about reelection, but it is precisely that worry that keeps presidents reasonably concerned about what the American people want.

Making the System Less Democratic

The second kind of critic of the Constitution thinks the government does too much, not too little. Though the separation of powers at one time may have slowed the growth of government and moderated the policies it adopted, in the last few decades government has grown helter-skelter. The problem, these critics argue, is not that democracy is a bad idea but that democracy can produce bad, or at least unintended, results if the government caters to the special-interest claims of the citizens rather than to their long-term values.

To see how these unintended results might occur, imagine a situation in which every citizen thinks the government grows too big, taxes too heavily, and spends too much. Each citizen wants the government made smaller by reducing the benefits other people get—but not by reducing the benefits he or she gets. In fact such citizens may even be willing to see their own benefits cut, provided everybody else's are cut as well, and by a like amount.

But the political system attends to individual wants, not general preferences. It gives aid to farmers, contracts to industry, grants to professors, pensions to the elderly, and loans to students. As someone once said, the government is like an adding machine: during elections candidates campaign by promising to do more for whatever group is dissatisfied with what the incumbents are doing for it. As a result most elections bring to office men and women who are committed to doing more for somebody. The grand total of all these additions is more for everybody. Few politicians have an incentive to do less for anybody.

To remedy this state of affairs, these critics suggest various mechanisms, but principally a constitutional amendment that would either set a limit on the amount of money the government could collect in taxes each year or require that each year the government have a balanced budget (that is, not spend more than it takes in in taxes), or both. In some versions of these plans an extraordinary majority (say, 60 percent) of Congress could override these limits, and the limits would not apply in wartime.

The effect of such amendments, the proponents claim, would be to force Congress and the president to look at the big picture—the grand total of what they are spending—rather than just to operate the adding machine by pushing the "add" button over and over again. If they could only spend so much during a given year, they would have to allocate what they spend among all rival claimants. For example, if more money were to be spent on the poor, less could then be spent on the military, or vice versa.

Some critics of an overly powerful federal government think these amendments will not be passed or may prove unworkable; instead they favor enhancing the president's power to block spending by giving him a **line-item veto**. Most state governors can veto a particular part of a bill and approve the rest, using a line-item veto. The theory is that such a veto would better equip the president to stop unwarranted spending without vetoing the other provisions of a bill. In 1996 President Clinton signed the Line Item Veto Act, passed by the 104th Congress. But despite its name, the new law did not give the president full line-item veto power (only a change in the Constitution could confer that power). Instead, the law gave the president authority to selectively eliminate individual items in large appropriations bills, expansions in certain income-transfer programs, and tax breaks (giving the president what budget experts call *enhanced rescission authority*). But it also left Congress free to craft bills in ways that would give the president few opportunities to veto (or *rescind*) favored items. For example, Congress can still force the president to accept or reject an entire appropriations bill simply by tagging on this sentence: "Appropriations provided under this act (or

As governor of New Jersey, Christine Todd Whitman can veto specific items in a spending bill passed by the legislature.

title or section) shall not be subject to the provisions of the Line Item Veto Act." A federal court has declared that this law is unconstitutional. The Supreme Court will act after the line item veto is used.

Finally, some of these critics of a powerful government feel that the real problem arises not from an excess of "adding-machine" democracy but from the growth in the power of the federal courts, as described in Chapter 14. What these critics would like to do is devise a set of laws or constitutional amendments that would narrow the authority of federal courts.

The opponents of these suggestions argue that constitutional amendments to restrict the level of taxes or to require a balanced budget are unworkable, even assuming—which they do not—that a smaller government is desirable. There is no precise, agreed-upon way to measure how much the government spends or to predict in advance how much it will receive in taxes during the year; thus, defining and enforcing a "balanced budget" is no easy matter. Since the government can always borrow money, it might easily evade any spending limits. It has also shown great ingenuity in spending money in ways that never appear as part of the regular budget.

The line-item veto may or may not be a good idea. We will not know until it has been in effect at the federal level for a number of years since the states, where some governors have long had the veto, are quite different from the federal government in power and responsibilities. We might well discover that the president will use it not to spend less but to spend more—by threatening, for example, to veto something of modest cost that Congress wants in order to get Congress to vote for a far more costly item that the president wants.

Finally, proposals to curtail judicial power are thinly veiled attacks, the opponents argue, on the ability of the courts to protect essential citizen rights. If Congress and the people do not like the way the Supreme Court has interpreted the Constitution, they can always amend the Constitution to change a specific ruling; there is no need to adopt some across-the-board limitation on court powers.

Who Is Right?

Some of the arguments of these two sets of critics of the Constitution may strike you as plausible or even

entirely convincing. Whatever you may ultimately decide, decide nothing for now. One cannot make or remake a constitution based entirely on abstract reasoning or unproven factual arguments. Even when the Constitution was first written in 1787, it was not an exercise in abstract philosophy but rather an effort to solve pressing, practical problems in the light of a theory of human nature, the lessons of past experience, and a close consideration of how governments in other countries and at other times had worked.

Just because the Constitution is over two hundred years old does not mean that it is out of date. The crucial questions are these: How well has it worked over the long sweep of American history? How well has it worked compared to the constitutions of other democratic nations?

The only way to answer those questions is to study American government closely—with special attention to its historical evolution and to the practices of other nations. That is what this book is about. Of course, even after close study, people will still disagree about whether our system should be changed. People want different things and evaluate human experience according to different beliefs. But if we first understand how, in fact, the government works and why it has produced the policies it has, we can then argue more intelligently about how best to achieve our wants and give expression to our beliefs.

SUMMARY

The Framers of the Constitution sought to create a government capable of protecting both liberty and order. The solution they chose—one without precedent at that time—was a government that was based on a written constitution that combined the principles of popular consent, the separation of powers, and federalism.

Popular consent was embodied in the procedure for choosing the House of Representatives but limited by the indirect election of senators and the Electoral College system for selecting the president. Political authority was to be shared by three branches of government in a manner deliberately intended to produce conflict among these branches. This conflict, motivated by the self-interest of the people occupying each branch, would, it was hoped, prevent tyranny, even by a popular majority.

Federalism came to mean a system in which both the national and state governments had independent authority. Allocating powers between the two levels of government and devising means to ensure that neither large nor small states would dominate the national government required the most delicate compromises at the Philadelphia convention. The decision to do nothing about slavery was another such compromise.

In the drafting of the Constitution and the struggle over its ratification in the states, the positions people took were chiefly determined not by their economic interests but by a variety of factors. Among these were profound differences of opinion over whether the state governments or the national government would be the best protector of personal liberty.

KEY TERMS

unalienable rights   *p. 21*

Articles of Confederation   *p. 23*

Constitutional Convention   *p. 24*

Shays's Rebellion   *p. 25*

The *Federalist* Papers   *p. 28*

Great Compromise   *p. 31*

republic   *p. 32*

judicial review   *p. 33*

federalism   *p. 33*

separation of powers   *p. 34*

checks and balances   *p. 34*

faction   *p. 35*

Federalists   *p. 35*

Antifederalists   *p. 35*

coalition   *p. 37*

writ of habeas corpus   *p. 37*

bill of attainder   *p. 37*

ex post facto law   *p. 37*

bill of rights   *p. 38*

amendment   *p. 44*

line-item veto   *p. 47*

SUGGESTED READINGS

Bailyn, Bernard. *The Ideological Origins of the American Revolution.* Cambridge, Mass.: Harvard University Press, 1967. A brilliant account of how the American colonists formed and justified the idea of independence.

Becker, Carl L. *The Declaration of Independence.* New York: Vintage, 1942. The classic account of the meaning of the Declaration.

Farrand, Max. *The Framing of the Constitution of the United States.* New Haven, Conn.: Yale University Press, 1913. A good, brief account of the Philadelphia convention, by the editor of Madison's notes on the convention.

Federalist papers. By Alexander Hamilton, James Madison, and John Jay. The definitive edition, edited by Jacob E. Cooke, was published in Middletown, Conn., in 1961, by the Wesleyan University Press.

Goldwin, Robert A., and William A. Schambra, eds. *How Capitalistic Is the Constitution?* Washington, D.C.: American Enterprise Institute, 1982. Essays from different viewpoints discussing the relationship between the Constitution and the economic order.

———. *How Democratic Is the Constitution?* Washington, D.C.: American Enterprise Institute, 1980. Collection of essays offering different interpretations of the political meaning of the Constitution.

McDonald, Forrest. *Novus Ordo Seclorum.* Lawrence: University of Kansas Press, 1985. A careful study of the intellectual origins of the Constitution. The Latin title means "New World Order," which is what the Framers hoped they were creating.

Robinson, Donald L., ed. *Reforming American Government.* Boulder, Colo.: Westview Press, 1985. Collection of essays advocating constitutional reform.

Storing, Herbert J. *What the Anti-Federalists Were For.* Chicago: University of Chicago Press, 1981. Close analysis of the political views of those opposed to the ratification of the Constitution.

Wood, Gordon S. *The Creation of the American Republic.* Chapel Hill, N.C.: University of North Carolina Press, 1969. A detailed study of American political thought before the Philadelphia convention.

———. *The Radicalism of the American Revolution.* New York: Alfred P. Knopf, 1992. Magisterial study of the nature and effects of the American Revolution and the relationship between the socially radical revolution and the Constitution.

3

Federalism

- ★ Contrast of federal and unitary systems
- ★ Intent of Founders to disperse power
- ★ "Necessary and proper" clause
- ★ *McCulloch* v. *Maryland*
- ★ Dual federalism
- ★ National supremacy
- ★ Politics of federal grants
- ★ Intergovernmental lobbies
- ★ Block grants and revenue sharing
- ★ Federal aid and federal control
- ★ Mandates and conditions of aid
- ★ Congress: representatives *to* Washington, not *of* Washington
- ★ Increased nationalization

Since the adoption of the Constitution in 1787, the single most persistent source of political conflict has been the relations between the national and state governments. The political conflict over slavery, for example, was intensified because some state governments condoned or supported slavery, while others took action to discourage it. The proponents and opponents of slavery were thus given territorial power centers from which to carry on the dispute. Other issues, such as the regulation of business and the provision of social welfare programs, were in large part fought out, for well over a century, in terms of "national interests" versus "states' rights." While other nations, such as Great Britain, were debating the question of whether the national government *ought* to provide old-age pensions or regulate the railroads, the United States debated a different question—whether the national government *had the right* to do these things. Even after these debates had ended—almost invariably with a decision favorable to the national government—the administration and financing of the programs that resulted have usually involved a large role for the states.

Today an effort is under way to scale back the size and activities of the national government and to shift responsibility for a wide range of domestic programs from Washington to the states. In recent years the effort to devolve onto the states the national government's functions in areas such as welfare, health care, and job training has become known as **devolution**. In the 104th Congress (1994–1996), Republican majorities in the House and Senate made proposals, several of them enacted into law, to accelerate the devolution of national power. Many of these proposals involved giving the states **block grants**—money from the national government for programs in certain general areas that the states can use at their discretion within broad guidelines set by Congress.

In 1908 Woodrow Wilson observed that how we structure the relationship between the national government and the states "is the cardinal question of our constitutional system," a question that cannot be

51

Republican candidates for Congress gather to endorse the Contract with America that promised more devolution.

settled by "one generation, because it is a question of growth, and every successive stage of our political and economic development gives it a new aspect, makes it a new question."[1]

As the nation approaches the twenty-first century, is the American political system in the early stages of a "devolution revolution" that will make the states, not the national government, the dominant force in domestic affairs? Do most Americans support devolution? Why do some leaders hope for this historic change as ardently as others oppose it? What, if any, differences are recently enacted devolution reforms likely to make in who governs and to what ends? Before one can begin to address these questions, it is important to master the basic concepts and understand the political history of federalism.

Governmental Structure

Federalism refers to a political system in which there are local (territorial, regional, provincial, state, or municipal) units of government, as well as a national government, that can make final decisions with respect to at least some governmental activities and whose existence is specially protected.[2] Almost every nation in the world has local units of government of some kind, if for no other reason than to decentralize the administrative burdens of governing. But these governments are not federal unless the local units exist independently of the preferences of the national government and can make decisions on at least some matters without regard to those preferences.

The United States, Canada, Australia, India, Germany, and Switzerland are federal systems, as are a few other nations. France, Great Britain, Italy, and Sweden are not: they are **unitary systems,** because such local governments as they possess can be altered or even abolished by the national government and cannot plausibly claim to have final authority over any significant governmental activities.

The special protection that subnational governments enjoy in a federal system derives in part from the constitution of the country but also from the habits, preferences, and dispositions of the citizens and the actual distribution of political power in society. The constitution of the former Soviet Union in theory created a federal system, as claimed by that country's full name—the Union of Soviet Socialist Republics—but for most of their history, none of these "socialist republics" were in the slightest degree independent of the central government. Were the American Constitution the only guarantee of the independence of the American states, they would long since have become mere administrative subunits of the government in Washington. Their independence results in large measure from the commitment of Americans to the idea of local self-government and from the fact that Congress consists of people who are selected by and responsive to local constituencies.

"The basic political fact of federalism," writes David B. Truman, "is that it creates separate, self-sustaining centers of power, prestige, and profit."[3] Political power is locally acquired by people whose careers depend for the most part on satisfying local interests. As a result, though the national government has come to have vast powers, it exercises many of those powers through state governments. What many of us forget when we think about "the government in Washington" is that it spends much of its money and enforces most of its rules not on citizens directly but on other, local units of government. A large part of the welfare system, all of the interstate highway system, virtually every aspect of programs to improve cities, the largest part of the effort to supply jobs to the unemployed, the entire program to clean up our water, and even much of our military manpower (in the form of the National Guard) are enterprises in which the national government does not govern so much as it seeks, by regulation, grant, plan, argument, and cajolery, to get the states to govern in accordance with nationally defined (though often vaguely defined) goals.

In France welfare, highways, education, the police, and the use of land are all matters that are directed nationally. In the United States highways and some welfare programs are largely state functions (though they make use of federal money), while education, policing, and land-use controls are primarily local (city, county, or special-district) functions.

Federalism: Good or Bad?

A measure of the importance of federalism is the controversy that surrounds it. To some, federalism means allowing states to block action, prevent

On the Evolving Meaning of Federalism

*I*t is customary in textbooks to distinguish among three forms of government—the unitary, the federal, and the confederal—and to claim that the United States is an instance of the federal form.

These three terms describe different places in which political sovereignty can be located. **Sovereignty** means supreme or ultimate political authority: a sovereign government is one that is legally and politically independent of any other government. A unitary system is one in which sovereignty is wholly in the hands of the national government, so that the states and localities are dependent on its will. A **confederation** or **confederal system** is one in which the states are sovereign and the national government is allowed to do only that which the states permit. A **federal system** is one in which sovereignty is shared, so that on some matters the national government is supreme and on others the states are supreme.

These definitions, though neat and systematic, do not correspond either to the intentions of the Founders or to the realities of American politics. The Founders at the Philadelphia convention, and later in the *Federalist* papers, did not make precise distinctions among these three kinds of governments. Indeed, there is some evidence that they took *confederal* and *federal* to mean much the same thing. Nor did they establish a government in which there was a clear and systematic division of sovereign authority between the national and state governments. They created something quite new—a government that combined some characteristics of a unitary regime with some of a confederal one.

In this text little is made of the conventional definitions and distinctions. Instead a federal regime is defined in the simplest possible terms—as one in which local units of government have a specially protected existence and can make some final decisions over some governmental activities. Where "sovereignty" is located is a matter that the Founders did not clearly answer, and no one else has been able to answer since.

progress, upset national plans, protect powerful local interests, and cater to the self-interest of hack politicians. Harold Laski, a British observer, described American states as "parasitic and poisonous,"[4] and William H. Riker, an American political

Federalism has permitted experimentation. Women were able to vote in the Wyoming territory in 1888, long before they could do so in most states.

litical power is widely available (as among the fifty states, three thousand counties, and many thousands of municipalities in the United States), it is obvious that in different places different people will make use of that power for different purposes. There is no question that allowing states and cities to make autonomous, binding political decisions will allow some people in some places to make those decisions in ways that maintain racial segregation, protect vested interests, and facilitate corruption. It is equally true, however, that this arrangement also enables other people in other places to pass laws that attack segregation, regulate harmful economic practices, and purify politics, often long before these ideas gain national support or become national policy.

For example, in a unitary political system, such as that of France, a small but intensely motivated group could not have blocked civil rights legislation for as long as some southern senators blocked it in this country. But by the same token it would have been equally difficult for another small but intensely motivated group to block plans to operate a nuclear power plant in their neighborhood, as citizens have done in this country but not in France. An even more dramatic illustration involved the efforts of citizens in England, France, and the United States to prevent the Concorde supersonic transport from landing at airports near certain populated areas. Such groups had no success in England or France, where the national government alone makes these decisions. But they enjoyed considerable (albeit temporary) success in the United States, where they were able to persuade the New York Port Authority to deny landing rights to the Concorde. British and French officials were incredulous that such matters could be decided by local authorities. (Eventually the courts ruled that these restrictions had to be lifted.)

The existence of independent state and local governments means that different political groups pursuing different political purposes will come to power in different places. (While groups opposed to the Concorde had the most influence in New York, those welcoming it were most influential in Dallas.) The smaller the political unit, the more likely it is to be dominated by a single political faction. James Madison understood this fact perfectly and used it to argue (in *Federalist* No. 10) that it would be in a large (or "extended") republic, such as the United

scientist, argued that "the main effect of federalism since the Civil War has been to perpetuate racism."[5] By contrast another political scientist, Daniel J. Elazar, believes that the "virtue of the federal system lies in its ability to develop and maintain mechanisms vital to the perpetuation of the unique combination of governmental strength, political flexibility, and individual liberty, which has been the central concern of American politics."[6]

So diametrically opposed are the Riker and the Elazar views that one wonders whether they are talking about the same subject. They are, of course, but they are stressing different aspects of the same phenomenon. Whenever the opportunity to exercise po-

Critical Thinking

Federalism American-Style: Should Who Gets What Depend on Where?

Ronald A. Harmelin learned about federalism the hard way. On June 27, 1991, the U.S. Supreme Court ruled 5 to 4 that the life-without-parole prison sentence imposed on him by the state of Michigan did not violate the Constitution. In 1978 Michigan adopted a law requiring a mandatory life sentence for persons convicted of possessing more than 650 grams (about one and one-half pounds) of cocaine. Mr. Harmelin had 672.5 grams of cocaine in the trunk of his car when the police stopped him for running a red light. When he was convicted in 1986, Michigan was the only state to impose a mandatory life sentence for the possession of this amount of cocaine. For the same crime under the federal sentencing guidelines he would have received about ten years. In Alabama and some other states he would have received only about five years.

Politics, argued the political scientist Harold Lasswell, is about deciding "who gets what." In a federal system, many decisions about who gets what depend on who lives where. Criminal justice furnishes some of the most dramatic examples: a conviction for first-degree murder in some states means the death penalty, but a conviction for the same crime in other states normally means only ten years (or fewer) behind bars.

Criminal justice is not the only area in which who gets what depends on who lives where. States differ widely in the benefits they pay to persons on public assistance, the degree to which they restrict minors' access to abortion, the extent to which they regulate corporations in the name of environmental protection, the restrictions (if any) they place upon parents wishing to legally educate their children at home (through "home-schooling" ordinances), and much more.

Federalism permits intrastate as well as interstate differences both in where certain laws are applied and in per capita spending on public services. For example, in 1996 Pennsylvania and Tennessee were two of twenty-seven states that permitted citizens who meet certain basic requirements to carry firearms. But while Tennessee's "right-to-carry" permit program applied statewide, Pennsylvania's did not extend to persons in big cities such as Philadelphia.

Likewise, a study by the Congressional Research Service documented big intrastate gaps in public school expenditures. In at least ten states the average annual expenditures per pupil in the ten wealthiest school districts were twice or more the expenditures of the ten poorest school districts. For example, in New York the ten wealthiest school districts spent an annual average of about ten thousand dollars per student while the ten poorest spent barely four thousand dollars per student. Similarly, average an-nual spending per pupil in Texas ranges from about twenty-seven hundred dollars in some school districts to nearly ten thousand dollars in others.

Much else depends on the state and local government under which you happen to live or under whose jurisdiction you happen to be passing: whether you can legally drive faster than fifty-five miles per hour on designated highways without risking a speeding ticket, whether you can purchase a bottle of beer at a neighborhood restaurant or have to go dry, whether you can get divorced quickly or have to show grounds, and whether your property taxes are light or heavy.

Other countries that have federal systems limit the extent of such differences more than we do in the United States. What criteria should be used in deciding which matters of public law and policy are allowed to vary, and to what degree, among and between states and localities? Who should decide? Congress? Federal and state judges? Governors? State legislatures? City officials? Trying to answer such questions is one way to begin to come to grips with the pros and cons of federalism American-style.

SOURCES: *Governing* (April 1993): 23; Jill Zuckerman, "The Next Education Crisis," *Congressional Quarterly Weekly* (March 27, 1993): 749–754; Linda Greenhouse, "Mandatory Life Term Is Upheld in Drug Cases," *New York Times* (June 28, 1991).

States as a whole, that one would find the greatest opportunity for all relevant interests to be heard. When William Riker condemns federalism, he is thinking of the fact that in some places the ruling factions in cities and states have opposed granting equal rights to blacks. When Daniel Elazar praises federalism, he is recalling that, in other states and cities, the ruling factions have taken the lead (long in advance of the federal government) in developing measures to protect the environment, extend civil rights, and improve social conditions. If you live in California, whether you like federalism depends in part on whether you like the fact that California has, independent of the federal government, cut property taxes, strictly controlled coastal land use, heav-

ily regulated electric utilities, and increased (at one time) and decreased (at another time) its welfare rolls.

Increased Political Activity

Federalism has many effects, but its most obvious effect has been to facilitate the mobilization of political activity. Unlike Don Quixote, the average citizen does not tilt at windmills. He or she is more likely to become involved in organized political activity if he or she feels there is a reasonable chance of having a practical effect. The chances of having such an effect are greater where there are many elected officials and independent governmental bodies, each with a relatively small constituency, than where there are few elected officials, most of whom have the nation as a whole for a constituency. In short a federal system, by virtue of the decentralization of authority, lowers the cost of organized political activity; a unitary system, because of the centralization of authority, raises the cost. We may disagree about the purposes of organized political activity, but the fact of widespread organized activity can scarcely be doubted—or if it can be doubted, it is only because you have not yet read Chapters 6 and 9.

It is impossible to say whether the Founders, when they wrote the Constitution, planned to produce such widespread opportunities for political participation. Unfortunately they were not very clear (at least in writing) about how the federal system was supposed to work, and thus most of the interesting questions about the jurisdiction and powers of our national and state governments had to be settled by a century and a half of protracted, often bitter, conflict.

FIGURE 3.1 Lines of Power in Three Systems of Government

UNITARY SYSTEM

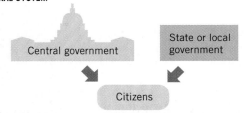

Power centralized.
State or regional governments derive authority from central government.
Examples: United Kingdom, France.

FEDERAL SYSTEM

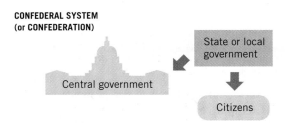

Power divided between central and state or local governments.
Both the government and constituent governments act directly upon the citizens.
Both must agree to constitutional change.
Examples: Canada, United States since adoption of Constitution.

CONFEDERAL SYSTEM
(or CONFEDERATION)

Power held by independent states.
Central government is a creature of the constituent governments.
Example: United States under the Articles of Confederation.

The Founding

The goal of the Founders seems clear: federalism was one device whereby personal liberty was to be protected. (The separation of powers was another.) They feared that placing final political authority in any one set of hands, even in the hands of persons popularly elected, would so concentrate power as to risk tyranny. But they had seen what happened when independent states tried to form a compact, as under the Articles of Confederation; what the states

The States and the Constitution

The Framers made some attempt to define the relations between the states and the federal government and how states were to relate to one another. The following points were made in the original Constitution—before the Bill of Rights was added.

RESTRICTIONS ON POWERS OF THE STATES

States may not make treaties with foreign nations, coin money, issue paper currency, grant titles of nobility, pass a bill of attainder or an ex post facto law,* or, without the consent of Congress, levy any taxes on imports or exports, keep troops and ships in time of peace, or enter into an agreement with another state or with a foreign power.

[Art. I, sec. 10]

GUARANTEES BY THE FEDERAL GOVERNMENT TO THE STATES

The national government guarantees to every state a "republican form of government" and protection against foreign invasion and (provided the states request it) protection against domestic insurrection.   [Art. IV, sec. 4]

An existing state will not be broken up into two or more states or merged with all or part of another state without that state's consent.   [Art. IV, sec. 3]

* For definitions of *bill of attainder* and *ex post facto law,* see the Glossary.

Congress may admit new states into the Union.

[Art. IV, sec. 3]

Taxes levied by Congress must be uniform throughout the United States: they may not be levied on some states but not others.   [Art. I, sec. 8]

The Constitution may not be amended to give states unequal representation in the Senate.   [Art. V]

RULES GOVERNING HOW STATES DEAL WITH EACH OTHER

"Full faith and credit" shall be given by each state to the laws, records, and court decisions of other states. (For example, a civil case settled in the courts of one state cannot be retried in the courts of another.)   [Art. IV, sec. 1]

The citizens of each state shall have the "privileges and immunities" of the citizens of every other state. (No one is quite sure what this is supposed to mean.)   [Art. IV, sec. 2]

If a person charged with a crime by one state flees to another, he or she is subjected to extradition—that is, the governor of the state that finds the fugitive is supposed to return the person to the governor of the state that wants him or her.   [Art. IV, sec. 2]

---

put together, they could also take apart. The alliance among the states that existed from 1776 to 1787 was a confederation: that is, a system of government in which the people create state governments, which, in turn, create and operate a national government (see Figure 3.1). Since the national government in a confederation derives its powers from the states, it is dependent on their continued cooperation for its survival. By 1786 that cooperation was barely forthcoming.

A Bold, New Plan

A federation—or a "federal republic," as the Founders called it—derives its powers directly from the people, as do the state governments. As the Founders envisioned it, both levels of government, the national and the state, would have certain powers, but neither would have supreme authority over the other. Madison, writing in *Federalist* No. 46, said that both the state and federal governments "are in fact but different agents and trustees of the people, constituted with different powers." In *Federalist* No. 28 Hamilton explained how he thought the system would work: the people could shift their support between state and federal levels of government as needed to keep the two in balance. "If their rights are invaded by either, they can make use of the other as the instrument of redress."

It was an entirely new plan, for which no historical precedent existed. Nobody came to the Philadelphia convention with a clear idea of what a federal (as opposed to a unitary or a confederal) system would look like, and there was not much discussion at Philadelphia of how the system would work in practice. Few delegates then used the word *federalism* in the sense in which we now employ it (it was originally used as a synonym for *confederation* and only later came to stand for something different).[7] The Constitution does not spell out the powers that the states are to have, and until the Tenth Amendment was added at the insistence of various states, there was not even a clause in it saying (as did the amendment) that "the powers not delegated to the United States by the Constitution, nor prohibited by it to the states, are reserved to the states respectively, or to the people." The Founders assumed from the outset that the federal government would have only those powers given to it by the Constitution; the Tenth Amendment was an afterthought, added to make that assumption explicit and allay fears that something else was intended.[8]

The Tenth Amendment has rarely had much practical significance, however. From time to time the Supreme Court has tried to interpret that amendment as putting certain state activities beyond the reach of the federal government, but invariably the Court has later changed its mind and allowed Washington to regulate such matters as the hours that employees of a city-owned mass-transit system may work. The Court did not find that running such a transportation system was one of the powers "reserved to the states."[9]

Elastic Language

The need to reconcile the competing interests of large and small states and of northern and southern states, especially as they affected the organization of Congress, was sufficiently difficult without trying to spell out exactly what relationship ought to exist between the national and state systems. For example, Congress was given the power to regulate commerce "among the several states." The Philadelphia convention would have gone on for four years rather than four months if the Founders had decided that it was necessary to describe, in clear language, how one was to tell where commerce *among* the states ended and commerce wholly *within* a single state began. The Supreme Court, as we shall see, devoted over a century to that task before giving up.

Though some clauses bearing on federal-state relations were reasonably clear (see the accompanying box), other clauses were quite vague. The Founders knew, correctly, that they could not make an exact and exhaustive list of everything the federal government was empowered to do—circumstances would change, new exigencies would arise. Thus they added the following elastic language to Article I: Congress shall have the power to "make all laws which shall be necessary and proper for carrying into execution the foregoing powers."

The Founders themselves carried away from Philadelphia different views of what federalism meant. One view was championed by Hamilton. Since the people had created the national government, since the laws and treaties made pursuant to the Constitution were "the supreme law of the land" (Article VI), and since the most pressing needs were the development of a national economy and the conduct of foreign affairs, Hamilton thought that the national government was the superior and leading force in political affairs and that its powers ought to be broadly defined and liberally construed.

The other view, championed by Jefferson, was that the federal government, though important, was the product of an agreement among the states; and though "the people" were the ultimate sovereigns, the principal threat to their liberties was likely to come from the national government. (Madison, a strong supporter of national supremacy at the convention, later became a champion of states' rights.) Thus the powers of the federal government should be narrowly construed and strictly limited. As Madison put it in *Federalist* No. 45, in language that probably made Hamilton wince, "The powers delegated by the proposed Constitution to the federal government are few and defined. Those which are to remain in the State governments are numerous and indefinite."

Hamilton argued for national supremacy, Jefferson for states' rights. Though their differences were greater in theory than in practice (as we shall see in Chapter 12, Jefferson while president sometimes acted in a positively Hamiltonian manner), the differing interpretations they offered of the Constitution were to shape political debate in this country until well into the 1960s.

The Debate on the Meaning of Federalism

The Civil War was fought, in part, over the issue of national supremacy versus states' rights, but it settled only one part of that argument—namely, that the national government was supreme, its sovereignty derived directly from the people, and thus the states could not lawfully secede from the Union. Virtually every other aspect of the national-supremacy issue continued to animate political and legal debate for another century.

The Supreme Court Speaks

As arbiter of what the Constitution means, the Supreme Court became the focal point of that debate. In Chapter 14 we shall see in some detail how the Court made its decisions. For now it is enough to know that during the formative years of the new Republic, the Supreme Court was led by a staunch and brilliant advocate of the Hamilton position, Chief Justice John Marshall. In a series of decisions he and the Court powerfully defended the national-supremacy view of the newly formed federal government.

The most important decision was in a case, seemingly trivial in its origins, that arose when James McCulloch, the cashier of the Baltimore branch of the Bank of the United States, which had been created by Congress, refused to pay a tax levied on that bank by the state of Maryland. He was hauled into state court and convicted of failing to pay a tax. In 1819 McCulloch appealed all the way to the Supreme Court in a case known as *McCulloch* v. *Maryland.*

Thomas Jefferson (1743–1826) was not at the Constitutional Convention. His doubts about the new national government led him to oppose the Federalist administration of John Adams and to become an ardent champion of states' rights.

The Court, in a unanimous opinion, answered two questions in ways that expanded the powers of Congress and confirmed the supremacy of the federal government in the exercise of those powers.

The first question was whether Congress had the right to set up a bank, or any other corporation, since such a right is nowhere explicitly mentioned in the Constitution. Marshall said that, though the federal government possessed only those powers enumerated in the Constitution, the "extent"—that is, the meaning—of those powers required interpretation. Though the word *bank* is not in that document, one finds there the power to manage money: to lay and collect taxes, issue a currency, and borrow funds. To carry out these powers Congress may reasonably decide that chartering a national bank is "necessary and proper." Marshall's words were carefully chosen to endow the **"necessary and proper" clause** with the widest possible sweep:

> *Let the end be legitimate, let it be within the scope of the Constitution, and all means which are appropriate, which are plainly adapted to that end, which are not prohibited, but consistent with the letter and spirit of the Constitution, are constitutional.*[10]

The second question was whether a federal bank could lawfully be taxed by a state. To answer it, Marshall went back to first principles. The government of the United States was not established by the states, but by the people, and thus the federal government was supreme in the exercise of those powers conferred upon it. Having already concluded that chartering a bank was within the powers of Congress, Marshall then argued that the only way for such powers to be supreme was for their use to be immune from state challenge and for the products of their use to be protected against state destruction. Since "the power to tax involves the power to destroy," and since the power to destroy a federal agency would confer upon the states using it supremacy over the federal government, the states may not tax any federal instrument. Hence the Maryland law was unconstitutional.

McCulloch won, and so did the federal government. Half a century later, the Court decided that what was sauce for the goose was sauce for the gander. It held that, just as state governments could not tax federal bonds, the federal government could not tax the interest people earn on state and municipal bonds. In 1988 the Supreme Court changed its mind and decided that Congress was now free, if it wished, to tax the interest on such state and local bonds. Municipal bonds, which for nearly a century were a tax-exempt investment protected, so their holders thought, by the Constitution, were now protected only by politics. So far Congress hasn't wanted to tax them.[11]

Nullification

The Supreme Court can decide a case without settling the issue. The struggle over states' rights versus national supremacy continued to rage in Congress, during presidential elections, and ultimately on the battlefield. The issue came to center on the doctrine of **nullification.** When Congress passed laws (in 1798) to punish newspaper editors who published stories critical of the federal government, James Madison and Thomas Jefferson opposed the laws, suggesting (in statements known as the Virginia and Kentucky Resolutions) that the states had the right to "nullify" (that is, declare null and void) a federal law that, in the states' opinion, violated the Constitution. The laws expired before the claim of nullification could be settled in the courts.

Later the doctrine of nullification was revived by John C. Calhoun of South Carolina, first in opposition to a tariff enacted by the federal government

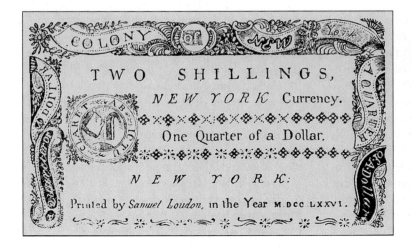

At one time the states could issue their own paper money, such as this New York currency worth 25 cents in 1776. Under the Constitution this power was reserved to Congress.

and later in opposition to federal efforts to restrict slavery. Calhoun argued that if Washington attempted to ban slavery, the states had the right to declare such acts unconstitutional and thus null and void. This time, the issue was settled—by war. The northern victory in the Civil War determined once and for all that the federal union is indissoluble and that states cannot declare acts of Congress unconstitutional, a view later confirmed by the Supreme Court.[12]

Dual Federalism

After the Civil War the debate about the meaning of federalism focused on the interpretation of the commerce clause of the Constitution. Out of this debate there emerged the doctrine of **dual federalism,** which held that though the national government was supreme in its sphere, the states were equally supreme in theirs, and that these two spheres of action should and could be kept separate. Applied to commerce, the concept of dual federalism implied that there was such a thing as *inter*state commerce, which Congress could regulate, and *intra*state commerce, which only the states could regulate, and that the Court could tell which was which.

For a long period the Court tried to decide what was interstate commerce based on the kind of business that was being conducted. Transporting things between states was obviously interstate commerce, and so subject to federal regulation. Thus federal laws affecting the interstate shipment of lottery tickets,[13] prostitutes,[14] liquor,[15] and harmful foods and drugs[16] were upheld. On the other hand, manufacturing,[17] insurance,[18] and farming[19] were in the past considered *intra*state commerce, and so only the state governments were allowed to regulate them.

Such product-based distinctions turned out to be hard to sustain. For example, if you ship a case of whiskey from Kentucky to Kansas, how long is it in interstate commerce (and thus subject to federal law), and when does it enter intrastate commerce and become subject only to state law? For a while the Court's answer was that the whiskey was in interstate commerce so long as it was in its "original package,"[20] but that only precipitated long quarrels as to what was the original package, and how one is to treat things, like gas and grain, that may not be shipped in packages at all. And how could one distinguish between manufacturing and transportation when one company did both or when a single manufacturing corporation owned factories in different states? And if an insurance company sold policies to customers both inside and outside a given state, were there to be different laws regulating identical policies that happened to be purchased from the same company by persons in different states?

In time the effort to find some clear principles that distinguished interstate from intrastate commerce was pretty much abandoned. Commerce was like a stream flowing through the country, drawing to itself contributions from thousands of scattered enterprises and depositing its products in millions of individual homes. The Court began to permit the federal government to regulate almost anything that affected this stream, so that by the 1940s not only had farming and manufacturing been redefined as part of interstate commerce,[21] but even the janitors and window washers in buildings that housed companies engaged in interstate commerce were now said to be part of that stream.[22]

The current Court interpretation of various laws pertaining to commerce is immensely complex, difficult to summarize, and impossible to explain. (For example, lawyers are said to engage in interstate commerce but professional baseball players are not, so that federal antitrust laws affect the former but not the latter.)[23] It would be only a mild overstatement, however, to say that the doctrine of dual federalism is virtually extinct and that, provided it has a good reason for wanting to do so, Congress can pass a law that will regulate constitutionally almost any kind of economic activity anywhere in the country.

Federal-State Relations

Though constitutionally the federal government may be supreme, politically it must take into account the fact that the laws it passes have to be approved by members of Congress selected from, and responsive to, state and local constituencies. Thus what Washington lawfully may do is not the same thing as what it politically may wish to do. For example, in 1947 the Supreme Court decided that the federal government and not the states had supreme authority over

Thinking   *The Tenth Amendment: Sleeping Giant?*

The Tenth Amendment to the Constitution reads, "The powers not delegated to the United States by the Constitution, nor prohibited by it to the States, are reserved to the States respectively, or to the people."

In the one hundred years after Chief Justice John Marshall left the Court in 1835, the Tenth Amendment was frequently invoked by proponents of states' rights to limit powers expressly granted to Congress, including the powers to regulate interstate commerce, to enforce the equal-protection clause of the Fourteenth Amendment, and to impose and collect taxes. But after the late 1930s and President Franklin D. Roosevelt's New Deal, the Tenth Amendment was virtually forgotten. In 1993, the U.S. Advisory Commission on Intergovernmental Relations declared that a series of U.S. Supreme Court decisions stretching into the 1980s had "reduced the status of the states to that of 'interest groups' operating and competing in the national political process."

But in the 1992 case *New York* v. *United States*, the Court struck down a federal law that required the states to regulate low-level radioactive waste produced within their borders, holding that the law infringed on state sovereignty: "States are not mere political subdivisions of the United States." Likewise, in the 1995 case *United States* v. *Lopez*, the Court invalidated the 1990 Gun-Free School Zones Act. The Court ruled that making it a federal crime to carry a gun within one thousand feet of a school

could not be justified as a rational extension of congressional authority to regulate interstate economic activity, for the statute "would convert congressional authority under the commerce clause to a general police power of the sort retained by the states." In 1997, the Court refused to allow Congress, in the Brady bill, to require local law enforcement officers to do background checks on people trying to buy guns (*Printz* v. *United States*).

Moreover, in recent years a number of state leaders have asserted Tenth Amendment rights. For example, after the 1994 elections, thirty of the nation's Republican governors met and signed "The Williamsburg Resolve," drafted by Governor George Allen of Virginia: "Here and in other colonial capitals, the nation's founders first debated the idea of independence and the fundamental principles of freedom. . . . Chief among [the checks and balances the founders established] were to be the State governments, whose co-equal role was expressly acknowledged in the Tenth Amendment to the Constitution." And in 1995 Colorado legislators passed this joint resolution: "The state of Colorado hereby claims sovereignty under the Tenth Amendment to the Constitution of the United States over all other powers not otherwise enumerated and granted to the federal government by the United States Constitution, including at least sovereignty over its people and its natural resources."

Clearly, the Tenth Amendment is no longer a political sleeper, but is it a sleep-

ing giant? How, if at all, might renewed interest in its twenty-eight words change the course of federal-state relations? If the doctrine of nullification (states' declaring acts of Congress unconstitutional) is null and void, then what do champions of the Tenth Amendment mean by "state sovereignty" and the states' "co-equal role"? How, if at all, might adherence to the Tenth Amendment narrow the scope of congressional power to regulate interstate commerce and thereby revive the doctrine of dual federalism (the idea that the national government and the states are each supreme in their respective spheres)? Is there any activity you can think of that does not somehow involve "interstate commerce"? Getting dressed in the morning—in a shirt made in China and shipped from outside the state? Buying a watch in one state—containing parts made in another?

Find out whether the Tenth Amendment has been debated by leaders in your home state. What arguments have they made about it, and which points, pro and con, do you find most persuasive?

SOURCES: Edward S. Corwin, *The Constitution and What It Means Today* (Princeton, NJ: Princeton University Press, 1978), p. 443; *Federal Regulation of State and Local Governments* (U.S. Advisory Commission on Intergovernmental Relations, July 1993), p. 7; Linda Greenhouse, "Blowing the Dust Off the Constitution That Was," *New York Times*, May 28, 1995, sec. 4, pp. 1, 6; W. John Moore, "A Landmark Decision? Maybe Not," *National Journal*, May 6, 1995, p. 1131; *The American Enterprise*, March/April 1995, p. 30.

oil beneath the ocean off the nation's coasts.[24] Six years later, after an intense debate, Congress passed and the president signed a law transferring title to these tidelands oil reserves back to the states.

Grants-in-Aid

The best illustration of how political realities modify legal authority can be found in federal **grants-in-aid.** The first of these programs began even before the Constitution was adopted, in the form of land grants made by the national government to the states in order to finance education. (State universities all over the country were built with the proceeds from the sale of these land grants; hence the name *land-grant colleges.*) Land grants were also made to support the building of wagon roads, canals, railroads, and flood-control projects. These measures were hotly debated in Congress (President Madison thought some were unconstitutional), even though the use to which the grants were put was left almost entirely to the states.

Cash grants-in-aid began almost as early. In 1808 Congress gave $200,000 to the states to pay for their militias, with the states in charge of the size, deployment, and command of these troops. However, grant-in-aid programs remained few in number and small in price until the twentieth century, when scores of new ones came into being. In 1915 less than $6 million was spent per year in grants-in-aid; by 1925 over $114 million was spent; by 1937 the figure was nearly $300 million.[25] The greatest growth began in the 1960s: between 1960 and 1966 federal grants to the states doubled; from 1966 to 1970 they doubled again; between 1970 and 1975 they doubled yet again. By 1985 they amounted to over $100 billion a year and were spent through more than four hundred separate programs. The five largest programs accounted for over half the money spent and reflected the new priorities that federal policy had come to serve: housing assistance for low-income families, Medicaid, highway construction, services to the unemployed, and welfare programs for mothers with dependent children and for the disabled.

The grant-in-aid system, once under way, grew rapidly because it helped state and local officials resolve a dilemma. On the one hand they wanted

Some of the nation's greatest universities, such as the University of California at Berkeley, began as land-grant colleges.

access to the superior taxing power of the federal government. On the other hand prevailing constitutional interpretation, at least until the late 1930s, held that the federal government could not spend money for purposes not authorized by the Constitution. The solution was obviously to have federal money put into state hands: Washington would pay the bills, the states would run the programs.

There were four reasons why federal money seemed, to state officials, so attractive. First, the money was there. During most of the nineteenth century and the early decades of the twentieth, the federal government was taking in more money than it was spending. The high-tariff policies of the Republicans produced a large budget surplus; in the 1880s Washington literally had more money than it knew what to do with. Some went to pay off a big part of the national debt, some was given to Civil War veterans as a pension, and some went to the states or was otherwise used for internal improvements.[26]

By the mid-twentieth century, when budget surpluses had pretty much become a thing of the past, a second reason for turning to Washington became evident: the federal income tax. Inaugurated in the 1920s, it proved to be a marvelously flexible tool of public finance, for it automatically brought in more money as economic activity (and thus personal income) grew.

Third, the federal government, unlike the states, managed the currency and thus could print more money whenever it needed it. (Technically it borrowed this money, and of course it paid interest on what it had borrowed, but it was under no obligation to pay it all back, because, as a practical matter, it had borrowed from itself.) The size of the federal public debt stayed more or less constant, or even declined, in the second half of the nineteenth century. By the mid-twentieth century people no longer worried about the national debt so much, or at least they worried about it for reasons other than the fear of being in debt. Thus the federal government came to accept, as a matter of policy, the proposition that when it needed money, it would print it. States could not do this: if they borrowed (and many could not), they had to pay it all back, in full.

These three economic reasons for the attractiveness of federal grants were probably not as important as a fourth reason: politics. Federal money seemed to a state official to be "free" money. If Alabama could get Washington to put up the money for improving navigation on the Tombigbee River, the citizens of the entire nation, not just those of Alabama, would pay for it. Of course, if Alabama gets money for that purpose, every state will want it (and will get it). Even so, it was still an attractive political proposition: the governor of Alabama did not have to propose, collect, or take responsibility for federal taxes. Indeed, the governor could denounce the federal government for being profligate in its use of the people's money. Meanwhile he would cut the ribbon opening the new dam on the Tombigbee.

That every state had an incentive to ask for federal money to pay for local programs meant, of course, that it would be very difficult for one state to get money for a given program without every state's getting it. The senator from Alabama who votes for the project to improve navigation on the Tombigbee will have to vote in favor of projects improving navigation on every other river in the country if the senator expects his or her Senate colleagues to support such a request. Federalism as practiced in the United States means that when Washington wants to send money to one state or congressional district, it must send money to many states and districts.

In 1966, for example, President Lyndon Johnson proposed a "Model Cities" plan, under which federal funds would be spent on experimental programs in a small number of large cities that had especially acute problems. When the bill went to Congress, it quickly became clear that no such plan could be passed unless the number of cities to benefit was increased. Senator Edmund Muskie of Maine, whose support was crucial, would not vote for a bill that did not make Augusta, Bangor, and Portland eligible for aid originally intended to help New York, Chicago, and Philadelphia.[27]

FIGURE 3.2 The Changing Purposes of Federal Grants to State and Local Governments

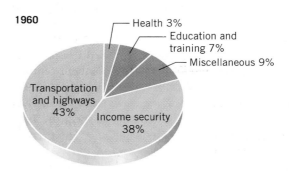

1960

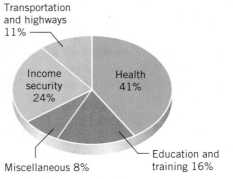

1995

SOURCE: *Budget of the U.S. Government, Fiscal Year 1996*, Table 12.3.

Meeting National Needs

Until the 1960s most federal grants-in-aid were conceived by or in cooperation with the states and were designed to serve essentially state purposes. Large blocs of voters and a variety of organized interests would press for grants to help farmers, build highways, or support vocational education. During the 1960s, however, an important change occurred: the federal government began devising grant programs based less on what states were demanding and more on what federal officials perceived to be important *national* needs (see Figure 3.2). Federal officials, not state and local ones, were the principal proponents of grant programs to aid the urban poor, combat crime, reduce pollution, and deal with drug abuse. Some of these programs even attempted to bypass the states, providing money directly to cities or even to local citizen groups. These were worrisome developments for governors, who were accustomed to being the conduit for money on its way from Washington to local communities.

TABLE 3.1 Federal Aid to State and Local Governments, 1955–1995

Year	Total Federal Aid (in billions)[a]	Federal Aid as a Percentage of	
		Federal Outlays	State and Local Outlays
1955	$15.1	4.7%	10.1%
1960	29.1	7.6	14.7
1965	41.8	9.2	15.3
1970	73.6	12.3	19.2
1975	105.4	15.0	23.0
1980	127.6	15.5	26.3
1985	113.0	11.2	21.0
1990	119.7	10.8	20.0
1995	175.3 (est.)	15.3 (est.)	NA

[a] In constant 1987 dollars.

SOURCE: Total aid figures, percentages of federal outlays, and 1995 estimates from *Budget of the U.S. Government, Fiscal Year 1993*, Table 12.1, part 5, 164–165. Percentages of state and local outlays 1955–1985 from *Budget of the U.S. Government, Fiscal Year 1991*, Table 12.1, A-321. Percentage of state and local outlays in 1990 from *Budget of the U.S. Government, Fiscal Year 1994*, 79.

FIGURE 3.3 Federal Aid to State and Local Governments, 1980–1994

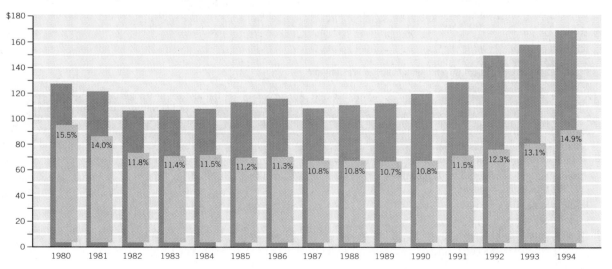

Total federal aid to state and local governments, in billions of constant 1987 dollars, and the aid as a percentage of total federal spending, for each fiscal year.

Total aid (scale at left)

Percentage of federal spending

NOTE: Data for 1992, 1993, and 1994 are estimated.

SOURCE: *Budget of the U.S. Government, Fiscal Year 1991 Supplement*, Table 12.1, 164–165.

The rise in federal activism in setting goals and the efforts, on occasion, to bypass state officials occurred at a time when the total amount of federal aid to states and localities had become so vast that many jurisdictions were completely dependent on it for the support of vital services. Whereas federal aid amounted to less than 2 percent of state and local spending in 1927, by 1970 it amounted to 19 percent and by 1980 to 26 percent (see Table 3.1 and Figure 3.3, page 65). Some older, larger cities had become what one writer called "federal-aid junkies," so dependent were they on these grants. In 1978 in Detroit 77 percent of the revenue the city raised came from Washington.[28]

The Intergovernmental Lobby

State and local officials, both elected and appointed, began to form an important new lobby—the "intergovernmental lobby," made up of mayors, governors, superintendents of schools, state directors of public health, county highway commissioners, local police chiefs, and others who had come to count on federal funds.[29] The five largest of these lobbies employed, in 1990, over four hundred people and spent about $45 million (see Table 3.2), nearly half of which came from the federal government. Even this has proved insufficient. After all, national organiza-

tions of governors or mayors can press for more federal money but not for increased funding for any particular state or city. Thus over thirty-one individual states, more than two dozen counties, and over one hundred cities have opened their own offices in Washington. Some are small, some share staff with other communities, but a few are quite large. Texas alone employs two dozen people in Washington to look after its interests.

The purpose of this intergovernmental lobby was the same as that of any private lobby—to obtain more federal money with fewer strings attached. For a while the cities and states did in fact get more money, but by 1980 federal grants had stopped growing.

Categorical Grants versus Revenue Sharing

The effort to loosen the strings took the form of shifting, as much as possible, the federal aid from **categorical grants** to block grants or to **revenue sharing.** A categorical grant is one for a specific purpose defined by federal law: to build an airport or a college dormitory, for example, or to make welfare payments to low-income mothers. Such grants usually require that the state or locality put up money to "match" some part of the federal grant, though

TABLE 3.2 **State and Local Governments Lobby in Washington**

Organization	Number of Employees 1990	Approximate Budget 1990	Percentage of Budget from Federal Governments	
			1980	1990
National Governors' Association (55 state and territorial governors)	100	$10 million	42%	33%
National Conference of State Legislatures (50 state legislatures)	140	$10 million	36	15
National League of Cities (14,700 cities)	65	$8 million	43	2
U.S. Conference of Mayors (1,000 large cities)	50	$7 million	60	35
National Association of Counties (2,000 counties)	70	$10 million	30	9

SOURCE: Compiled by Xandra Kayden.

Federal aid now supports almost every local government program, including school lunches.

the amount of matching funds can be quite small. (In the federal highway program Washington pays about 90 percent of the construction costs and the states only about 10 percent.) Governors and mayors complained about these categorical grants because their purposes were often so narrow that it was impossible for a state to adapt federal grants to local needs. A mayor seeking federal money to build parks might have discovered that the city could get money only if it launched an urban renewal program that entailed bulldozing several blocks of housing or small businesses.

One response to this problem was to consolidate several categorical or project grant programs into a single block grant devoted to some general purpose and with fewer restrictions on its use. Block grants (sometimes called "special revenue sharing" or "broad-based aid") began in the mid-1960s, when such a grant was created in the health field. Though many block grants were proposed between 1966 and 1980, only five were enacted. Of the three largest, one consolidated various categorical grant programs aimed at cities (Community Development Block Grants); another created a program to aid local law enforcement (Law Enforcement Assistance Act); and a third authorized new kinds of locally managed programs for the unemployed (CETA, or the Comprehensive Employment and Training Act). In 1981 President Reagan persuaded Congress to raise the number of block grants to nine. In 1987 block grants accounted for about 12 percent of all federal aid programs.

Revenue sharing (sometimes called *general revenue sharing,* or *GRS*) was even more permissive. Adopted in 1972 with the passage of the State and Local Fiscal Assistance Act, GRS provided for the distribution of about $6 billion a year in federal funds to the states and localities, with no requirement as to matching funds and freedom to spend the money on almost any governmental purpose. Distribution of the money was determined by a statistical formula that took into account population, local tax effort, and the wealth of the state in a way intended to send more money to poorer, heavily taxed states and less to richer, lightly taxed ones. In 1986 the program was ended after having distributed about $85 billion over a fourteen-year period.

In theory block grants and revenue sharing were supposed to give the states and cities considerable freedom in deciding how to spend the money while helping to relieve their tax burdens. To some extent they did. However, neither the goal of "no strings" nor the one of fiscal relief was really attained. First, the amount of money available from block grants and revenue sharing did not grow as fast as the states had hoped nor as quickly as did the money available through categorical grants. Second, the federal government steadily increased the number of strings attached to the spending of this supposedly "unrestricted" money. Thus, between 1993 and 1995 the number of federal grants to state and local governments increased from 599 to 633. The entire growth was in categorical grants (from 578 to 618); no new block grants were established. In 1995 as in 1975, roughly 85 to 90 percent of total federal grant dollars were in categorical programs.

The Slowdown in "Free" Money

Block grants grew more slowly than categorical grants because of the different kinds of political coalitions supporting each. Congress and the federal bureaucracy liked categorical grants for the same reason the states disliked them—the specificity of these programs enhanced federal control over how the money was to be used. Federal officials, joined by liberal interest groups and organized labor, tended to distrust state governments. Whenever Congress wanted to address some national problem, its natural inclination was to create a categorical grant program so that it, and not the states, would decide how the money would be spent.

Moreover, even though governors and mayors like block grants and revenue sharing, these programs cover such a broad range of activities that no single interest group has a vital stake in pressing for their enlargement. Revenue sharing, for example, provided a little money to many city agencies but rarely provided all or even most of the money for any single agency. Thus no single agency acted as if the expansion of revenue sharing were a life-and-death matter. Categorical grants, on the other hand, are often a matter of life and death for many agencies—state departments of welfare, of highways, and of health, for example, are utterly dependent on federal aid. Accordingly the administrators in charge of these programs will press strenuously for their expansion. Moreover, categorical programs are supervised by special committees of Congress, and as we shall see in Chapter 11, many of these committees have an interest in seeing their programs grow.

As a result of the political differences between categorical grants and block grants or revenue sharing, the amount spent on the former tends to increase faster than the amount spent on the latter. Between 1975 and 1978 the amount spent on revenue sharing increased by 11 percent, but that spent on categorical grants increased by 56 percent.[30] One observer explained: "You dilute the constituency when you make aid more general. Say you had a program to control a disease. You'd get everyone in the country interested in that disease to focus on that one subject, and a congressman to become the champion of it. . . . There just is not that much sympathy to increase revenue sharing."[31] So little support did general revenue sharing have that, in their debate over the 1986 budget, almost the only thing Democrats and Republicans could agree on was abolishing revenue sharing, which they did.

Not only did general revenue sharing lack a constituency, but it was a wasteful way of trying to help poor communities. The waste resulted from the fact that *every* community—some thirty-nine thousand in all—got revenue-sharing money whether it was rich or poor. Paw Paw, West Virginia, a town devastated by a loss of jobs, received only $11,874 from revenue sharing, but that amounted to more than one-third of all the tax money it collected, and was enough to pay the salary of its lone police officer. Beverly Hills, California, a city so affluent and exclusive that, as the joke goes, the police department has an unlisted phone number, also got revenue-sharing money.

Rivalry Among the States

The more important that federal money becomes to the states, the more likely they are to compete among themselves for the largest share of it. For a century or better, the growth of the United States—in population, business, and income—was concentrated in the industrial Northeast. In recent decades, however, that growth—at least in population and employment, if not in income—has shifted to the South, Southwest, and Far West. This change has precipitated an intense debate over whether the federal government, by the way it distributes its funds and awards its contracts, is unfairly helping some regions and states at the expense of others. Journalists and politicians have dubbed the struggle as one between "Snowbelt" (or "Frostbelt") and "Sunbelt" states.

Whether in fact there is anything worth arguing about is far from clear: the federal government has had great difficulty in figuring out where it ultimately spends what funds for what purposes. For example, a $1 billion defense contract may go to a company with headquarters in California, but much of the money may actually be spent in Connecticut or New York, as the prime contractor in California buys from subcontractors in the other states. It is even less clear whether federal funds actually affect the growth rate of the regions. The uncertainty about the facts has not prevented a debate about the issue, however. That debate focuses on the formulas written into federal laws by which block grants are allocated. These formulas take into account such factors as a county's or city's population, personal income in the area, and housing quality. A slight change in a formula can shift millions of dollars in grants in ways that favor either the older, declining cities of the Northeast or the newer, still-growing cities of the Southwest.

With the advent of grants based on distributional formulas (as opposed to grants for a particular project), the results of the census, taken every ten years, assume monumental importance. A city or state shown to be losing population may, as a result, forfeit millions of dollars in federal aid. There are over one hundred programs (out of some five hundred federal grant programs in all) that distribute money on the basis of population. When the director of the census in 1960 announced figures showing that many big cities had lost population, he was generally ignored. When he made the same announcement in 1980, after the explosion in federal grants, he was roundly denounced by the mayors of those cities.

Senators and representatives now have access to computers that can tell them instantly the effect on their states and districts of even minor changes in a formula by which federal aid is distributed. These formulas rely on objective measures, but the exact measure is selected with an eye to its political consequences. There is nothing wrong with this in principle, since any political system must provide some benefits for everybody if it is to stay together. Given the competition among states in a federal system, however, the struggle over allocation formulas becomes especially acute. The results are sometimes plausible, as when Congress decides to distribute money intended to help disadvantaged local school systems in large part on the basis of the proportion of poor children in each school district. But sometimes the results are a bit strange, as when the formula by which federal aid for mass transit is determined gives New York, a city utterly dependent on mass transit, a federal subsidy of two cents per transit passenger but gives Grand Rapids, a city that relies chiefly on the automobile, a subsidy of forty-five cents per passenger.[32]

Federal Aid and Federal Control

So important has federal aid become for state and local governments that mayors and governors, along with others, began to fear that Washington was well on its way to controlling other levels of government. "He who pays the piper calls the tune," they muttered. In this view the constitutional protection of state government to be found in the Tenth Amendment was in jeopardy as a result of the strings being attached to the grants-in-aid on which the states were increasingly dependent.

Block grants and revenue sharing were efforts to reverse this trend by allowing the states and localities freedom (considerable in the case of block grants; almost unlimited in the case of revenue sharing) to spend money as they wished. But as we have seen, these new devices did not in fact reverse the trend. Until 1978 block grants and revenue sharing increased until they amounted to 27 percent of all federal grants to states and localities but then began to decline, so that by 1986 they accounted for only 18 percent of such aid. Categorical grants—those with strings attached—continued to grow even faster.

There are two kinds of federal controls on state governmental activities. The traditional control tells the state government what it must do if it wants to get some grant money. These strings are often called **conditions of aid.** The newer form of control tells the state government what it must do, period. These rules are called **mandates.** Sometimes the mandates

TABLE 3.3	Major Mandate Enactments Regulating State and Local Governments, 1982–1991
1982	Surface Transportation Assistance Act
	Voting Rights Act Amendments
1983	Social Security Amendments
1984	Child Abuse Amendments
	Hazardous and Solid Waste Amendments
	Highway Safety Amendments
	Voting Accessibility for the Elderly and Handicapped Act
1985	Consolidated Omnibus Budget Reconciliation Act
1986	Age Discrimination in Employment Act Amendments
	Asbestos Hazard Emergency Response Act
	Commercial Motor Vehicle Safety Act
	Education of the Handicapped Act Amendments
	Emergency Planning and Community Right-to-Know Act
	Handicapped Children's Protection Act
	Safe Drinking Water Act Amendments
1987	Civil Rights Restoration Act
	Water Quality Act
1988	Drug-Free Workplace Act
	Fair Housing Act Amendments
	Lead Contamination Control Act
	Ocean Dumping Ban Act
1990	Americans with Disabilities Act
	Cash Management Improvement Act
	Clean Air Act Amendments
	Education of the Handicapped Act Amendments
	Older Workers Benefit Protection Act
1991	Social Security Fiscal Budget Reconciliation Act

SOURCE: Adapted from Timothy J. Conlan and David R. Beam, "Federal Mandates: The Record of Reform and Future Prospects," *Intergovernmental Perspective* (Fall 1992): 8.

must be observed only if the state takes any federal grants, but sometimes the mandates have nothing to do with federal aid—they apply to all state governments whether or not they accept grants.

Mandates

Most mandates concern civil rights and environmental protection. States may not discriminate in the operation of their programs, no matter who pays for them. Initially the antidiscrimination rules applied chiefly to distinctions based on race, sex, age, and ethnicity, but of late they have been broadened to include physical and mental disabilities as well. Various pollution-control laws require the states to comply with federal standards for clean air,

pure drinking water, and sewage treatment.[33]

Stated in general terms, these mandates seem reasonable enough. It is hard to imagine anyone arguing that state governments should be free to discriminate against people because of their race or national origin. In practice, however, some mandates create administrative and financial problems, especially when the mandates are written in vague language, thereby giving federal administrative agencies the power to decide for themselves what state and local governments are supposed to do.

In 1980 there were thirty-six mandates affecting state and local governments, twenty-two of them enacted in the 1970s. Both the Reagan administration and the Bush administration opposed the growth of mandates. Nevertheless, between 1981 and 1986 some 140 regulations, representing nearly six thousand new requirements on state and local government, were added to eighteen existing mandates. And between 1982 and 1991 Congress passed twenty-seven additional mandates (see Table 3.3).

All mandates are not created equal. Some mandates take the form of regulatory statutes and amendments that expand on previous legislation; the 1982 Voting Rights Act Amendment was based on federal civil rights laws dating back to the 1960s. Other mandates represent new areas of federal involvement. For example, the 1986 Handicapped Children's Protection Act introduced federal regulations intended to improve the life prospects of disabled youngsters. Some mandates are easy to understand, simple to administer, and relatively inexpensive; for example, the 1988 Ocean Dumping Ban Act, which prohibits any additional dumping of municipal sewage sludge in ocean waters. However, many mandates are hard to interpret, difficult to administer, and have high or uncertain costs. The 1990 Americans with Disabilities Act (ADA), which required businesses and state and local governments to provide the disabled with equal access to services, employment, buildings, and transportation systems, was one of twenty mandates signed into law by President Bush in 1990. Unfortunately the ADA was enacted with no clear-cut definition of "equal access," no unambiguous blueprint of how it was to be administered, and no reliable estimates of how much it would cost to implement.

Republican leaders in the 104th Congress promised to roll back mandates. They took special aim at requirements from Washington that dictate actions by state and local governments without providing the money to carry them out. For example, in 1993 the U.S. Conference of Mayors claimed that it cost 314 cities $6.5 billion to comply with just ten federal laws that contained such "unfunded mandates."[34] In 1995 Congress passed and President Clinton signed a law that directed the Congressional Budget Office to identify any bill, amendment, or conference report that would impose a new mandate of more than $50 million on state and local governments. But the law neither repealed existing unfunded mandates nor prohibited new ones, and it exempted all anti-discrimination legislation.

Mandates are not the only way in which the federal government imposes costs on state and local governments. According to a 1994 study by the U.S. Advisory Commission on Intergovernmental Relations, certain federal tax and regulatory policies make it difficult or expensive for state and local governments to raise revenues, borrow funds, or privatize public functions. Other federal laws expose state and local governments to financial liability, and numerous federal court decisions and administrative regulations require state and local governments to do or not do various things, either by statute or through an implied constitutional obligation.[35]

It is clear that the federal courts have helped fuel the growth of mandates. As interpreted in this century by the United States Supreme Court, the Tenth Amendment provides state and local officials no protection against the march of mandates. Indeed, many of the more controversial mandates result not from congressional action but from court decisions. For example, many state prison systems have been, at one time or another, under the control of federal judges who required major changes in prison construction and management in order to meet standards the judges derived from their reading of the Constitution.

School-desegregation plans are of course the best-known example of federal mandates. Those involving busing—an unpopular policy—have typically been the result of court orders rather than of federal law or regulation.

Judges—usually, but not always, in federal courts—have ordered Massachusetts to change the way it hires fire fighters, required Philadelphia to institute new procedures to handle complaints of police brutality, and altered the location in which Chicago was planning to build housing projects. Note that in most of these cases nobody in Washington was placing a mandate on a local government; rather a local citizen was using the federal courts to change a local practice.

The Supreme Court has made it much easier of late for citizens to control the behavior of local officials. A federal law, passed in the 1870s to protect newly freed slaves, makes it possible for a citizen to sue any state or local official who deprives that citizen of any "rights, privileges, or immunities secured by the Constitution and laws" of the United States.[36] In 1980 the Court decided that this law permitted a citizen to sue a local official if the official deprived the citizen of *anything* to which the citizen was entitled under federal law (and not just those federal laws protecting civil rights).[37] For example, a citizen can now use the federal courts to obtain from a state welfare office a payment to which he or she may be entitled under federal law. No one yet knows how this development will affect the way local government operates.

Conditions of Aid

By far the most important federal restrictions on state action are the conditions attached to the grants the states receive. In theory accepting these conditions is voluntary—if you don't want the strings, don't take the money. But when the typical state depends for a quarter or more of its budget on federal grants, many of which it has received for years and on which many of its citizens depend for their livelihoods, it is not clear exactly how "voluntary" such acceptance is. During the 1960s some strings were added, the most important of which had to do with civil rights. But beginning in the 1970s the number of conditions proliferated. One study of federal grant programs in five large states found that between 1951 and 1978 over a thousand conditions had been added to these programs; nearly 90 percent had been added after 1971.[38]

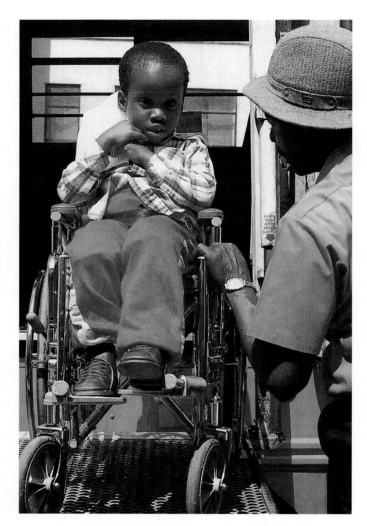

With more federal aid has come more federal control. City transportation systems getting federal money must be accessible to disabled persons.

Some conditions are specific to particular programs. For example, if a state does not establish a highway-beautification program, it will lose 10 percent of its federal highway aid money.[39] Others are general, covering most or all grants. For instance, if a state builds something with federal money, it must first conduct an environmental-impact study, it must pay construction workers the "prevailing wage" in the area, it often must provide an opportunity for citizen participation in some aspects of the design or location of the project, and it must ensure

that the contractors who build the project have nondiscriminatory hiring policies.

The states and the federal government, not surprisingly, disagree about the costs and benefits of such rules. Members of Congress and federal officials feel they have an obligation to develop uniform national policies with respect to important matters and to prevent states and cities from misspending federal tax dollars. State officials, on the other hand, feel these national rules fail to take into account diverse local conditions, require the states to do things that the states must then pay for, and create serious inefficiencies.

The dispute over the best way to make city transit facilities accessible to disabled persons illustrates the difficulty of reconciling national objectives and a decentralized system of government. In 1973 Congress passed the Rehabilitation Act, which forbids discrimination against disabled people in any program receiving federal aid. Since there was virtually no discussion of this provision as the bill moved through Congress, no one was quite certain what it would mean when applied to a city transit system receiving federal money. Narrowly read, the law might mean only that the city could not refuse to hire an otherwise qualified disabled person to work in the transit system. Broadly read, it might mean that the buses and subway cars in the city had to be made physically accessible to disabled persons.

Under pressure from organizations representing the disabled, various federal agencies decided that the law should be given the broader interpretation. Accordingly they issued regulations requiring that city transit systems receiving federal aid equip their buses and subway cars with devices to lift wheelchairs on board.

Disabled people were pleased with these rules, believing that the benefits to them were well worth the cost. State and local officials took a different view. The then mayor of New York City, Edward Koch, argued that rebuilding existing buses and subways and buying new ones would make each trip by a wheelchair user cost thirty-eight dollars. It would be cheaper, he said, for the city to give free taxicab rides to every disabled person, but the federal regulations would not permit that. Billions would be spent by cities for a program to benefit 2 percent of the transit users, deserving though they may be.[40]

(In 1981 the Reagan administration relaxed the requirement that buses be able to lift wheelchairs aboard.)

What local officials discovered, in short, was that "free" federal money was not quite free after all. In the 1960s federal aid seemed to be entirely beneficial; what mayor or governor would not want such money? But just as local officials found it attractive to do things that another level of government then paid for, in time federal officials learned the same thing. Passing laws to meet the concerns of national constituencies—leaving the cities and states to pay the bills and manage the problems—began to seem attractive to Congress.

One's perspective depends on what office one holds, as is revealed by this statement of Mayor Koch, who once had been a congressman from New York:

> As a member of Congress I voted for many of the laws imposing grant conditions, and did so with every confidence that we were enacting sensible permanent solutions to critical problems. It took a plunge into the mayor's job to drive home how misguided my congressional outlook had been. The bills I voted for came to the floor in a form that compelled approval. After all, who can vote against clean air and water or better access and education for the handicapped? But as I look back it is hard to believe I could have been taken in by the simplicity of what the Congress was doing and by the flimsy empirical support . . . offered to persuade the members that the proposed solution would work throughout the country.[41]

As is evident from the mayor's remarks, the tensions in the federal system do not arise from one level of government or another being callous or incompetent, but from the kinds of political demands with which each must cope. Because of these competing demands, federal and local officials find themselves in a bargaining situation in which each side is trying to get some benefit (solving a problem, satisfying a pressure group) while passing on to the other side most of the costs (taxes, administrative problems).

The bargains struck in this process used to favor the local officials, because members of Congress

Federal Mandates: Golf Courses and Alarm Boxes

During the debate on the Americans with Disabilities Act (ADA), no one mentioned golf courses. Nevertheless, the ADA has changed the way that public golf courses are administered. There is an Association of Disabled American Golfers and a National Blind Golfers Association. The March 1993 issue of *Golf Course News* offered the following guidelines to public golf course operators, who must comply with the ADA:

- Reserve one or two handicapped parking spaces near the bag drop rather than next to the clubhouse.
- Cut out spots on raised curbs so carts can pass through.
- Build ramps to tees where possible.
- Provide a spot for disabled golfers to get in and out of the bunker.
- Keep bunker grades no more than one foot of elevation for every five feet of length.
- Install a Telecommunication Device for the Deaf (TDD) in the reservation office so the hearing impaired can make tee-time reservations by phone.

Likewise, no one mentioned alarm boxes during the debate over the ADA. But in 1996 Federal District Court Judge Robert W. Sweet ordered the New York City Fire Department to halt its plan to replace the city's 16,300 antiquated alarm boxes with public telephones wired to an emergency system. Judge Sweet ruled that because deaf and hearing-impaired people may be unable to use the phones to call for help, the plan violated the ADA's guarantee of "equal access to public services." Rather than appeal his ruling, New York Mayor Rudolph W. Giuliani directed city officials to meet with Judge Sweet and try to persuade him that the new phone system was usable by the deaf, who could tap a special fire alarm code over the system.

SOURCES: Joanne Desky, "Park Facilities Meet ADA Challenges: Even Public Golf Course Managers Must Comply," *PA Times*, 16, no. 5 (May 1, 1993): 1, 16; Don Vannatta, Jr., "U.S. Judge Says Removing Alarm Boxes Discriminates Against the Deaf," *New York Times*, February 14, 1996, p. B3.

were essentially servants of local interests: they were elected by local political parties, they were part of local political organizations, and they supported local autonomy. Beginning in the 1960s, however, changes in American politics that will be described

When George McGovern was a senator (left), he voted for many federal regulations
that he later found burdensome when he became an innkeeper in Connecticut (right).

in later chapters—especially the weakening of political parties, the growth of public-interest lobbies in Washington, and the increased activism of the courts—shifted the orientation of many in Congress toward favoring Washington's needs over local needs.

Various presidents have tried to reverse this trend, but with little success. President Nixon proclaimed the "new federalism" and helped create revenue sharing and block grants, but as we shall see, federal mandates and conditions of aid grew rather than declined during his administration.

In 1981 President Reagan asked Congress to consolidate eighty-three categorical grants into six large block grants, none of which would seriously restrict how the states could spend the money. Congress went along in name only—it consolidated fifty-seven programs into nine small block grants, each of which had many restrictions attached. The debate over this plan showed that what is at stake is not simply differing views on how best to "streamline" or make "more efficient" the way in which federal money supports local programs, but rather competing philosophies of governance.

The Reagan administration believed that giving money without strings to the states was good because state governments are generally more conservative than the federal government. The reasons are that state governments must have balanced budgets (and thus cannot spend on social programs by running up deficits) and that liberal interest groups are less influential at the state level than at the national level. The critics of the Reagan view distrusted state governments for the very reason he admired them— they are less responsive to liberal causes. And members of Congress, whether they are liberal or conservative, are exposed to the demands of state officials who wish to have particular federal programs that benefit them protected by "categorization."

In general, the states did not respond to Reagan-era block grants and budget cuts simply by slashing programs. A state-by-state study led by Richard P. Nathan found that "state and local government responses to the 1981 federal aid cuts—through replacement funding, through a wide variety of financial coping and delaying measures, and through administrative reforms"— actually produced "higher service levels than otherwise would have been the case."[41] Likewise, another study concluded that, on balance, the Reagan block grants had promoted greater state flexibility in program design, reduced administrative costs, and necessitated little reduction in services despite the fact that states had to operate with about 13 percent fewer federal dollars.[42]

nomic recession, would slash benefits and services for the poor and push millions of women and children into poverty. Others argued that devolving welfare would free the states to streamline welfare bureaucracies, push millions of able-bodied adults into economic self-sufficiency, and help cure any number of social problems, from family disintegration to teenage pregnancy, that were ostensibly fueled by the existing welfare system.

But how devolved was welfare before 1996, and how much did state welfare benefits and programs vary before the new law was passed? The best one-word answer is "lots." For example, in 1995 the maximum monthly AFDC and food stamp benefit for a family of three ranged from $1,223 in Alaska to $424 in Mississippi. In ten states the benefit was $800 or above, while in thirteen states it was $600 or below. Expenditures for low-income housing and medical coverage also varied greatly, as did the quality and range of state and local welfare-related social services (child care, remedial education, job training).

In fact, "who gets what" on welfare in this country has long depended largely on "who lives where." But should it? Should it be possible under federal law for poor U.S. citizens living in one state to receive much in the way of public cash assistance and services while equally poor U.S. citizens in another state receive less?

Any judgment about devolving welfare, like any judgment about the worth of federalism itself, is fundamentally about important competing values. And very few of us have consistent values. If we favor equal treatment of individuals by government, we will prefer uniform national policies instead of diverse state ones. But if we also favor personal liberty and local diversity, we also will support devolution and be suspicious of Washington.

As you think about devolving welfare, and as you wrestle with other key issues of federalism and public policy, consult the Constitution. You will discover that the Founders did not produce a document that drew clear lines between national and state responsibilities. They left them vague and subject to political determination. Over two hundred years of political history have not clarified them very much or made it possible to devise some "rational" scheme for deciding which government will do what.

If you doubt it, just ask President Clinton. He came to office in 1992 armed with a detailed blueprint for sorting out Washington's proper role. The blueprint listed criminal justice as an area in which "no federal role is justified" and welfare as one in which "federal action is strongly justified." By 1996, however, the president had approved major expansions in the federal role in crime control and signed into law the further devolution of welfare.

104th Congress did not succeed in turning Medicaid into a block grant program. But, as the "Devolving Welfare" feature above explains, they did succeed with AFDC and a number of related programs. And they did put the devolution of Medicaid and other important federal programs squarely on the national political agenda, possibly to stay.

What's Driving Devolution?

The drive for devolution has complex roots, but three reasons stand out: the beliefs of devolution's proponents, the realities of deficit politics, and the views of most citizens. According to R. Kent Weaver, the House Republicans who spearheaded the devolution effort harbored a "deep-seated ideological mistrust of the federal government reinforced by the belief that governments closer to the people were more responsive to popular sentiment, and more likely to constrain the growth of programs that were wasteful and redistributive."[43] At the same time, by 1994 many governors of both parties were convinced that the time had come to let state capitals take the lead in figuring out how best to address social problems and administer public health and welfare programs.

Medicaid versus AFDC

Medicaid is the eight-hundred-pound gorilla of federal-state relations. For example, in 1995 the federal contribution to Medicaid totaled $89 billion—roughly 40 percent of all federal grants to state and local governments and more than six times as much as the federal government spent on Aid to Families with Dependent Children (AFDC). At the state level, Medicaid expenditures rose from about 11 percent of all state spending in 1988 to 20 percent in 1994. Indeed, by 1996 about half of every new dollar of state revenue was being spent on Medicaid. Many leading health policy experts agreed that Washington—in particular, the Health Care Finance Administration (HCFA), the federal agency that oversees and regulates state health care programs—was largely to blame for Medicaid's spiraling costs and administrative inefficiencies. In the 1990s, HCFA granted many states waivers to experiment with new approaches to Medicaid. In 1994, Florida's assistant secretary for Medicaid, Gary Clarke, summarized the case for devolving Medicaid:

> The federal rules on Medicaid are 694 pages long. The federal/state Medicaid manual encompasses six large texts. One chapter alone has been re-vised twelve times [in the last five months]. For every problem, [the federal] government thinks there ought to be a new statute or regulation.

Thus, the case for devolving Medicaid would appear to be at least as compelling as the case for devolving AFDC. Yet the devolution of Medicaid in the 104th Congress ended with waivers, while the devolution of AFDC ended the program and replaced it with a big new welfare block grant (see "Devolving Welfare" on pages 76–77). Why?

One answer is that who governs and to what ends often depends on whose ox is being gored—or whose program is being cut and redesigned.

Take AFDC. In 1992 President Clinton campaigned successfully on a pledge to "end welfare as we know it." In 1994 Republicans won control of Congress after pledging in their "Contract with America" to "discourage illegitimacy and teen pregnancy" by denying increased aid to mothers who have more children while on welfare, denying benefits to mothers under eighteen altogether, requiring welfare recipients to find work within two years, and cutting welfare spending overall. In abolishing AFDC, both the Democratic president and the Republican Congress were responding to polls showing that upwards of 65 percent of Americans supported reducing welfare payments and shifting responsibility for welfare programs to the states.

Moreover, as suggested by the accompanying table, the general public had come to perceive welfare as a perverse, Washington-run system of government hand-outs that had created a permanent and undeserving underclass. Various congressional defenders of AFDC attempted to rebut this perception. For example, they stressed that the program provided cash assistance to 4.2 million single mothers and 9.4 million children, and that most adults who received AFDC for five years or more were poor minority women who did not have a high school education.

Despite its much bigger budgetary drain and much tighter bureaucratic stranglehold on the states, Medicaid was not substantially cut *or* devolved. A key reason is that Medicaid recipients include not just the poor but also the middle-class and elderly Americans who rely on the program for long-term nursing home care. A 1996 study commissioned by the American Association of Retired Persons (AARP), one of the most power-

But deficit politics also played a role. Congressional Republicans sought not only to fund entitlement programs with block grants instead of categorical grants but also to make major cuts in entitlement spending. For example, one of their bills would have reduced Medicaid spending by $163 billion and various welfare entitlements by $175 billion over seven years. In the words of Richard P. Nathan, there is probably no way any big "federal deficit-reduction targets can be met without striking a deal whereby governors get more power in exchange for going along with growth caps on grants-in-aid.

ful lobbying organizations in the country, made clear that "Medicaid performs a substantial safety net function for the middle class as well as for the poor." As we will see in Chapter 6, middle-class and older Americans vote and otherwise participate in political activities more than poor and younger Americans.

Thus during the 1994 congressional elections Medicaid, unlike AFDC, figured only tangentially in the Republicans' "Contract with America." Once in power, Republicans gradually backed off any all-encompassing plans for cutting Medicaid. As R. Kent observed, they feared alienating middle-class voters and appearing "callous in meeting the needs of clientele for whom the public shows substantial sympathy," namely, elderly but not affluent people in nursing homes.

Find out more about Medicaid and AFDC. How, if at all, have the programs overlapped? (Hint: In 1994 about $17 billion in federal dollars and another $13 billion in state spending went to AFDC recipients on Medicaid.) Do you know anyone who has received benefits from either or both programs? How big is the nation's elderly (over age 65) population, and is it growing? Which agencies administer health and other programs for the elderly in your home state? If you represented your district in the House and were running for re-election, how likely do you think you would be to vote "yes" on far-reaching proposals to reduce Medicaid benefits while giving the states autonomy over the program? Why? Finally, how might who governs on Medicaid, and to what ends, change over the next decade or so?

SOURCES: Gary Clarke, as quoted in National Commission on State and Local Public Service, *Frustrated Federalism: Rx for State and Local Health Reform* (Albany, NY: Rockefeller Institute of Government, 1993), p. 27; Joshua M. Weiner et al., *Spending Down on Medicaid* (Washington, D.C.: American Association of Retired Persons, June 1996); R. Kent Weaver, "Deficits and Devolution in the 104th Congress," unpublished draft, Brookings Institution, April 1996, pp. 17, 25, 29.

Percentage saying item is a "very serious" problem	Blacks	Whites
People abuse the system by staying on too long and not trying hard enough to get off.	72%	72%
Welfare is passed on from generation to generation, creating a permanent underclass.	62	68
The system gives people benefits without requiring them to do work in return.	60	66
People cheat and commit fraud to get welfare benefits.	69	62
Welfare encourages teenagers to have kids out of wedlock.	59	61
The system costs taxpayers too much.	55	59
The system does not give people the skills and help they need to get off welfare.	66	53
The system gives out benefits too easily, without making sure applicants deserve them.	50	51

SOURCE: Chart adapted from *The Values We Live By: What Americans Want From Welfare Reform* (New York, NY: Public Agenda Foundation, 1996), p. 40. Reprinted with permission.

Once you put a growth cap on these programs, you have to give the states added flexibility to meet them. Whether you call this a block grant or not does not matter. The result is programs that look and function like block grants."[44]

As Figure 3.4 (page 81) suggests, most Americans favor devolution, at least in principle. But it remains unclear how deep public sentiment in favor of devolution runs when "shifting responsibility to the states" also means cutting specific program benefits. For example, when asked in 1995 which federal programs "should be cut back in order to reduce the fed-

The federal government helps shape the character of cities by giving money to build parts of the federal highway system.

eral budget deficit," most Americans opposed cuts in Medicaid (73 percent), environmental spending (67 percent), unemployment insurance (64 percent), and many other programs. The one main exception was AFDC (only 35 percent opposed cutting it).[45]

Congress and Federalism

It is not yet clear whether the devolution movement will gain momentum, stall, or be reversed. But whatever the movement's fate, the United States will not become a wholly centralized nation. There remains more political and policy diversity in America than one is likely to find in any other large industrialized nation. The reason is not only that state and local governments have retained certain constitutional protections but also that members of Congress continue to think of themselves as the representatives of localities *to* Washington and not as the representatives *of* Washington to the localities. As we shall see in Chapter 11, American politics, even at the national level, remains local in its orientation.

But if this is true, why do these same members of Congress pass laws that create so many problems for, and stimulate so many complaints from, mayors and governors? One reason is that members of Congress represent different constituencies from the same localities. For example, one member of Congress from Los Angeles may think of the city as a collection of businesspeople, homeowners, and taxpayers, while another may think of it as a group of blacks, Hispanics, and nature lovers. If Washington wants to simply send money to Los Angeles, these two representatives could be expected to vote together. But if Washington wants to impose mandates or restrictions on the city, they might very well vote on opposite sides, each voting as his or her constituents would most likely prefer.

Another reason is that the organizations that once linked members of Congress to local groups have eroded. As we shall see in Chapter 7, the political parties, which once allowed many localities to speak with a single voice in Washington, have decayed to the point where most members of Congress now operate as free agents, judging local needs and national moods independently. In the 1960s these needs and moods seemed to require creating new grant programs; in the 1970s they seemed to require voting for new mandates; in the 1980s they seemed to require letting the cities and states alone to experiment with new ways of meeting their needs.

There are exceptions. In some states the parties continue to be strong, to dominate decision making in the state legislatures, and to significantly affect the way their congressional delegation behaves. Democratic members of Congress from Chicago, for example, typically have a common background in party politics and share at least some allegiance to important party leaders.

But these exceptions are becoming fewer and fewer. As a result, when somebody tries to speak "for" a city or state in Washington, that person has

FIGURE 3.4   Devolution in the Polls: The States Over Washington

QUESTION

Which do you favor—concentration of power in the federal government or in the state government?

QUESTION

Would you still favor shifting responsibility for programs from the federal government to state governments if it meant your state taxes would increase to offset a decrease in your federal taxes?

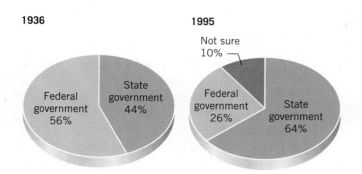

1936

1995

Not sure 10%

Federal government 56%

State government 44%

Federal government 26%

State government 64%

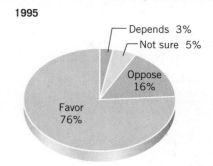

1995

Depends 3%

Not sure 5%

Oppose 16%

Favor 76%

QUESTION

What if some of the tax dollars that go to the federal government now went to your state government instead? Generally speaking, do you think that would result in better government services, or in worse government services, or wouldn't it have much impact on the quality of government services?

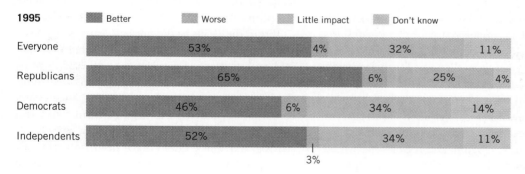

1995   ■ Better   ■ Worse   ■ Little impact   ■ Don't know

	Better	Worse	Little impact	Don't know
Everyone	53%	4%	32%	11%
Republicans	65%	6%	25%	4%
Democrats	46%	6%	34%	14%
Independents	52%	3%	34%	11%

* Asked of those who favored giving states more responsibility (75%). Survey by the Hart and Teeter research Companies for the Council for Excellence in Government, March 16–18, 1995.

SOURCE: Polling results on devolution as compiled by Richard P. Nathan, Director, Rockefeller Institute at SUNY-Albany, with the assistance of the Roper Center for Public Opinion Research at the University of Connecticut. Data for bottom graph: Survey by the *Los Angeles Times,* January 19–22, 1995, as published in *The Public Perspective* (Storrs, CT: The Roper Center for Public Opinion Research, University of CT), April/May 1995, p. 28. © The Public Perspective. Reprinted by permission.

little claim to any real authority. The mayor of Philadelphia may favor one program, the governor of Pennsylvania may favor another, and individual local and state officials—school superintendents, the insurance commissioner, public-health administrators—may favor still others. In bidding for federal aid, those parts of the state or city that are best organized often do the best, and increasingly the best-organized groups are not the political parties but rather specialized occupational groups such as doctors or schoolteachers. If one is to ask, therefore, why a member of Congress does not listen to his or her state anymore, the answer is, "What do you mean by *the state*? Which official, which occupational group, which party leader speaks for the state?"

FIGURE 3.5   From Which Level of Government Do You Feel You Get the Most for Your Money?

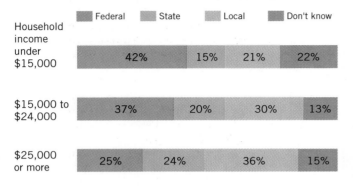

SOURCE: Advisory Commission on Intergovernmental Relations (1982): *Changing Public Attitudes on Governments and Taxes,* as cited in David C. Nice, *Federalism: The Politics of Intergovernmental Relations* (New York: St. Martin's Press, 1987), p. 210.

Finally, Americans differ in the extent to which we like federal as opposed to local decisions. As Figure 3.5 shows, when people are asked which level of government gives them the most for their money, relatively poor citizens are likely to mention the federal government first, whereas relatively well-to-do citizens are more likely to mention local government. If we added to income other measures of social diversity—race, religion, and region—we would probably see even sharper differences of opinion about which level of government works best. It is this social diversity, and the fact that it is represented not only by state and local leaders but also by members of Congress as well, that keeps federalism alive and makes it so important. Americans simply do not agree on enough things, or even on which level of government ought to decide on those things, to make possible a unitary system.

SUMMARY

States participate actively both in determining national policy and in administering national programs. Moreover, they reserve to themselves or the localities within them important powers over public services, such as schooling and law enforcement, and important public decisions, such as land-use control, that in unitary systems are dominated by the national government.

How one evaluates federalism depends in large part on the value one attaches to the competing criteria of equality and participation. Federalism means that citizens living in different parts of the country will be treated differently, not only in spending programs, such as welfare, but in legal systems that assign in different places different penalties to similar offenses or that differentially enforce civil rights laws. But federalism also means that there are more opportunities for participation in making decisions: in influencing what is taught in the schools and in deciding where highways and government projects are to be built. Indeed, differences in public policy—that is, unequal treatment—are in large part the result of participation in decision making. It is difficult, perhaps impossible, to have more of one of these values without having less of the other.

From the 1930s to the present, American politics and public policy became decidedly more nationalized, with the federal government, and especially the federal courts, imposing increasingly uniform standards on the states in the form of both mandates and conditions of aid. Efforts begun in the 1960s and 1970s to reverse this trend by shifting to revenue sharing and block grants have been only partially successful. In the mid-1990s, a political movement to devolve power from Washington to the states gained momentum. But whether this devolution revolution will effect large and lasting changes in federal-state relations remains to be seen.

KEY TERMS

devolution   *p. 51*

block grants   *p. 51*

federalism   *p. 52*

unitary systems   *p. 52*

sovereignty   *p. 53*

confederation or confederal system   *p. 53*

federal system   *p. 53*

"necessary-and-proper" clause   *p. 60*

nullification   *p. 60*

dual federalism   *p. 61*

grants-in-aid   *p. 63*

categorical grants   *p. 66*

revenue sharing   *p. 66*

conditions of aid   *p. 69*

mandates   *p. 69*

SUGGESTED READINGS

Beer, Samuel H. *To Make a Nation: The Rediscovery of American Federalism.* Cambridge, Mass.: Harvard University Press, 1993. The definitive study of the philosophical bases of American federalism.

Diamond, Martin. "The Federalist's View of Federalism." In *Essays in Federalism,* edited by George C. S. Benson. Claremont, Calif.: Institute for Studies in Federalism of Claremont Men's College, 1961, 21–64. A profound analysis of what the Founders meant by federalism.

Elazar, Daniel J. *American Federalism: A View from the States.* 2d ed. New York: Crowell, 1972. A sympathetic analysis of historical development and present nature of American federalism.

Grodzins, Morton. *The American System.* Chicago: Rand McNally, 1966. Argues that American federalism has always involved extensive sharing of functions between national and state governments.

Melnick, R. Shep. *Between the Lines: Interpreting Welfare Rights.* Washington, D.C.: Brookings Institution, 1994. An examination of how trends in statutory interpretation have affected broader policy developments, including the expansion of the agenda of national government, the persistence of divided government, and the resurgence and decentralization of Congress.

Peterson, Paul E., Barry G. Rabe, and Kenneth K. Wong. *When Federalism Works.* Washington, D.C.: Brookings Institution, 1986. A careful analysis of how various federal grant-in-aid programs actually work.

Pressman, Jeffrey L., and Aaron B. Wildavsky. *Implementation.* Berkeley: University of California Press, 1973. An excellent case study of how federalism affected the implementation of a single economic development project in Oakland, California.

Riker, William H. *Federalism: Origin, Operation, Significance.* Boston: Little, Brown, 1964. An explanation and critical analysis of federalism here and abroad.

Wright, Deil S. *Understanding Intergovernmental Relations.* 2d ed. Monterey, Calif.: Brooks/Cole, 1982. Useful survey of how state and local officials try to influence federal policies.

4

American Political Culture

★ Tocqueville's observations

★ Culture and the political system

★ Americanism

★ Culture and the economic system

★ Sources of political culture

★ Legitimization of an opposition party

★ Influence of religious heritage

★ The culture war

★ Trust in government

★ Increase in cynicism

★ Political efficacy

★ Support for civil liberties

If the Republic, created in 1787, had depended for its survival entirely on the constitutional machinery designed by the Founders, it probably would not have endured. That machinery has been copied by many other nations, notably those of Latin America, but in virtually no other country have such devices as federalism, an elected president, a bicameral legislature, and the separation of powers produced a political system capable of both effective government and the protection of liberty. In many nations (such as Argentina, Brazil, and the Philippines) that adopted the American model, there have been, at best, brief periods of democratic rule interrupted by military takeovers, the rise to power of demagogues, or the spread of wholesale corruption. The Constitution of the United States, like an old wine, has rarely survived an ocean crossing.

Alexis de Tocqueville, the perceptive French observer of American politics, noticed this as early as the 1830s. One reason a democratic republic took root in the United States but not in other countries that copied its constitution was that this country offered more abundant and fertile soil in which the roots could grow.[1] The vast territory of the United States created innumerable opportunities for people to acquire land and make a living. No feudal aristocracy monopolized the land, the government imposed only minimal taxes, and few legal restraints existed. As one place after another filled up, people kept pushing west to find new opportunities. A nation of small, independent farmers, unlike the traditional European one of landless peasants and indentured servants, could make democracy work.

But other nations that were similarly favored did not achieve the same result. As Tocqueville noted, much of South America contains fertile lands and rich resources, but democracy has not flourished there.[2] Had he returned to the United States fifty years later, when the frontier was no longer expanding and Americans were crowding into big cities, he would have found that democratic government was still more or less intact.

The Constitution and the physical advantages of the land cannot by themselves explain the persist-

85

Alexis de Tocqueville (1805–1859) was a young French aristocrat who came to the United States to study the American prison system. He wrote the brilliant *Democracy in America* (2 vols., 1835–1840), a profound analysis of our political culture.

ence of the nation's democratic institutions. In addition we must consider the customs of the people—what Tocqueville called their "moral and intellectual characteristics"[3] and what modern social scientists call our political culture.

Political Culture

If you travel abroad, you will quickly become aware that other people often behave differently from Americans. Spaniards may eat dinner at 10:00 P.M., whereas Americans eat at 6:00 or 7:00 P.M. Italians may close their shops for three hours in the middle of the day, while American shops are open continuously from 9:00 to 5:00. The Germans address people more formally than Americans, using last names

when we would use first names. Japanese business executives attach a lot of importance to working together as a group, while their American counterparts often are more individualistic. In these and countless other ways, we can observe cultural differences among people.

Such differences are not limited to eating, shopkeeping, or manners. They include differences in political culture as well. A **political culture** is a distinctive and patterned way of thinking about how political and economic life ought to be carried out (see the accompanying box). Beliefs about economic life are part of the political culture because politics affects economics.

Americans do not judge their political and economic systems in the same way. As we shall see, this difference makes them somewhat unique, for in many other nations people apply the same standards to both systems. For example, Americans think it very important that everybody should be equal politically, but they do not think it important that everybody should be equal economically. By contrast people in some other nations believe that the principle of equality should be applied to both economic and political life.

The Political System

There are at least five important elements in the American view of the political system:

- *Liberty:* Americans are preoccupied with their rights. They believe they should be free to do pretty much as they please, with some exceptions, so long as they don't hurt other people.

- *Equality:* Americans believe everybody should have an equal vote and an equal chance to participate and succeed.

- *Democracy:* Americans think government officials should be accountable to the people.

- *Civic duty:* Americans generally feel people ought to take community affairs seriously and help out when they can.[4]

- *Individual responsibility:* A characteristically American view is that, barring some disability, individuals are responsible for their own actions and well-being.

The Meaning of Political Culture

A political culture is a patterned set of ways of thinking about how politics and governing ought to be carried out. A nation, if it is made up of people who are quite similar to one another, may have a single political culture, part of what is sometimes referred to as a "national character." Most nations are not homogeneous, however, being made up instead of distinctive regions, religions, and ethnic groups. Each of these parts may have a distinctive political subculture. The American South, for example, has a political culture that differs in important ways from that of the Northeast.

Because a political culture consists of our fundamental assumptions about how the political process should operate, we often take it for granted or are completely unaware of how important these assumptions are. For instance, we assume that a person who loses an election should not try to prevent the winner from taking office, that it is wrong to use public office to enrich oneself or one's family, and that nobody should have a greater claim to political authority simply because he or she comes from a rich or wellborn family. In many other societies these are not widely shared assumptions, and in some societies the opposite is often believed.

A political culture is not the same as a **political ideology**. The concept of ideology will be explained in Chapter 5. As used there, it will refer to more or less consistent sets of views concerning the policies government ought to pursue. A doctrinaire conservative, liberal, or radical has an ideology. Up to a point people can disagree on ideology (what government should do) but still share a common political culture and viewpoint about how government ought to be operated. Some ideologies, however, are so critical of the existing state of affairs that they require a fundamental change in the way politics is carried on, and thus they embody a different political culture as well.

America has both a shared political culture and some distinctive subcultures associated with various ethnic and reiigious groups.

At the height of immigration to this country there was a striking emphasis on creating a shared political culture. Schoolchildren, whatever their national origin, were taught to salute this country's flag.

By vast majorities Americans believe that every citizen should have an equal chance to influence government policy and to hold public office, and they oppose the idea of letting people have titles, such as "Lord" or "Duke," as in England. By somewhat smaller majorities they believe that people should be allowed to vote even if they can't read or write or vote intelligently.[5] Though Americans recognize that people differ in their abilities, they overwhelmingly agree with the statement that "teaching children that all people are really equal recognizes that all people are equally worthy and deserve equal treatment."[6]

At least three questions can be raised about this political culture. First, how do we know that the American people share these beliefs? For most of our history there were no public opinion polls, and even after they became commonplace, they were rather crude tools for measuring the existence and meaning of complex, abstract ideas. There is in fact no way to prove that such values as those listed above are important to Americans. But neither is there good reason for dismissing the list out of hand. One can infer, as have many scholars, the existence of certain values by a close study of the kinds of books Americans read, the speeches they hear, the slogans to which they respond, and the political

choices they make, as well as by noting the observations of insightful foreign visitors. Personality tests as well as opinion polls, particularly those asking similar questions in different countries, also supply useful evidence, some of which will be reviewed in the following paragraphs.

Second, if these values are important to Americans, how can we explain the existence in our society of behavior that is obviously inconsistent with them? For example, if white Americans believe in equality of opportunity, why did so many of them for so long deny that equality to black Americans? That people act contrary to their professed beliefs is an everyday fact of life: people believe in honesty, yet they steal from their employers and sometimes underreport their taxable income. Besides values, self-interest and social circumstances also shape behavior. Gunnar Myrdal, a Swedish observer of American society, described race relations in this country as "an American dilemma" resulting from the conflict between the "American creed" (a belief in equality of opportunity) and American behavior (denying blacks full citizenship).[7] But the creed remains important because it is a source of change: as more and more persons become aware of the inconsistency between their values and their behavior, that behavior slowly changes.[8] Race relations in this country would take a very different course if instead of an abstract but widespread belief in equality there were an equally widespread belief that one race is inherently inferior to another. (No doubt some Americans believe that, but most do not.)

Third, if there is agreement among Americans on certain political values, why has there been so much political conflict in our history? How could a people who agree on such fundamentals fight a bloody civil war, engage in violent labor-management disputes, take to the streets in riots and demonstrations, and sue each other in countless court battles? Conflict, even violent struggles, can occur over specific policies even among those who share, at some level of abstraction, common beliefs. Many political values may be irrelevant to specific controversies: there is no abstract value, for example, that would settle the question of whether steelworkers ought to organize unions. More important, much of our conflict has occurred precisely because we have strong beliefs that happen, as each of us interprets them, to be in conflict. Equality of opportunity seems an attractive idea, but sometimes it can be pursued only by curtailing personal liberty, another attractive idea. The states went to war in 1861 over one aspect of that conflict—the rights of slaves versus the rights of slaveowners.

Indeed, the Civil War illustrates the way certain fundamental beliefs about how a democratic regime ought to be organized have persisted despite bitter conflict over the policies adopted by particular governments. When the southern states seceded from the Union, they formed not a wholly different government but one modeled, despite some important differences, on the United States Constitution. Even some of the language of the Constitution was duplicated, suggesting that the southern states believed not that a new form of government or a different political culture ought to be created but that the South was the true repository of the existing constitutional and cultural order.[9]

Perhaps the most frequently encountered evidence that Americans believe themselves bound by common values and common hopes has been the persistence of the word *Americanism* in our political vocabulary. Throughout the nineteenth and most of the twentieth centuries, *Americanism* and *American*

When in the 1950s a committee of the House of Representatives investigated alleged subversion, it was called the committee on *"Un-American"* activities—a term that seemed strange to nations that did not understand the great appeal of the concept of "Americanism."

way of life were familiar terms not only in Fourth of July speeches but also in everyday discourse. For many years the House of Representatives had a committee called the House Un-American Activities Committee. There is hardly any example to be found abroad of such a way of thinking: there is no "Britishism" or "Frenchism," and when Britons and French people become worried about subversion, they call it a problem of internal security, not a manifestation of "un-British" or "un-French" activities.

The Economic System

Americans judge the economic system using many of the same standards by which they judge the political one, albeit with some very important differences. As it is in American politics, liberty is important in the U.S. economy. Thus Americans support the idea of a free-enterprise economic system, calling the nation's economy "generally fair and efficient" and denying that it "survives by keeping the poor down."[10] However, there are limits to how much freedom they think should exist in the marketplace. People support government regulation of business in order to keep some firms from becoming too powerful and to correct specific abuses.[11]

Americans are more willing to tolerate economic inequality than political inequality. They believe in maintaining "equality of opportunity" in the economy but not "equality of results." If everyone has an equal opportunity to get ahead, then it is all right for people with more ability to earn higher salaries, and it is all right for wages to be set based on how hard people work rather than on their economic needs.[12] Although Americans are quite willing to support education and training programs to help disadvantaged people get ahead, they are strongly opposed to anything that looks like preferential treatment (for example, hiring quotas) in the workplace.[13]

The leaders of very liberal political groups, such as civil rights and feminist organizations, are more willing than the average American to support preferential treatment in the hiring and promoting of minorities and women. They do so because, unlike most citizens, they believe that whatever disadvantages blacks and women face are the result of failures of the economic system rather than the fault of individuals.[14] Even so, these leaders strongly support the idea that earnings should be based on ability and oppose the idea of having any top limit on what people can earn.[15]

This popular commitment to economic individualism and personal responsibility may help explain how Americans think about particular public policies, such as welfare and civil rights. Polls show that Americans are willing to help people "truly in need" (this includes the elderly and the disabled) but not those deemed "able to take care of themselves" (this includes, in the public's mind, people "on welfare"). Also, Americans dislike preferential hiring programs and the use of quotas to deal with racial inequality.

At the core of these policy attitudes is a widely (but not universally) shared commitment to economic individualism and personal responsibility. Some scholars, among them Donald Kinder and David Sears, interpret these individualistic values as "symbolic racism"—a kind of plausible camouflage for antiblack attitudes.[16] But other scholars, such as Paul M. Sniderman and Michael Gray Hagen, argue that these views are not a smoke screen for bigotry or insensitivity but a genuine commitment to the ethic of self-reliance.[17] Since there are many Americans on both sides of this issue, debates about welfare and civil rights tend to be especially intense. What is striking about the American political culture is that in this country the individualist view of social policy is by far the most popular.[18]

Views about specific economic policies change. Americans now are much more inclined than they once were to believe that the government should help the needy and regulate business. But the commitment to certain underlying principles has been remarkably enduring. In 1924 most of the high school students in Muncie, Indiana, said that "it is entirely the fault of the man himself if he cannot succeed" and disagreed with the view that differences in wealth showed that the system was unjust. In 1977, over half a century later, the students in this same high school were asked the same questions again, with the same results (see Table 4.1)[19]

Comparing America with Other Nations

The best way to learn what is distinctive about the American political culture is to compare it with that of other nations. This comparison shows that Americans have somewhat different beliefs about the political system, the economic system, and religion.

TABLE 4.1 Responsibility for Success or Failure

Statement	Percentage of High School Students Agreeing	
	1924	1977
It is entirely the fault of the man himself if he cannot succeed.	47%	47%
The fact that some men [in 1977: people] have so much more money than others shows there is an unjust condition in this country that ought to be changed.	30	34

SOURCE: Theodore Caplow and Howard M. Bahr, "Half a Century of Change in Adolescent Attitudes: Replication of a Middletown Survey by the Lynds," *Public Opinion Quarterly* 43 (Spring 1979): 1–17, Table 1. Copyright © 1979, reprinted by permission of University of Chicago Press.

Political System

Sweden has a well-developed democratic government, with a constitution, free speech, an elected legislature, competing political parties, and a reasonably honest and nonpartisan bureaucracy. But the Swedish political culture is significantly different from ours; it is more deferential than participatory. Though almost all adult Swedes vote in national elections, few participate in politics in any other way. They defer to the decisions of experts and specialists who work for the government, rarely challenge governmental decisions in court, believe leaders and legislators ought to decide issues on the basis of "what is best" more than on "what the people want," and value equality as much as (or more than) liberty.[20] Whereas Americans are contentious, Swedes value harmony; while Americans tend to assert their rights, Swedes tend to observe their obligations.

The contrast in political cultures is even greater when one looks at a nation, such as Japan, with a wholly different history and set of traditions. One study compared the values expressed by a small number of upper-status Japanese with those of some similarly situated Americans. Whereas the Americans emphasized the virtues of individualism, competition, and equality in their political, economic, and social relations, the Japanese attached greater value to maintaining good relations with colleagues, having decisions made by groups, preserving social harmony, and displaying respect for hierarchy. Americans were more concerned than the Japanese with rules and with treating others fairly but impersonally, with due regard for their rights. The Japanese, on the other hand, stressed the importance of being sensitive to the personal needs of others, avoiding conflict, and reaching decisions through discussion rather than the application of rules.[21] These cultural differences affect in profound but hard-to-measure ways the workings of the political and economic systems of the two countries, making them function quite differently despite the fact that both are industrialized, capitalist nations.

It is easy to become carried away by the more obvious differences among national cultures and to overgeneralize from them. Thinking in stereotypes about the typical American, the typical Swede, or the typical Japanese is as risky as thinking of the typical white or the typical black American. This can be especially misleading in nations, such as the United States and Canada, that have been settled by a variety of ethnic and religious groups (English-speaking versus French-speaking Canadians, for example, or Jewish, Protestant, and Catholic Americans). But it is equally misleading to suppose that the operation of a political system can be understood entirely from the nation's objective features—its laws, economy, or physical terrain.

In 1959–1960 Gabriel Almond and Sidney Verba published a study of political culture in five nations. In general they found that Americans, and to a lesser degree citizens of Great Britain, had a stronger sense of **civic duty** (a belief that one has an obligation to participate in civic and political affairs) and a stronger sense of **civic competence** (a belief that one can affect government policies) than did the citizens of Germany, Italy, or Mexico. Over half of all Americans and a third of all Britons believed that the average citizen ought to "be active in one's community," compared to only a tenth in Italy and a fifth in Germany. Moreover, many more Americans and Britons than Germans, Italians, or Mexicans believed that they could "do something" about an unjust national law or local regulation.[22] Since 1960 nobody has asked people in these five countries the same questions, and hence we do not know whether these views have changed in recent years. But in a 1995 study of citizen participation in politics, Verba and others reported that while America lagged behind Austria, the Netherlands, West Germany, and the United Kingdom in voter participation, when it came to campaigning, attending political meetings, becoming active in the local community, and contacting government officials, Americans were as active—or substantially more active—than citizens elsewhere.[23]

Nevertheless, today the American people have less trust in government than they once did. But even so, popular confidence in political institutions remains higher here than in many places abroad. In 1987 a survey in the United States and four European nations showed that Americans and Britons were much more likely than people in West Germany, France, or Spain to say that they had a "great deal of" or "some" confidence in their country's armed forces, police, and legislature. With respect to the nation's judicial system and labor

TABLE 4.2   Popular Confidence in Institutions in Europe and America, 1987

Institution	*Percentage Saying They Have a "Great Deal of" or "Some" Confidence*				
	U.S.	Great Britain	West Germany	France	Spain
Armed forces	86%	79%	69%	59%	36%
Police	88	80	80	72	44
Congress (Parliament)	83	52	64	55	30
Schools	82	53	82	82	59
Church	85	56	66	53	38
Business	84	55	44	30	26
Press / media / TV	69	38	41	48	46
Labor unions	52	29	43	36	26
Judicial system	77	56	72	62	35

SOURCE: Laurence Parisot, "Attitudes About the Media: A Five-Country Comparison," *Public Opinion* (January–February 1988): 18. Reprinted with the permission of the American Enterprise Institute for Public Policy Research, Washington, D.C.

unions, Americans displayed less confidence but still more than did Europeans (see Table 4.2).[24]

By the same token, Americans were more likely to say that they were "very proud" of their national identity and that, if a war came, they would be "willing to fight" for their country (see Table 4.3).[25] Of course Americans know that their country has a lot of faults. But even the most disaffected voters believe the United States needs to change only certain policies, not its system of government.[26]

A television picture of a U.S. serviceman captured by the enemy (here, Michael Durant, a prisoner of war in Somalia) powerfully unites the nation.

Economic System

The political culture of Sweden is not only more deferential than ours but also more inclined to favor equality of results over equality of opportunity. Sidney Verba and Gary Orren compared the views of Swedish and American trade union and political party leaders on a variety of economic issues. In both countries the leaders were chosen from either blue-collar unions or the major liberal political party (the Democrats in the United States, the Social Democrats in Sweden).

The results (as you can see in Table 4.4) are quite striking. By margins of four or five to one, the Swedish leaders were more likely to believe in giving workers equal pay than were their American counterparts. Moreover, by margins of at least three to one, the Swedes were more likely than the Americans to favor putting a top limit on incomes.[27]

Just what these differences in beliefs mean in dollars-and-cents terms was revealed by the answers to another question. Each group was asked what should be the ratio between the income of an executive and that of a menial worker (a dishwasher in Sweden, an elevator operator in the United States). The Swedish leaders said the ratio should be a little over two to one. That is, if the dishwasher earned $200 a week, the executive should earn no more than $440 to $480 a week. But the American leaders were ready to let the executive earn between $2,260

TABLE 4.3   Patriotism in America and Europe, 1991

	Percentage Agreeing				
Statement	U.S.	Germany	Great Britain	Italy	France
I am very patriotic.	88%	77%	72%	69%	64%
We should all be willing to fight for our country whether it is right or wrong.	55	28	56	39	37

SOURCE: Adapted from *The Public Perspective* (November/December 1991): 6. Reprinted by permission of *The Public Perspective,* a publication of the Roper Center for Public Opinion Research, University of Connecticut.

and $3,040 per week when the elevator operator was earning $200.

Americans, compared to people in many other countries, are more likely to think that freedom is more important than equality and less likely to think that hard work goes unrewarded or that the government should guarantee citizens a basic standard of living (see Table 4.5, page 94). These cultural differences make a difference in politics. In fact there is less income inequality in Sweden than in the United States—the government sees to that.

The Role of Religion

In the 1830s Tocqueville was amazed at how religious Americans were in comparison to his fellow Europeans. As political sociologist Seymour Martin Lipset has observed, "from the early nineteenth century down to the present, the United States has been among the most religious countries in the world."[28] The average American is more likely than the average European to believe in God, to pray on a daily basis, and to acknowledge clear standards of right and wrong (see Table 4.6, page 94). Surveys in forty-five countries conducted from 1990 to 1993 revealed that America was the only industrial nation in which over 80 percent of citizens identified themselves as religious. Only 1 percent of Americans claimed they were atheist (see Table 4.7, page 95).

Religious beliefs have always played a significant role in American politics. The religious revivalist movement of the late 1730s and early 1740s (known as the First Great Awakening) transformed the political life of the American colonies. Religious ideas fueled the break with England, for violating, in the words of the Declaration of Independence, "the laws of nature and nature's God." Religious leaders were central to the struggle over slavery in the nineteenth century and the temperance movement of the early twentieth century.

Both liberals and conservatives have used the pulpit to promote political change. The civil rights

TABLE 4.4   Commitment to Income Equity in Sweden and the United States

	Political-Party Leaders		Blue-Collar Union Leaders	
	Sweden (Social Democrats)	U.S. (Democrats)	Sweden	U.S.
Favor equality of results (%)	21%	9%	14%	4%
Favor equal pay (%)	58	12	68	11
Favor top limit on income (%)	44	17	51	13
Fair income ratio of executive to menial worker[a]	2 : 1	15 : 1	2 : 1	11 : 1

[a] In Sweden, menial worker was a dishwasher; in U.S., menial worker was an elevator operator.
SOURCE: Reprinted by permission of the publisher from *Equality in America: The View from the Top* by Sidney Verba and Gary R. Orren, Cambridge, Mass.: Harvard University Press, Copyright © 1985 by the Presidents and Fellows of Harvard College.

TABLE 4.5 Attitudes Toward Economic Equality in America and Europe, 1991

Statement	Percentage Agreeing				
	U.S.	Great Britain	Germany	Italy	France
It is government's responsibility to take care of the very poor who can't take care of themselves.	23%	62%	50%	66%	62%
Hard work guarantees success.	63	46	38	51	46
Government should *not* guarantee every citizen food and basic shelter.	34	9	13	14	10

SOURCE: Adapted from *The Public Perspective* (November/December 1991): 5, 7. Reprinted by permission of *The Public Perspective,* a publication of the Roper Center for Public Opinion Research, University of Connecticut.

movement of the 1950s and 1960s was led mainly by black religious leaders, most prominently Martin Luther King, Jr. In the 1980s, a conservative religious group known as the Moral Majority advocated constitutional amendments that would allow prayer in public schools and ban abortion. In the 1990s, another conservative religious group, the Christian Coalition, attracted an enormous amount of media attention and became a prominent force in many national, state, and local elections. If history is any guide, religious beliefs will continue to shape American political culture well into the next century.

The Sources of Political Culture

That Americans bring a distinctive way of thinking to their political life is easier to demonstrate than to explain. But even a brief, and necessarily superficial, effort to understand the sources of our political culture can help make its significance clearer.

The American Revolution, as we discussed in Chapter 2, was essentially a war fought over liberty: an assertion by the colonists of what they took to be their rights. Though the Constitution, produced eleven years after the Revolution, had to deal with other issues as well, its animating spirit reflected the effort to reconcile personal liberty with the needs of social control. These founding experiences, and the political disputes that followed, have given to American political thought and culture a preoccupation with the assertion and maintenance of rights. This tradition has imbued the daily conduct of U.S. politics with a kind of adversarial spirit quite foreign to the political life of countries that did not undergo a libertarian revolution or that were formed out of an interest in other goals, such as social equality, national independence, or ethnic supremacy.

The adversarial spirit of the American political culture reflects not only our preoccupation with rights but also our long-standing distrust of authority and of people wielding power. The colonies' ex-

TABLE 4.6 Religious Belief in America and Europe, 1991

Statement	Percentage Agreeing				
	U.S.	Great Britain	Germany	Italy	France
I never doubt the existence of God.	60%	31%	20%	56%	29%
Prayer is an important part of my daily life.	77	37	44	69	32
There are clear guidelines about what is good and evil.	79	65	54	56	64

SOURCE: Adapted from *The Public Perspective* (November/December 1991): 5, 8. Reprinted by permission of *The Public Perspective,* a publication of the Roper Center for Public Opinion Research, University of Connecticut.

TABLE 4.7 Religion in Industrial Nations, 1990–1993

Statement	Percentage Answering Yes							
	U.S.	Sweden	France	W. Germany	Britian	Spain	Canada	Mexico
Would you say you are . . .								
A religious person?	82	29	48	54	55	64	69	72
Not a religious person?	15	56	36	27	37	27	26	22
A convinced atheist?	1	7	11	2	4	4	3	2
Not sure	2	9	5	17	4	5	2	4

SOURCE: Adapted from *The Public Perspective*, reporting data from surveys conducted from 1990 to 1993 by the Inter-University Consortium for Political and Social Research. *The Public Perspective* (Storrs, CT: The Roper Center for Public Opinion Research, University of CT), April/May 1995, p. 2. © The Public Perspective. Reprinted by permission.

periences with British rule was one source of that distrust. But another, older source was the religious belief of many Americans, which saw human nature as fundamentally depraved. To the colonists, all of mankind suffered from original sin, symbolized by Adam and Eve eating the forbidden fruit in the Garden of Eden. Since no one was born innocent, no one could be trusted with power. Thus, the Constitution had to be designed in such a way as to curb the darker side of human nature. Otherwise, everyone's rights would be in jeopardy.

The contentiousness of a people animated by a suspicion of government and devoted to individualism could easily have made democratic politics so tumultuous as to be impossible. After all, one must be willing to trust others with power if there is to be any kind of democratic government, and sometimes those others will be people not of one's own choosing. The first great test case took place around 1800 in a battle between the Federalists, led by John Adams and Alexander Hamilton, and the Democratic-Republicans, led by Thomas Jefferson and James Madison. The two factions deeply distrusted each other: the Federalists had passed laws designed to suppress Jeffersonian journalists; Jefferson suspected the Federalists were out to subvert the Constitution; and the Federalists believed Jefferson intended to sell out the country to France. But as we shall see in Chapter 7, the threat of civil war never materialized, and the Jeffersonians came to power peacefully. Within a few years the role of an opposition party became legitimate, and people abandoned the idea of making serious efforts to suppress their opponents. By happy circumstance people came to accept

that liberty and orderly political change could coexist.

The Constitution, by creating a federal system and dividing political authority among competing institutions, provided ample opportunity for widespread—though hardly universal—participation in politics. The election of Jefferson in 1800 produced no political catastrophe, and those who had predicted one were, to a degree, discredited. But other, more fundamental features of American life contributed to the same end. One of the most important of these was religious diversity.

Religion plays a larger role in the lives of Americans than it does in the lives of the citizens of most other Western countries.

The absence of an established or official religion for the nation as a whole, reinforced by a constitutional prohibition of such an establishment and by the migration to this country of people with different religious backgrounds, meant that religious diversity was inevitable. Since there could be no orthodox or official religion, it became difficult for a corresponding political orthodoxy to emerge. Moreover, the conflict between the Puritan tradition, with its emphasis on faith and good works, and the Catholic church, with its devotion to the sacraments and priestly authority, provided a recurrent source of cleavage in American public life. The differences in values between these two groups showed up not only in their religious practices but also in areas involving the regulation of manners and morals, and even in people's choice of political party. For more than a century candidates for state and national office were deeply divided over whether the sale of liquor should be prohibited, a question that arose ultimately out of competing religious doctrines.

Even though there was no established church, there was certainly a dominant religious tradition—Protestantism, and especially Puritanism. The Protestant churches provided people with both a set of beliefs and an organizational experience that had profound effects on American political culture. Those beliefs encouraged, or even required, a life of personal achievement as well as religious conviction: a believer had an obligation to work, save money, obey the secular law, and do good works. Max Weber explained the rise of capitalism in part by what he called the Protestant ethic—what we now sometimes call the **work ethic**.[29] Such values had political consequences, as people holding them were motivated to engage in civic and communal action.

Churches offered ready opportunities for developing and practicing civic and political skills. Since most Protestant churches were organized along congregational lines—that is, the church was controlled by its members, who put up the building, hired the preacher, and supervised the finances—they were, in effect, miniature political systems, with leaders and committees, conflict and consensus. Developing a participatory political culture was undoubtedly made easier by the existence of a participatory religious culture. Even some Catholic churches in early America were under a degree of lay control.

Parishioners owned the church property, negotiated with priests, and conducted church business.

All aspects of culture, including the political, are preserved and transmitted to new generations primarily by the family. Though some believe that the weakening of the family unit has eroded the extent to which it transmits anything, particularly culture, and has enlarged the power of other sources of values—the mass media and the world of friends and fashion, leisure and entertainment—there is still little doubt that the ways in which we think about the world are largely acquired within the family. In Chapter 5 we shall see that the family is the primary source of one kind of political attitude—identification with one or another political party. Even more important, the family shapes in subtle ways how we think and act on political matters. Erik Erikson, the psychologist, noted certain traits that are more characteristic of American than of European families—the greater freedom enjoyed by children, for example, and the larger measure of equality among family members. These familial characteristics promote a belief, carried through life, that every person has rights deserving protection and that a variety of interests have a legitimate claim to consideration when decisions are made.[30]

The combined effect of religious and ethnic diversity, an individualistic philosophy, fragmented political authority, and the relatively egalitarian American family can be seen in the absence of a high degree of **class consciousness** among Americans. Class consciousness means thinking of oneself as a worker whose interests are in opposition to those of management, or vice versa. In this country most people, whatever their jobs, think of themselves as "middle class."

If any group of Americans were likely to think and act in terms of their economic class, one would suppose it would be the unemployed. Nonetheless, a careful study in 1976 showed that, though unemployed people feel deprived, the great majority do not identify with other unemployed persons or think that their interests as a class are in opposition to those of management. The political views of the unemployed do not seem to differ much from those of the employed, and even when the former think in class terms, their political views do not seem to be affected. Moreover, we know that even in the late 1930s, when the country was in the grip of a massive

The changing American family. At the top is an extended
family in Black River Falls, Wisconsin, around 1900;
on the lower left a single-parent family; on the lower right
a nuclear family in contemporary America.

depression, only a small minority of the unemployed expressed a strong sense of class consciousness.[31]

Though the writings of Horatio Alger are no longer popular, Americans still seem to believe in the message of those stories—that the opportunity for success is available to people who work hard. This may help explain why the United States is the only large industrial democracy without a significant socialist party and why the nation has been slow to adopt certain welfare programs.

The Culture War

Almost all Americans share some elements of a common political culture. Why, then, is there so much cultural conflict in American politics? For many years, the most explosive political issues have included abortion, gay rights, drug use, school prayer, and pornography. Viewed from a Marxist perspective, politics in the United States is utterly baffling: instead of two economic classes engaged in a bitter struggle over wealth, we have two cultural classes locked in a war over values.

As chancellor of the New York City public school system, Joseph Fernandez supported condom distribution and a curriculum that recognized nontraditional families. His contract was not renewed.

To say that there are two cultural classes is, of course, an oversimplification, but to say that there is a culture war is not an exaggeration.[32] Groups supporting and opposing the right to abortion have had many angry confrontations in recent years. The latter have been arrested while attempting to block access to abortion clinics; some clinics have been fire-bombed; and at least one physician has been killed. A controversy over what schoolchildren should be taught about homosexuals was responsible, in part, for the firing of the head of the New York City school system; in other states there have been fierce arguments in state legislatures and before the courts over whether gay and lesbian couples should be allowed to adopt children. Although most Americans want to keep heroin, cocaine, and other drugs illegal, a significant number of people want to legalize (or at least decriminalize) their use. The Supreme Court has ruled that children cannot pray in public schools, but this has not stopped many parents and school authorities from trying to reinstate school prayer, or at least prayerlike moments of silence. The discovery that a federal agency, the National Endowment for the Arts, had given money to support exhibitions and performances that many people thought were obscene led to a furious congressional struggle over the future of the agency. The 1992 presidential election centered, in part, on a passionate argument over which candidate best exemplified "family values."

The culture war differs from other political disputes (over such matters as taxes, business regulations, and foreign policy) in several ways: money is not at stake, compromises are almost impossible to arrange, and the conflict is more profound. It is animated by deep differences in people's beliefs about private and public morality—that is, about the standards that ought to govern individual behavior and social arrangements. It is about what kind of country we ought to live in, not just about what kinds of policies our government ought to adopt.

To simplify, there are two opposed camps, the **orthodox** and the **progressive**. On the orthodox side are people who believe that morality is as important as, or more important than, self-expression and that moral rules derive from the commands of God or the laws of nature—commands and laws that are relatively clear, unchanging, and independent of individual preferences. On the progressive side are people who think that personal freedom is as important as, or more important than, certain traditional moral rules and that those rules must be evaluated in light of the circumstances of modern life—circumstances that are quite complex, changeable, and dependent on individual preferences.

Most conspicuous among the orthodox are fundamentalist Protestants and born-again Christians, and so critics who dislike orthodox views often dismiss them as the fanatical expressions of "the Religious Right." But many people who hold orthodox views are not fanatical or deeply religious or right-wing on most issues; they simply have strong views about drugs, pornography, and sexual morality. Similarly, the progressive side often includes members of liberal Protestant denominations (for example, Episcopalians and Unitarians) and people with no strong religious beliefs, and so their critics often denounce them as immoral, anti-Christian radicals who have embraced the ideology of secular humanism, the belief that moral standards do not require religious justification. But in all likelihood few progressives are immoral or anti-Christian, and most do not regard secular humanism as their defining ideology.

Moreover, the culture war is occurring not just between different religious denominations but also within them. Catholic, Protestant, and Jewish leaders with an orthodox perspective tend to assign great importance to two-parent families, condemn pornography, denounce homosexuality, oppose ratification of the Equal Rights Amendment to the Constitution, and think the United States is in general a force for good in the world. Leaders of the same faiths who have a progressive outlook are more likely to say that many legitimate alternatives to the traditional two-parent family exist, that pornography and homosexuality are private matters protected by individual rights, and that the United States has been at best a neutral and at worst a bad force in world affairs.[33] This conflict between the orthodox and progressive view of American culture is similar to, and has many of the same causes, as the cleavage (described in Chapter 5) between the traditional middle class and the new middle class.

American history has always had conflicts of this sort, but they have acquired special importance today as a result of two major changes in American society. The first is the great increase in the proportion of people who consider themselves progressive. Once almost everyone was religiously orthodox, even if politically liberal; today fewer are. The second factor is the rise of media (such as television and direct-mail advertising) that make it easy to wage a cultural war on a large scale. In the past, preachers, writers, and lecturers could reach at most a few hundred people at a time; today, television evangelists, radio talk-show hosts, and the authors of direct-mail messages can wage a furious war of words reaching tens of millions of people and recruiting hundreds of thousands of followers. A cultural war that once enlisted only a few activists can now mobilize mass armies.

The tensions generated by the culture war affect our views as to how well our government works, how much influence ordinary people can have over it, and how large a measure of freedom we ought to grant to our opponents. Trust in government, a sense of political efficacy, and tolerance for views we dislike are always fragile under the best of circumstances. Have the cultural tensions of recent decades made matters worse? In the rest of this chapter we shall try to answer these questions.

Mistrust of Government

In 1979 President Jimmy Carter, taking note of numerous public opinion polls that showed a dramatic decline in the proportion of Americans who said they had a great deal of confidence in our system, made a nationwide television address on the subject of "the American malaise," which he defined as a crisis of confidence evident in Americans' "growing disrespect" for government, schools, churches, and other institutions.

Though it probably wasn't a politically astute speech—Americans don't like to be told they suffer from a malaise, and the following year they voted against Carter and for a man, Ronald Reagan, who offered a much more upbeat assessment of the American condition—it was based on some solid factual evidence. As can be seen in Figure 4.1, various measures of mistrust in government rose steadily for about fifteen years beginning in the mid-1960s. By 1976 nearly twice as many Americans as in 1958 thought that there were "quite a few" crooks in

FIGURE 4.1   The Growth of Mistrust of Government

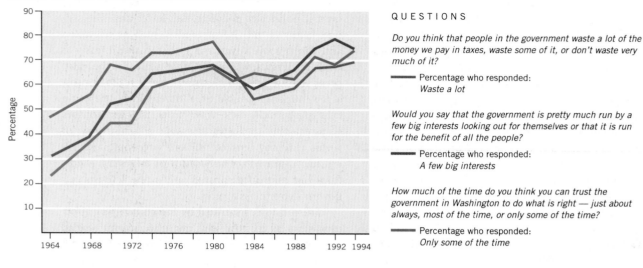

QUESTIONS

Do you think that people in the government waste a lot of the money we pay in taxes, waste some of it, or don't waste very much of it?

━━━ Percentage who responded:
Waste a lot

Would you say that the government is pretty much run by a few big interests looking out for themselves or that it is run for the benefit of all the people?

━━━ Percentage who responded:
A few big interests

How much of the time do you think you can trust the government in Washington to do what is right — just about always, most of the time, or only some of the time?

━━━ Percentage who responded:
Only some of the time

SOURCES: Survey Research Center, University of Michigan. Supplied by the SRC/CPS American National Election Studies, University of Michigan. 1990, 1992, and 1994 figures supplied by ICPSR American National Election Studies, University of Michigan.

The trust and confidence that Americans felt in their government was especially high in the 1950s, during the period Eisenhower was president.

government, that government was run for the benefit of a "few big interests," that "a lot" of tax money was wasted, and that we can expect government to do the right thing only "some of the time."[34]

In part this decline in trust was the result of some dramatic events. The largest single increase in mistrust occurred between 1972 and 1974—the time of the Watergate scandal, when close aides to President Nixon authorized a burglary of the Democratic party headquarters and the president himself participated in the cover-up of the bungled break-in. But the decline began long before Watergate (or the war in Vietnam) and continued after both events were history.

This rising mistrust is worrisome, but it should be viewed in context. There is evidence that the mistrust is chiefly aimed not at our *system* of government but at specific leaders and policies.[35] We have already seen that Americans have more confidence in their governmental institutions than do citizens of many other countries. Even in 1972–1974, when distrust of government was especially high, 86 percent of those interviewed in a national survey agreed with the following statement: "I am proud of many things about our form of government."[36]

The impassioned conflict over American involvement in Vietnam brought out protesters on both sides, each side seeking to associate important symbols ("peace" and "patriotism") with its cause.

Moreover, there are reasons for thinking that the current level of trust in government is close to the historical norm and that the much higher levels of trust of the late 1950s and early 1960s were unusual. Though polling was then in its infancy, there is evidence that Americans in the 1930s were not much more trustful of their government than they are now.[37] Between the 1930s and the 1960s this nation overcame an economic depression and won World War II, events that gave to citizens an unusually high degree of confidence in the capacity of their government. The 1960s and 1970s, when that confidence weakened, were years of great turmoil—the civil rights movement, the war in Vietnam, a sharp rise in

TABLE 4.8 Confidence in People Running American Institutions, 1966–1996

	Percentage saying they have "a great deal of confidence" in "people in charge of running" various institutions				
Institution	1966	1971–1979	1980–1989	1990–1996	Change 1966–1996
Congress	42%	16%	19%	10%	55%
U.S. Supreme Court	50	29	29	28	76
Federal bureaucracy	41	19	20	12	70
The press	29	23	18	16	44
Major companies	55	22	18	18	69

SOURCE: Calculated from survey data compiled by Louis Harris and Associates, 1966–1996.

Intense press coverage of scandals has deepened popular distrust of government. Here, special counsel Kenneth Starr talks about his investigation of the Whitewater affair.

crime rates, the assassination of various leaders, urban riots and campus demonstrations, and economic inflation. Small wonder that people thought that things were getting out of hand and that political leaders ought to take some of the blame.

The decline in popular confidence in government that began in the 1960s was part and parcel of a general loss of confidence in almost all institutions. As we can see in Table 4.8 on page 101, the percentage of Americans saying they had "a great deal of confidence in" the people running major companies and the press also declined sharply between 1966 and the early 1990s.

There was a brief and small improvement in trust during the early Reagan years,[38] but that gain was washed out, and then some, by a big drop in the early 1990s. Owing to the combined effects of an

economic recession, political scandals (such as the revelation that members of the House of Representatives were writing checks without having money in the House bank to cover them), and the continued growth in such problems as crime, drug abuse, and the federal debt, Americans in record numbers expressed disgust at politics and politicians. Ross Perot, the Texas businessman who ran for president in 1992 as an independent, tried to capitalize on that anger. But there was no sign of a popular revolt against the system of government laid out in the Constitution.

In sum, Americans have not lost confidence in themselves or in their governmental system, but they no longer so readily give to political leaders and their policies the kind of support they gave in the less troubled years of the 1950s.

Political Efficacy

Perhaps the most worrisome aspect of recent changes in the American political culture is the decline in the extent to which citizens feel that the political system will respond to their needs and beliefs. These changes are in what scholars call a citizen's sense of **political efficacy,** by which they mean a citizen's capacity to understand and influence political events.

This sense of efficacy has two parts—**internal efficacy** (the ability to understand and take part in political affairs) and **external efficacy** (the ability to make the system respond to the citizenry). Since the mid-1960s there has been a fairly sharp drop in the sense of external efficacy (or system responsiveness) but not much change in the sense of internal efficacy (personal competence).

As we can see in Figure 4.2, people today are not much different from people in 1952 with respect to whether they can understand what is going on in government (most find it too complicated to fathom) and whether they have much say in what the government does. But there has been a big change in how responsive people think the government is to their interests. In 1980 people were twice as likely as they were in the late 1950s to say that public officials don't "care much what people like me think." And in 1980 they were much more likely than they had been

FIGURE 4.2 Changes in the Sense of Political Efficacy

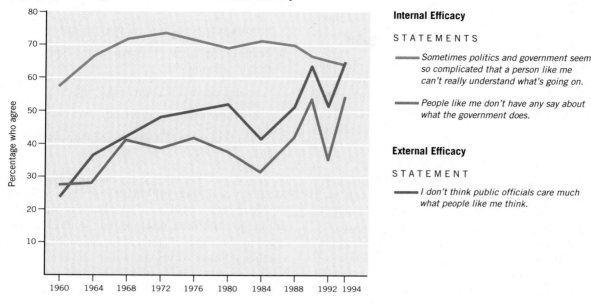

SOURCES: Center for Political Studies, University of Michigan, as reported in Seymour Martin Lipset and William Schneider, *The Confidence Gap: Business, Labor, and Government in the Public Mind* (New York: Free Press, 1983); 1990, 1992, and 1994 figures supplied by ICPSR American National Election Studies, University of Michigan.

(even as recently as 1968) to say "those we elect to Congress in Washington lose touch with the people pretty quickly" and "parties are only interested in people's votes, not their opinions."[39]

Unlike the increase in the mistrust of government, the increase in the feeling that government was unresponsive was not shaped by any particular events; the sense of external efficacy dropped more or less steadily throughout the 1960s and 1970s. What seems to have happened is that Americans gradually have come to the view that government has become too big and pervasive for it to be sensitive to citizen preferences. In 1964 less than a third of Americans thought the federal government was too powerful; in 1976 half did.[40]

Though Americans may feel less effective as citizens than they once did, their sense of efficacy remains much higher than it is among Europeans. In 1974 a poll taken in five nations found that the average American scored significantly higher on the efficacy scale than the average person in Austria, Germany, Great Britain, or the Netherlands. More-over, Americans were much more likely than Europeans to say that they regularly discussed politics, signed petitions, and worked to solve community problems.[41] Though Americans are less likely to vote than Europeans, they are more likely to do the harder chores that make up democratic politics.

Because Americans are less likely than they once were to hold their leaders in high esteem, to have confidence in government policies, and to believe the system will be responsive to popular wishes, some observers like to say that Americans today are more "alienated" from politics. It probably would be better to say that they are simply more realistic.

Political Tolerance

Democratic politics depends crucially on citizens' being reasonably tolerant of the opinions and actions of others. If unpopular speakers were always shouted down, if government efforts to censor newspapers were usually met with popular support or even public indifference, if peaceful demonstrations were regularly broken up by hostile mobs, if the losing candidates in an election refused to allow their victorious opponents to take office, then the essential elements of a democratic political culture would be missing, and democracy would fail. Democracy does not require perfect tolerance; if it did, the passions of human nature would make democracy forever impossible. But at a minimum citizens must have a political culture that allows the discussion of ideas and the selection of rulers in an atmosphere reasonably free of oppression.

Public opinion surveys show that the overwhelming majority of Americans agree with such concepts as freedom of speech, majority rule, and the right to circulate petitions—at least in the abstract.[42]

But when we get down to concrete cases, a good many Americans are not very tolerant of groups they dislike. Suppose you must decide which groups will be permitted to espouse their causes at meetings held in your community's civic auditorium. Which of these groups would *you* allow to run such a meeting?

Americans may not vote at as high a rate as citizens in European countries, but they probably sign more petitions than any other people anywhere.

1. Protestants holding a revival meeting

2. Right-to-life groups opposing abortion

3. People protesting a nuclear power plant

4. Feminists organizing a march for the Equal Rights Amendment

5. Gays organizing for homosexual rights

6. Atheists preaching against God

7. Students organizing a sit-in to shut down city hall

In a national opinion poll conducted by Herbert McClosky and Alida Brill in 1978–1979, a majority of Americans would have allowed the first four groups to hold their meetings but would have refused to allow the last three. (Similar findings from another opinion survey are shown in Figure 4.3.) Leaders in the communities where this survey was performed would have allowed the first five groups to meet. Lawyers and judges in these communities would have allowed all seven to meet.[43]

Clearly community leaders, and especially lawyers and judges, are more tolerant of specific political activities than are most citizens. But two things need to be said on behalf of the average citizen.

First, Americans are willing to allow many people with whom they disagree to do a great deal politically. In the McClosky-Brill study, for example, the general public supported the right of the movie industry to make movies on any subjects it chooses, upheld the right of reporters to keep confidential their sources of information, defended the right of newspapers and television stations to hire "radical reporters," believed that college officials should allow nonviolent protest demonstrations by students, and supported freedom of worship even for extremist religious groups.[44]

Second, Americans have become more tolerant over the last few decades. For instance, in the 1970s people were much more willing to allow communists, socialists, and atheists to meet and disseminate their views than they were in the early 1950s, even though Americans in the 1970s were probably no more sympathetic to these causes than they were in the 1950s.[45] Similarly, there has been a general increase in the willingness of citizens to say that they would vote for a Catholic, Jew, black, or woman for president (see Figure 4.4, page 106).

FIGURE 4.3 Public Tolerance for Advocates of Unpopular Ideas, 1954–1993

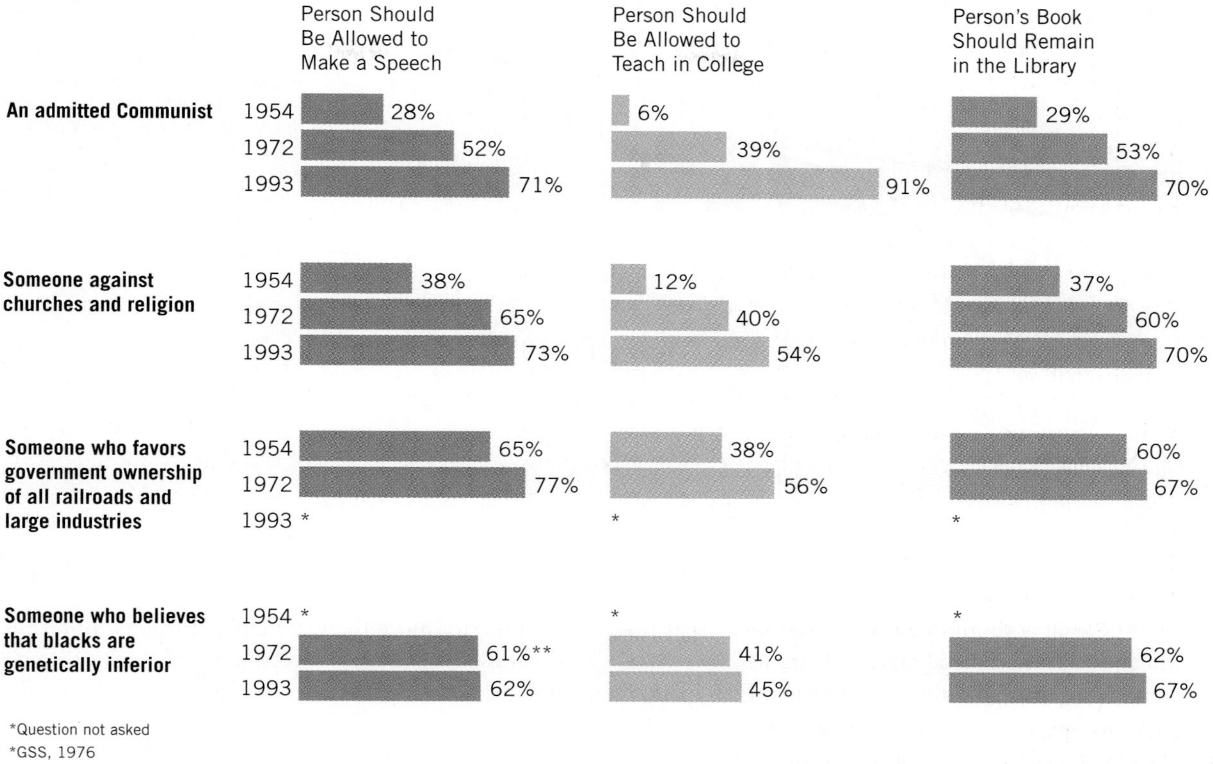

		Person Should Be Allowed to Make a Speech	Person Should Be Allowed to Teach in College	Person's Book Should Remain in the Library
An admitted Communist	1954	28%	6%	29%
	1972	52%	39%	53%
	1993	71%	91%	70%
Someone against churches and religion	1954	38%	12%	37%
	1972	65%	40%	60%
	1993	73%	54%	70%
Someone who favors government ownership of all railroads and large industries	1954	65%	38%	60%
	1972	77%	56%	67%
	1993	*	*	*
Someone who believes that blacks are genetically inferior	1954	*	*	*
	1972	61%**	41%	62%
	1993	62%	45%	67%

*Question not asked
*GSS, 1976

SOURCE: Adapted from Robert S. Erickson and Kent L. Tedin, *American Public Opinion*, 5th ed. Copyright © 1995 by Allyn and Bacon. Reprinted by permission.

Nonetheless, this majority tolerance for many causes should not blind us to the fact that for most of us there is some group or cause from which we are willing to withhold political liberties—even though we endorse those liberties in the abstract.

If most people dislike one or another group strongly enough to deny it certain political rights that we usually take for granted, how is it that such groups (and such rights) survive? The answer, in part, is that most of us don't act on our beliefs. We rarely take the trouble—or have the chance—to block another person from making a speech or teaching school. And among people who are in a position to deny other people rights—officeholders and political activists, for example—the level of political tolerance is somewhat greater than among the public at large.[46]

But another reason may be just as important. Most of us are ready to deny *some* group its rights, but we usually can't agree on which group that should be. Sometimes we can agree, and then the disliked group may be in for real trouble. There have been times (1919–1920, and again in the early 1950s) when socialists or communists were disliked by most people in the United States. The government on each occasion took strong actions against them. Today fewer people agree that these left-wing groups are a major domestic threat, and so their rights are now more secure.

Finally, the courts are sufficiently insulated from public opinion that they can act against majority sentiments and enforce constitutional protections (see Chapter 14). Most of us are not willing to give all rights to all groups, but most of us are not judges.

FIGURE 4.4 Changes in Levels of Political Tolerance

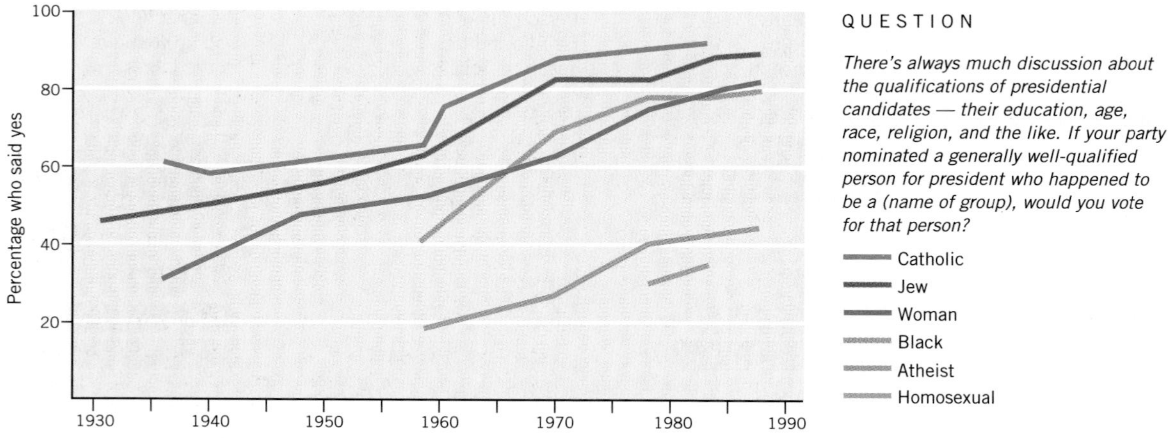

QUESTION

There's always much discussion about the qualifications of presidential candidates — their education, age, race, religion, and the like. If your party nominated a generally well-qualified person for president who happened to be a (name of group), would you vote for that person?

— Catholic
— Jew
— Woman
— Black
— Atheist
— Homosexual

SOURCE: Gallup poll data, various years, as compiled by Professor John Zaller, Department of Political Science, UCLA.

These facts should be a sober reminder that political liberty cannot be taken for granted. Men and women are not, it would seem, born with an inclination to live and let live, at least politically, and many—possibly most—never acquire that inclination. Liberty must be learned and protected. Happily the United States during much of its recent history has not been consumed by a revulsion for any one group that has been strong enough to place the group's rights in jeopardy.

Nor should any part of society pretend that it is always more tolerant than another. In the 1950s, for example, ultraconservatives outside the universities were attacking the rights of professors to say and teach certain things. In the 1960s and 1970s ultraliberal students and professors inside the universities were attacking the rights of other students and professors to say certain things.

SUMMARY

The American system of government is supported by a political culture that fosters a sense of civic duty, takes pride in the nation's constitutional arrangements, and provides support for the exercise of essential civil liberties (albeit out of indifference or diversity more than principle at times). In recent decades mistrust of government officials (though not of the system itself) has increased, and confidence in their responsiveness to popular feelings has declined.

Although Americans value liberty in both the political system and the economy, they believe equality is important only in the political realm. In economic affairs they wish to see equality of opportunity but accept inequality of results.

Not only is our culture generally supportive of democratic rule, it also has certain distinctive features that make our way of governing different from what one finds in other democracies. Americans are preoccupied with their rights, and this fact, combined with a political system that (as we shall see) encourages the vigorous exercise of rights and claims, gives to our political life an *adversarial* style. Unlike Swedes or Japanese, we do not generally reach political decisions by consensus, and we often do not defer to the authority of administrative agencies. American politics, more than that of many other nations, is shot through at every stage with protracted conflict.

But as we shall learn in the next chapter, that conflict is not easily described as always pitting liberals against conservatives. Not only do we have a lot of conflict, it is often messy conflict, a kind of political Tower of Babel. Foreign observers sometimes ask how we stand the confusion. The answer, of course, is that we have been doing it for over two hundred years. Maybe our Constitution is two centuries old not in spite of this confusion but because of it. We shall see.

KEY TERMS

political culture   *p. 86*

political ideology   *p. 87*

civic duty   *p. 91*

civic competence   *p. 91*

work ethic   *p. 96*

class consciousness   *p. 96*

orthodox   *p. 98*

progressive   *p. 98*

political efficacy   *p. 102*

internal efficacy   *p. 102*

external efficacy   *p. 102*

SUGGESTED READINGS

Almond, Gabriel, and Sidney Verba. *The Civic Culture.* Princeton, N.J.: Princeton University Press, 1963. A survey of the political cultures of five nations—the United States, Germany, Great Britain, Italy, and Mexico—as they were in 1959.

Devine, Donald J. *The Political Culture of the United States.* Boston: Little, Brown, 1972. Useful summary of several studies of American political values.

Hartz, Louis. *The Liberal Tradition in America.* New York: Harcourt Brace Jovanovich, 1955. A stimulating interpretation of American political thought since the Founding, emphasizing the notion of a liberal consensus.

Hochschild, Jennifer L. *What's Fair? American Beliefs About Distributive Justice.* Cambridge, Mass.: Harvard University Press, 1981. Revealing, in-depth interviews that compare the attitudes of rich and poor people toward inequality.

Lipset, Seymour Martin. *The First New Nation.* Rev. ed. New York: Norton, 1979. How the origins of American society gave rise to the partially competing values of equality and achievement and the ways in which these values shape political institutions.

McClosky, Herbert, and Alida Brill. *Dimensions of Tolerance: What Americans Believe About Civil Liberties.* New York: Russell Sage Foundation, 1983. How—and whether—different kinds of Americans learn political tolerance.

McClosky, Herbert, and John Zaller. *The American Ethos: Public Attitudes Toward Capitalism and Democracy.* Cambridge, Mass.: Harvard University Press, 1984. Study of the ways in which Americans evaluate political and economic arrangements.

Tocqueville, Alexis de. *Democracy in America.* Edited by Phillips Bradley. 2 vols. New York: Knopf, 1951. First published in 1835–1840, this was and remains the greatest single interpretation of American political culture.

Verba, Sidney, and Gary R. Orren. *Equality in America: The View from the Top.* Cambridge, Mass.: Harvard University Press, 1985. Elite views on political and economic equality.

Wald, Kenneth. *Religion and Politics in the United States,* 2nd ed. Washington, D.C.: Congressional Quarterly Press, 1992. A thoughtful look at how religious beliefs and organizations shape American politics.

PART TWO

Opinions, Interests, and Organizations

"The latent causes of faction are thus sown in the nature of man; and we see them everywhere brought into different degrees of activity, according to the different circumstances of civil society."

— FEDERALIST NO. 10

5

Public Opinion

★ Democracy and public opinion

★ Acquiring party identification from parents

★ Influence of religion, gender, and college on opinion

★ Conducting polls

★ Cleavages in public opinion

★ Liberal and conservative ideology

★ Activists and elite opinion

In the Gettysburg Address Abraham Lincoln said that the United States has a government "of the people, by the people, and for the people." That suggests that the government should do what the people want. If that is the case, it is puzzling that

- The federal government has had a large budget deficit, but the people want a balanced budget.
- Courts have ordered that children be bused in order to balance the schools racially, but the people opposed busing.
- The Equal Rights Amendment to the Constitution was not ratified, but polls showed that most people supported it.
- President Reagan sent aid to Nicaraguans fighting against the Marxist government there, but the people said they did not think our government should do this.
- Most people believe that there should be a limit on the number of terms to which U.S. senators and members of the U.S. House of Representatives can be elected, but Congress has not approved on term limits.

Some people, reflecting on the many gaps between what the government does and what the people want, may become cynical and think our system is democratic in name only. That would be a mistake. There are several very good reasons why government policy will often appear to be at odds with public opinion.

First, the Framers of the Constitution did not try to create a government that would do from day to day "what the people want." They created a government for the purpose of achieving certain substantive goals. The preamble to the Constitution lists six of these: "to form a more perfect union, establish justice, ensure domestic tranquility, provide for the common defense, promote the general welfare, and secure the blessings of liberty."

One means of achieving these goals was popular rule, as provided for by the right of the people to vote for members of the House of Representatives (and later for senators and presidential electors). But other means were provided as well: representative

Elderly Americans express—vocally—their opinions about Medicare benefits.

government, federalism, the separation of powers, a Bill of Rights, and an independent judiciary. These were all intended to be checks on public opinion. In addition, the Framers knew that in a nation as large and diverse as the United States there would rarely be any such thing as "public opinion"; rather, there would be many "publics" (that is, factions), holding many opinions. The Framers hoped that the struggle among these many publics would protect liberty (no one "public" would dominate) while at the same time permitting the adoption of reasonable policies that commanded the support of many factions.

Second, it is not as easy as one may suppose to know what the public thinks. We are so inundated these days with public opinion polls that we may imagine that they tell us what the public believes. That may be true on a few rather simple, clear-cut, and widely discussed issues, but it is not true with respect to most matters on which the government must act. The best pollsters know the limits of their methods, and the citizen should know them as well.

Third, the more people are active in and knowledgeable about politics, the more weight their opin-

ions carry in governmental circles. For most of us, politics ranks way down on the list of things to think about, well below our families, jobs, health, sweethearts, entertainment, and sports. Some people, however, are political activists, and so come to know as much about politics as the rest of us know about batting averages, soap operas, and car repair. Not only do these activists, or political elites, *know more* about politics than the rest of us, they *think differently* about it—they have different views and beliefs. The government attends more to the elite views than to popular views, at least on many matters.

In this chapter we shall take a close look at what "public opinion" is, how it is formed, the major cleavages in public opinion, and, especially, how political elites differ from ordinary citizens. In later chapters we shall examine the workings of political parties, interest groups, and government institutions and consider what impact they have on whether public opinion affects government policy.

What Is Public Opinion?

A few years ago some researchers at the University of Cincinnati asked twelve hundred local residents whether they favored passage of the Monetary Control Bill of 1983. About 21 percent said that they favored the bill, 25 percent said that they opposed it, and the rest said that they hadn't thought much about the matter or didn't know.

The members of Congress from Cincinnati would have been surprised to learn of this expression of public opinion from their constituents, for there was no such thing as the Monetary Control Bill. The researchers had made it up. Nor is there anything unusual about people in Cincinnati. A few years earlier, about 26 percent of the people questioned in a national survey also expressed opinions on the same nonexistent piece of legislation.[1]

Such ignorance (or the inclination to pretend that one is informed) is apparent not only when people are questioned about arcane bits of legislation. In 1986 a national survey found that only a third of the people polled could identify Caspar Weinberger (he was then the secretary of defense), and only 14 percent knew who William Rehnquist was (the chief justice of the United States Supreme Court). Robert Dole was running for president (and according to some polls, doing reasonably well), but only 12 percent of the people could identify him accurately.[2] Given this low level of name recognition, how much confidence should we place in polls that presumably tell us "what the American people think" about our defense policy, the posture of the Supreme Court, and presidential candidates?

Even if people have heard of a given person or issue, how a pollster words a question can dramatically affect the answer he or she gets. Suppose we want to know whether the public believes that the federal government should provide housing for people. In Table 5.1 we see the results obtained from asking that question in three different ways. In the first example people are asked whether they agree or disagree with a one-sided statement ("The federal government should see to it that all people have adequate housing"). A majority agree. In the second example we give people a choice between two statements, one favoring a federal housing policy (mentioned first) and the other favoring individual responsibility ("each person should provide for his own housing"). Given this choice, a small majority now opposes federal housing programs. In the third example the question is repeated, but this time with the individual responsibility option mentioned first. Now over 70 percent of the respondents oppose fed-

John Q. Public/ Middle America/ Silent Majority

John Q. Public is the average man or woman in the street, often portrayed by cartoonists as bespectacled and befuddled. The "little guy," the "common man" (or woman), John Doe or Jane Doe. John Q. Public is sometimes confused with James Q. Wilson, to whom he is only distantly related.

Middle America is a phrase coined by the late Joseph Kraft in 1968 to refer to Americans who have moved out of poverty but are not yet affluent and who cherish the traditional middle-class values.

The **silent majority** consists of those people, whatever their economic status, who uphold traditional values, especially against the counter-culture of the 1960s.

SOURCE: Adapted from *Safire's Political Dictionary* by William Safire. Copyright © 1968, 1972, 1978 by William Safire. Reprinted by permission of Random House, Inc. and the author.

TABLE 5.1 The Effects of Question Wording: The Issue of Public Housing

One-sided question		
Do you agree or disagree with the following statement: The federal government should see to it that all people have adequate housing.	Agree: government responsible	55.0%
	Disagree: government not responsible	45.0%
Two-sided question, government option first		
Some people feel that the federal government should see to it that all people have adequate housing, while others feel each person should provide for his own housing. Which comes *closest* to how you feel about this?	Government responsible	44.6%
	Government not responsible	55.4%
Two-sided question, government option second		
Some people feel that each person should provide for his own housing, while others feel the federal government should see to it that all people have adequate housing. Which comes *closest* to how you feel about this?	Government responsible	29.5%
	Government not responsible	70.5%

SOURCE: Howard Schuman and Stanley Presser, *Questions and Answers in Attitude Surveys* (New York: Academic Press, 1981), 70–71.

eral housing programs. Obviously just altering the order in which people are presented with options affects which option they choose and, in this case, changes what "public opinion" is on housing programs.

Moreover, opinions on public issues may not be stable—that is, they may not be firmly held. In a study conducted in 1980, the same people were asked the same questions in January and again in June of the same year. The first had to do with how tough we should be in dealing with the Soviet Union, the second with whether spending should be cut on things like health and education programs. As Table 5.2 shows, many people gave one opinion in January and then a different one in June. Of those who said in January that we should cooperate more with the Soviets, only one-quarter said in June that we should get together with them. Of those who said in January that the government should cut the services it provides, more than one-quarter said in June that they wanted to keep those services at the same level or expressed a middle-of-the-road position.

In sum, public opinion on many matters suffers from ignorance, instability, and sensitivity to the way questions are worded in polls. This does not mean that the American people are ignorant, unstable, or gullible, only that most Americans do not find it worth their while to spend the amount of time thinking about politics that they spend on their jobs, families, and friends. Moreover, just because people do not think much about politics does not mean that democracy is impossible, only that it can work best when people are given relatively simple, clear-cut choices—like the choice between Democrats and Republicans or between one presidential candidate and another.

Furthermore, our specific attitudes about particular matters may be much less important for the health of society than our underlying political culture—our commitment, discussed in Chapter 4, to liberty, equality, individualism, and civic duty. As we shall see, different people give different weight to the various parts of this culture, producing what can be described as a political ideology.

The Origins of Political Attitudes

Because our attitudes are often unstable or uninformed, some critics of American society have argued that we are brainwashed—duped by television or demagogic leaders into thinking one way or another. Often we are told that presidential candidates are "sold," as if they were boxes of soap flakes. Naturally these critics never say that *they* are brainwashed, only the rest of us.

TABLE 5.2   Response Stability over Repeated Interviews: Two Examples

AMERICAN RELATIONS WITH RUSSIA[a]
Some people feel it is important for us to try very hard to get along with Russia. Others feel it is a big mistake to try too hard to get along with Russia. Where would you place yourself on this scale, or haven't you thought about this?

| Attitudes in **June** 1980 | Attitudes in **January** 1980 | | | |
	Cooperate	Middle	Tougher	Unsure
Cooperate	**52%**	25%	13%	19%
Middle	14	**24**	17	16
Tougher	23	41	**60**	18
Unsure	10	11	11	**47**
Number	338	153	266	74

LEVEL OF GOVERNMENT SERVICES[b]
Some people think the government should provide fewer services, even in areas such as health and education, in order to reduce spending. Other people feel it is important for the government to continue the services it now provides even if it means no reduction in spending. Where would you place yourself on this scale, or haven't you thought about this?

| Attitudes in **June** 1980 | Attitudes in **January** 1980 | | | |
	Cut	Middle	Keep Same	Unsure
Cut	**54%**	38%	18%	34%
Middle	18	**24**	10	10
Keep same	11	25	**59**	15
Unsure	17	14	13	**41**
Number	362	122	208	138

[a] Respondents were asked to place themselves on a seven-point scale. In this table, points 1, 2, and 3 have been counted as "cooperate"; 4 is counted as "middle"; 5, 6, and 7 have been counted as "tougher." [b] Points 1, 2, and 3 have been counted as "cut"; 4 is counted as "middle"; 5, 6, and 7 have been counted as "keep same." SOURCE: National Election Studies, 1980 panel study. Reprinted from The American Enterprise, a Washington-based magazine of politics, business, and culture.

However shallow their analysis, the argument is a serious one. If the government (or the media) were able to manipulate our political attitudes, then democracy would be a joke. It is akin to what would happen in the marketplace if automobile dealers were able to "brainwash" us into buying Chevrolets, Fords, Chryslers, or Toyotas. The car manufacturers would no longer have to strive to achieve greater efficiency and produce better products; they would only have to "persuade" us what to like. We would be happy not because we owned a good car but because Madison Avenue *told* us we owned a good car.

Of course, advertising does affect our choice of candidates and policies, just as it affects our choice of automobiles. Otherwise, why would companies and politicians spend so much money on advertising? But there are real and important limits to the impact of that advertising. Those limits exist because we have learned, independently of government and the market, some things that help us make our own choices.

The Role of the Family

The best-studied (though not necessarily the most important) case of opinion formation is that of party identification. The majority of young people identify with their parents' political party. A study of high school seniors showed that, of these young men and women, almost all (91 percent) knew accurately the presidential preference of their parents, the great majority (71 percent) knew accurately their parents' party identification, and most shared that identification (only 9 percent identified with the party opposite to that of their parents).[3] (See Table 5.3.) This process begins fairly early in life: by the time they are in the fifth grade (age eleven), over half of all schoolchildren identify with one party or the other, and another fifth claim to be independents.[4]

Naturally, as people grow older they become more independent of their parents in many ways, including politically, but there nonetheless remains a great deal of continuity between youthful partisanship, learned from one's parents, and adult partisanship. One study of adults found that around 60 percent still had the party identification—Democrat, Republican, or independent—of their parents.

"Yes, son, we're Republicans."

Drawing by Richter; © 1991 The *New Yorker* Magazine, Inc.

Of those who differ with their parents, the overwhelming majority do so not by identifying with the opposite party but by describing themselves as "independents."[5]

The ability of the family to inculcate a strong sense of party identification has declined in recent years. The proportion of citizens who say they consider themselves to be Democrats or Republicans has become steadily smaller since the early 1950s. This drop has been greatest among those who *strongly* identify with one party or another. In 1952, fully 22 percent of voters said they were strong

TABLE 5.3 **Parent and Child Agreement in Party Identification**

Child	Parents		
	Democrat	Independent	Republican
Democrat	**66%**	29%	13%
Independent	27	**53**	36
Republican	7	17	**51**
Number	914	442	495

SOURCE: M. Kent Jennings and Richard G. Niemi, *The Political Character of Adolescence: The Influence of Families and Schools* (Princeton, N.J.: Princeton University Press, 1974), 41. Copyright © 1974 by Princeton University Press. Reprinted by permission.

Democrats and 13 percent said they were strong Republicans; by 1976 only 15 percent claimed to be strong Democrats and 9 percent to be strong Republicans. Accompanying this decline in partisanship has been a sharp rise in the proportion of citizens describing themselves as independents.

Part of this change results from the fact that young voters have always had a weaker sense of partisanship than older ones, and today there are proportionally a larger number of young voters than there were thirty years ago. But the youthfulness of the population cannot explain all the changes, for the decline in partisanship has occurred at all age levels. Moreover, those who reached voting age in the 1960s were less apt than those who matured in the 1950s to keep the party identification of their parents.[6]

Though we still tend to acquire some measure of partisanship from our parents, the meaning of that identification is far from clear. There are, after all, liberal and conservative Democrats, as well as liberal and conservative Republicans. So far the evidence suggests that children are more independent of their parents in policy preferences than in party identification. The correlation of children's attitudes with parental attitudes on issues involving civil liberties and racial questions is much lower than the correlation in their party identification. This may be because issues change from one generation to the next, because children are more idealistic than their parents, or because most parents do not communicate to their children clear, consistent positions on a range of political issues. The family dinner table is not a seminar in political philosophy but a place where people discuss jobs, school, dates, and chores.

In some families, however, the dinner table is a political classroom. Fairly clear political ideologies (a term we shall define in a later section) seem to be communicated to that small proportion of children raised in families where politics is a dominant topic of conversation and political views are strongly held. Studies of the participants in various student radical movements in the 1960s suggested that college radicals were often the sons and daughters of people who had themselves been young radicals; some commentators dubbed them the "red-diaper babies." Presumably, deeply conservative people come disproportionately from families that were also deeply conservative. This transfer of political beliefs from one generation to the next does not appear in large

TABLE 5.4 Religious Orientation

Political Opinion	Religious Orientation		
	Secular	In Between	Fundamentalist
Increase domestic spending	48%	41%	32%
Institute national health insurance	63	56	38
Guarantee good standard of living	38	23	21
Permit all abortions	70	50	14
Prohibit mandatory school prayers	67	60	51
Allow gays in the military	68	59	32
Encourage equal role for women	99	93	71
Fund more AIDS research	63	52	46
Cut defense spending	77	70	42
Oppose Gulf War	17	11	10
Increase aid to Russia	35	33	24
Percent Democratic (of party identifiers)	41	40	30
Percent liberal (of ideological identifiers)	48	38	7
Percent for Clinton (1992)	57	49	23

SOURCE: From Robert S. Erikson and Kent L. Tedin, *American Public Opinion*, 5th ed. Copyright © 1995 by Allyn and Bacon. Reprinted by permission.

national studies, because such a small proportion of the population is at either the far left or the far right of the political spectrum.

Religion

One way in which the family forms and transmits political beliefs is by its religious tradition. In general, Catholic families are somewhat more liberal on economic issues than white Protestant ones, while Jewish families are much more liberal on both economic and social issues than families of either Catholics or Protestants.[7]

There are two theories as to why this should be so. The first has to do with the **social status** of religious groups in America. When they immigrated to this country, Catholics and Jews were often poor and the object of discrimination. As a result they often affiliated themselves with whichever party and social doctrine seemed most sympathetic to their plight. In many places the Democratic party and a liberal social doctrine seemed to offer the most support. Today Catholics and Jews enjoy greater economic prosperity and face much less discrimination, and so their support for Democrats and liberal candidates has weakened.

The status explanation cannot be the whole story, for if it were simply a matter of low status and discrimination, born-again Christians, many of whom are poor and all of whom are treated with contempt by the national media, would be liberal Democrats.

The second theory emphasizes the content of the **religious tradition** more than the social status of its adherents. In this view the Jewish religion has always emphasized social justice as much as personal rectitude. By contrast evangelical Protestant denominations emphasize personal salvation (becoming "born again") more than questions of social policy. This difference in teachings has led Jews to be disproportionately liberal and fundamentalist Protestants to be disproportionately conservative on many social issues.

Whatever the reason, religious differences make for political differences. In Table 5.4 we can see how the religious beliefs of white voters affected their policy preferences in 1992. Fundamentalists believe that the Bible is God's word and literally true. They are more likely than those who doubt that the Bible

The Christian Coalition was for many years headed by Ralph Reed.

is inspired by God to oppose cuts in defense spending, to want cuts in domestic spending, to oppose abortions, and to favor prayer in schools. (These differences remain essentially the same even after you divide the respondents between those who have a lot of political information and those who have rather little.)

Interestingly, there are no significant differences in how people holding differing views of the Bible feel about economic issues, as opposed to social or foreign policy issues. Fundamentalists and nonfundamentalists have about the same opinion on government job guarantees and spending on government services. This suggests that both social status and religious tradition help explain the effect of religion on politics: the poor status of many fundamentalists inclines them to back liberal government economic policies, but the religious tradition of this group leads them to take a conservative position on social and foreign policy matters.

In the early 1990s a broad-based political movement arose to represent the views of conservative evangelical Christians. The movement was spearheaded by the Christian Coalition, an activist organ-

TABLE 5.5   The Gender Gap: Differences in Political Views of Men and Women

Issue	Men	Women
Federal spending for welfare programs should be increased.	13%	20%
Abortion should be permitted by law.	65	60
Sexual harassment is a very serious problem in the workplace.	24	38
This country would be better off if we just stayed home and did not concern ourselves with problems in other parts of the world.	21	33
The United States did the right thing in sending military forces to the Persian Gulf.	83	71
All things considered, the Persian Gulf War was worth it.	66	47
I voted for Clinton in 1992.	41	53
Generally speaking, I think of myself as a Democrat.	30	39
The United States should increase defense spending.	22	18
The United States should increase spending on solving the problems of the homeless.	66	78
Over the past year, America's ability to compete in the world economy has gotten better.	18	11

SOURCE: ICPSR American National Election Survey, 1992: Pre- and Post-Election Surveys.

ization founded by Pat Robertson and led by Ralph Reed. Unlike the older Moral Majority, the Christian Coalition took seriously the task of entering politics at the grassroots and recognized the need to build working alliances with mainstream politicians. Within a short time, people allied with the Christian Coalition have won power in many local Republican party organizations, and its national conferences have become important places for Republican presidential candidates to appear. Although the Christian Coalition is strongest in the South, Midwest, and West, it is unmistakably a national force in American politics. During the 1994 elections, for example, it distributed some 30 million voter guides nationwide, and affiliated local organizations may have distributed several million more. Recent opinion surveys show that since 1960, evangelical Christians have become more attached to Republican presidential candidates (except in 1976, when Jimmy Carter ran), while Jews and those without a religious orientation have been consistently supportive of the Democratic party.

The Gender Gap

In recent elections much has been made of the **gender gap**—that is, the differences in political views between women and men. In fact, such differences have existed for as long as we have records. What has changed about the gender gap is which party benefits from it.

During the 1950s women were more likely to be Republicans than men; since the late 1960s they have been more likely to be Democrats. The reason for the shift is that the political parties have changed their positions on the kinds of issues to which women respond differently than men—certain social questions (such as prohibition and gun control) and foreign policy (especially the threat of war). For example, in the 1930s and 1940s more women than men wanted to ban the sale of liquor and keep the country out of war; this helped the Republicans, who were then more sympathetic to such policies than the Democrats. In 1980 the aversion that women felt to any policy that might increase the risk of war hurt the Republicans, whom they saw being led by a candidate (Reagan) who was ready to send troops into combat (even so, in 1984 a clear majority of women voted for Reagan).[8]

The gender gap tends to disappear during years in which gender-sensitive policies—war, gun control, or pornography—are not in the limelight and to reemerge during those years in which these topics become hotly partisan. As we see in Table 5.5, the biggest male-female differences are over the use of force and in confidence in the future. The gender gap is not unique to the United States; it can be found throughout the world.

Analysts disagree about the electoral significance of the gender gap. One unresolved question is whether, other things being equal, female voters are more likely than male voters to support female candidates. For example, in 1992 there were ten U.S. Senate races with female candidates. As we see in Table 5.6, women gave a higher fraction of their

TABLE 5.6   **The Gender Gap in Selected U.S. Senate Races, 1992**

		Men	Women	Gender Gap[a]
Selected Senate races involving women				
California	Barbara Boxer (D)	43%	57%	28%
	Bruce Herschensohn (R)	51	37	
	Dianne Feinstein (D)	50	64	27
	John Seymour (R)	46	33	
Illinios	Carol Moseley Braun (D)	50	57	14
	Richard Williamson (R)	47	40	
Missouri	Geri Rothman-Serot (D)	39	48	17
	Christopher Bond (R)	58	50	
Pennsylvania	Lynn Yeakel (D)	42	52	19
	Arlen Specter (R)	54	45	
Selected Senate races not involving women				
Georgia	Wyche Fowler (D)	47	54	14
	Paul Coverdell (R)	53	46	
New York	Robert Abrams (D)	43	52	18
	Alfonse D'Amato (R)	54	45	
Oregon	Les AuCoin (D)	39	55	31
	Robert Packwood (R)	58	43	

a The gender gap is the difference between the margin of support women gave women (or Democratic) candidates and their opponents and the margin of support men gave women (or Democratic) candidates and their opponents.
SOURCE: Reprinted from *The American Enterprise,* a Washington-based magazine of politics, business, and culture (January/February 1993): 100.

votes to female candidates than did men in all of these races. But the size of the gender gap varied from race to race, and the gender gap was also a party gap. A hard-to-specify fraction of the gender gap in voting reflects the tendency of women to identify more strongly than men with the Democratic party.[9]

Schooling and Information

Studies going back over half a century seem to show that attending college has a big impact on political attitudes, usually making them more liberal. College students are more liberal than the population generally, and students at the most prestigious or selective colleges are the most liberal of all.[10] For example, the undergraduates at Harvard College in 1984 preferred Mondale to Reagan 61 percent to 28 percent, while the country at large favored Reagan over Mondale 59 percent to 41 percent.[11] Moreover, the longer students stay in college, the more liberal they are, with seniors more liberal than freshmen and graduate students more liberal than undergraduates.[12] Harvard seniors were more supportive of Mondale than were Harvard freshmen. Students studying the social sciences tend to be more liberal than those studying engineering or the physical sciences.[13] As we shall see in the next chapter, having gone to college increases the rate at which people participate in politics.

Why schooling should have this effect on attitudes is not clear. One possibility is that it has nothing to do with schooling but rather with the individual traits typically possessed by people who go to college and beyond. Some combination of temperament, intelligence, and family background may lead to greater liberalism, with the contents of a college education playing no role at all.

A second possibility is that college and postgraduate schooling expose people to more information

TABLE 5.7 Automobiles and Ideology: Kinds of Automobiles Owned by College Faculty Members Who Have Differing Political Ideologies (in percentages)

Automobile	Political Ideology				
	liberal 1	2	3	4	conservative 5
GM	12%	18%	18%	23%	29%
Ford	15	19	20	22	24
Chrysler	19	22	18	21	20
AMC	21	17	12	23	26
Japanese	22	22	17	20	18
Volkswagen	26	26	16	17	15
Fiat	27	18	30	11	13
Mercedes-Benz	32	19	21	17	11
Volvo	32	19	18	18	14
No car	31	28	23	11	7

NOTE: The more liberal the faculty member, the more likely he or she is to own no car or an imported car, especially a Volvo or a Mercedes-Benz. The more conservative the faculty member, the more likely he or she is to own an American car, especially a General Motors product.

SOURCE: Data from survey of faculty opinion by Everett Carll Ladd, Jr., and Seymour Martin Lipset, 1975. B. Bruce-Briggs, *The War against the Automobile* (New York: Dutton, 1977), 184.

about politics from all sources. College graduates, compared to high school graduates, read more newspapers and periodicals, join more organizations and social movements, and participate in more election campaigns and lobbying efforts. Their political beliefs may be shaped by these experiences as much as, or more than, by what they learn in the college classroom. In addition, evidence collected by John Zaller shows that the level of political information one has is the best single predictor of being liberal on some kinds of issues, such as civil liberties and civil rights.[14] Information on these matters, he suggests, is today produced by a predominantly liberal cultural elite (see Chapter 10). The longer you stay in school, the more you are exposed to the views of that elite.

The third possibility is that college somehow teaches liberalism. We know that professors are more liberal than members of other occupations, that professors at the most prestigious schools are more liberal than those at the less-celebrated ones, that professors in the social sciences are more liberal than those in engineering or business, and that younger faculty members are more liberal than older ones.[15]

(College faculty members often develop a lifestyle that reveals their political convictions. As shown in Table 5.7, a professor who drives a Volvo or Mercedes tends to be politically more liberal than one who drives a Chevrolet or Ford.)

The political disposition of professors is in part the result of the kinds of people who become college teachers, but it is also the result of the nature of intellectual work. Intellectuals require freedom to explore new or unpopular ideas and thus tend to be strong supporters of civil liberties. Intellectuals work with words and numbers to develop general or abstract ideas; frequently they do not take personal responsibility for practical matters. Thus they are often critical of people who do take such responsibility and who, in the management of complex human affairs, inevitably make compromises. Intellectuals are by training and profession skeptical of common opinions, and thus they are often critical of accepted values and existing institutions. They are interested in ideas and the ideal and thus are sometimes disdainful of the interests and institutions of society.

At one time the liberalizing effect of college had only a small impact on national politics, because so few persons were college graduates. In 1900 only 6 percent of Americans seventeen years of age had even graduated from high school, and less than 1 percent of twenty-three-year-olds were college graduates. By 1982, fully 71 percent of all Americans ages twenty-five and over were high school graduates, and 18 percent of those ages twenty-five and over were college graduates.[16] College, or the exposure to ideas and movements that one encounters there, has become, along with the family, an important source of political opinion for the American electorate.

Some people believe that college students today are more conservative than students were ten or twenty years ago. That is partly true and partly false. As indicated in Table 5.8, contemporary college freshmen are less likely to favor legalizing marijuana or abortion but more willing to support busing to integrate schools. Their opinions about government-sponsored environmental protection measures are unchanged.

How long the liberalizing effect of college persists depends on a number of factors. One study found that former college students still described themselves as more liberal than their parents seven years after graduation.[17] Another study found that students who changed in college from being conservative to being liberal tended to maintain that liberalism for at least twenty years if they acquired, after graduation, liberal friends and spouses.[18] College graduates who go on to get a postgraduate degree—say, a law degree or a Ph.D.—tend to become decidedly more liberal than those who stop with just a B.A. degree.[19] A scholar who tracked students graduating from college in 1969 found that those who had taken part in protests remained very liberal well into the 1980s, while nonprotesters became somewhat more conservative over the years.[20]

Cleavages in Public Opinion

The way in which political opinions are formed helps explain the cleavages that exist among these opinions and why these cleavages do not follow any single political principle but instead overlap and crosscut in bewildering complexity. If, for example, the United States lacked regional differences and was composed almost entirely of white Protestants who had never attended college there would still be plenty of political conflict—the rich would have different views from the poor; workers would have different views from farmers—but that conflict would be much simpler to describe and explain. It might even lead to political parties that were more clearly aligned with competing political philosophies than those we now have. In fact, some democratic nations in the world today do have a population very much like the one we have asked you to imagine, and the United States itself, during the first half of the nineteenth century, was overwhelmingly white, Protestant, and without much formal schooling.

Today, however, there are crosscutting cleavages based on race, ethnicity, religion, region, and education, in addition to those created by income and occupation. To the extent that politics is sensitive to public opinion, it is sensitive to a variety of different and even competing publics. Not all these publics have influence proportionate to their numbers or even to their numbers adjusted for the intensity of their feelings. As will be described later, a filtering process occurs that makes the opinions of some publics more influential than those of others.

TABLE 5.8   **The Changing College Student**

Since the 1970s college freshmen have become more conservative on some issues and more liberal on others.

Issue	Percentage Agreeing	
	1970s[a]	1993
Abolish death penalty	33%	22%
Legalize abortion	83	62
Legalize marijuana	47	28
Increase military spending	39	23
Criminals have too many rights	52	68
Government not doing enough to:		
Control pollution	91	84
Protect consumers	77	72

NOTE: We have no comparable figures for college seniors. Freshmen may change their opinions on these matters while in school.

[a] Exact year the question was asked in 1970s varies between 1970 and 1976, depending on the question.

SOURCE: Richard C. Braungart and Margaret M. Braungart, "Black Colleges: Freshmen Attitudes," *Public Opinion* (May–June 1989): 14. Reprinted with the permission of the American Enterprise Institute for Public Policy Research, Washington, D.C. Updated to 1993 from Alexander W. Astin, William S. Korn, and Ellyne R. Riggs, *The American Freshman* (Los Angeles, CA: UCLA Graduate School of Education, 1993), p. 25.

Whatever this state of affairs may mean for democracy, it creates a messy situation for political scientists. It would be so much easier if everyone's opinion on political affairs reflected some single feature of his or her life, such as income, occupation, age, race, or sex. Of course, some writers have argued that political opinion is a reflection of one such feature, social class, usually defined in terms of income or occupation, but that view, though containing some truth, is beset with inconsistencies: poor blacks and poor whites disagree sharply on many issues involving race; well-to-do Jews and well-to-do Protestants often have opposing opinions on social welfare policy; and low-income elderly people are much more worried about crime than are low-income graduate students. Plumbers and professors may have similar incomes, but they rarely have similar views, and businesspeople in New York City often take a very different view of government than businesspeople in Houston or Birmingham.

In some other democracies a single factor such as class may explain more of the differences in political attitudes than it does in the more socially heterogeneous United States. Most blue-collar workers

The Art of Public-Opinion Polling

A survey of public opinion—popu-larly called a **poll**—can provide us with a reasonably accurate measure of how people think, provided certain conditions are met. There are five key criteria that must be met in designing and interpreting surveys.

1. **The persons interviewed must be a random sample of the entire population.** In a **random sample** poll any given person, or any given voter or adult, has an equal chance of being interviewed. Most national surveys draw a sample of between a thousand and fifteen hundred persons by a process called stratified or multistage area sampling. The pollster makes a list of all the geographical units in the country (say, all the counties) and groups (or "stratifies") them by the size of their population. The pollster then selects at random units from each group or stratum in proportion to its total population. For example, if one stratum's total population is 10 percent of the national population, then 10 perent of the counties in the sample will be drawn from this stratum. Within each selected county, smaller and smaller geographical units (cities, towns, census tracts, blocks) are chosen, and then, within the smallest unit, individuals are selected at random (by, for example, choosing the occupant of every fifth house). The key is to stick to the sample and not let people volunteer to be inter-

viewed—volunteers often have views different from those who do not volunteer.

2. **The questions must be comprehensible.** The questions must ask people about things they have some knowledge of and some basis for forming an opinion about. Most people know, at least at election time, whom they would prefer as president; most people also have views about what they think the most important national problems are. But relatively few voters will have any opinion about our policy toward El Salvador (if indeed they have even heard of it) or about the investment tax credit. If everybody refused to answer questions about which they are poorly informed, no problem would arise, but unfortunately many of us like to pretend that we know things that in fact we don't or to be "helpful" to interviewers by inventing opinions on the spur of the moment.

3. **The questions must be asked fairly.** They should be worded in clear language, without the use of "loaded" or "emotional" words. They must give no indication of what the "right" answer is but offer a reasonable explanation, where necessary, of the consequences of each possible answer. For example, in 1971 a Gallup poll asked people whether they favored a proposal

"to bring home all U.S. troops [from Vietnam] before the end of the year." Two-thirds of the public agreed with that. Then the question was asked in a different way: Do you agree or disagree with a proposal to withdraw all U.S. troops by the end of the year "regardless of what happens there [in Vietnam] after U.S. troops leave"? In this form, substantially less than half the public agreed.

4. **The answer categories offered to a person must be carefully considered.** This is no problem when there are only two candidates for office—say, Bill Clinton and Bob Dole—and you want only to know which one the voters prefer. But it can be a big problem when you want more complex information. For example, if you ask people (as does George Gallup) whether they "approve" or "disapprove" of how the president is handling his job, you will get one kind of answer—let us say that 55 percent approve and 45 percent disapprove. On the other hand, if you ask them (as does Louis Harris) how they rate the job the president is doing, "excellent, pretty good, only fair, or poor," you will get very different results. It is quite possible that only 46 percent will pick such positive answers as "excellent" or "pretty good," and the rest will pick the negative answers, "only fair" and

"poor." If you are president, you can choose to believe Mr. Gallup (and feel pleased) or Mr. Harris (and be worried). The differences in the two polls do not arise from the competence of the two pollsters but entirely from the choice of answers that they include with their questions.

5. **Not every difference in answers is a significant difference.** A survey is based on a sample of people. Select another sample, by equally randomized methods, and you might get slightly different results. This difference is called a **sampling error,** and its likely size can be computed mathematically. In general, the bigger the sample and the bigger the differences between the percentage of people giving one answer and the percentage giving another, the smaller the sampling error. If a poll of fifteen hundred voters reveals that 47 percent favor Bill Clinton, we can be 95 percent certain that the actual proportion of all voters favoring Clinton is within three percentage points of this figure—that is, it lies somewhere between 44 and 50 percent. In a close race an error of this size could be quite important. It could be reduced by using a bigger sample, but the cost of interviewing a sample big enough to make the error much smaller is huge.

As a result of sampling error and for other reasons, it is very hard for pollsters to predict the winner in a close election. Since 1952 every major national poll has in fact picked the winner of the presidential election, but there may have been some luck involved in such close races as the 1960 Kennedy-Nixon and the 1976 Carter-Ford contests. In 1980 the polls greatly underestimated the Reagan vote, partly because many voters made up their minds at the last minute and partly because a bigger percentage of Carter supporters decided not to vote at all. In contrast, pollsters did remarkably well in forecasting the results of the 1992 presidential election, a volatile three-way race between Bill Clinton, George Bush, and Ross Perot. Although they tended to overestimate Clinton's margin and to underestimate Perot's, twenty of the most frequently cited national polls came close to predicting the actual results. Polling is not an exact science, but done right, it is a highly skilled art.

in America think of themselves as being "middle-class," whereas most such workers in Britain and France describe themselves as "working-class." In England the working class prefers the Labour party by a margin of three to one, while in the United States workers prefer the Democratic party by less than two to one, and in 1980 and 1984 they gave most of their votes to Ronald Reagan.[21]

Social Class

Americans speak of "social class" with embarrassment. The norm of equality tugs at our conscience, urging us to judge people as individuals, not as parts of some social group (such as "the lower class"). Social scientists speak of "class" with confusion. They know it exists but quarrel constantly about how to define it: By income? Occupation? Wealth? Schooling? Prestige? Personality?

Let's face up to the embarrassment and skip over the confusion. Truck drivers and investment bankers look different, talk different, and vote different. There is nothing wrong with saying that the first group consists of "working-class" (or "blue-collar") people and the latter of "upper-class" (or "management") people. Moreover, though different definitions of class produce slightly different groupings of people, most definitions overlap to such an extent that it does not matter too much which we use.

However defined, public opinion and voting have been less determined by class in the United States than in Europe, and the extent of class cleavage has declined in the last few decades in both the United States and Europe. In the 1950s V. O. Key, Jr., found that differences in political opinion were closely associated with occupation. He noted that people holding managerial or professional jobs had distinctly more conservative views on social welfare policy and more internationalist views on foreign policy than did manual workers.[22]

During the next decade this pattern changed greatly. Opinion surveys done in the late 1960s showed that business and professional people had views quite similar to those of manual workers on such matters as the poverty program, health insurance, American policy in Vietnam, and government efforts to create jobs.[23]

The voting patterns of different social classes have also become somewhat more similar. Class vot-

ing has declined sharply since the late 1940s in the United States, France, Great Britain, and West Germany and declined moderately in Sweden.

Class differences remain, of course. Unskilled workers are more likely than affluent white-collar workers to be Democrats and to have liberal views on economic policy. And when economic issues pinch—for example, when farmers are hurting or steelworkers are being laid off—the importance of economic interests in differentiating the opinions of various groups rises sharply. Moreover, there is some evidence that during the Reagan administration, income once again began to make a large difference in the party affiliation of voters.

Why should social class, defined along income lines, have become less important over the long term? One reason has to do largely with schooling. At one time the income of people did not depend so heavily as it now does on having educational credentials. Most people had only a high school education, whatever their job might be, and only a small minority had a college or postgraduate degree. Today access to higher-paying jobs (outside of sports and entertainment) is increasingly restricted to people with extensive schooling. Since, as we have seen, college and (especially) postgraduate education tends to make people more liberal than they would otherwise be, the arrival of millions of college graduates, lawyers, and Ph.D.'s into the ranks of the financially affluent has brought into the upper classes a more liberal political outlook than once was the case.

Another reason is that the issues that now lead us to choose which party to support and that determine whether we think of ourselves as liberals or conservatives have increasingly become noneconomic issues. In recent years our political posture has been shaped by the positions we take on race relations, abortion, school prayer, arms control, and environmentalism, issues that do not clearly affect the rich differently from the poor (or at least do not affect them as differently as do the union movement, the minimum wage, and unemployment). Moral, symbolic, and foreign policy matters do not divide rich and poor in the same way as economic ones. Thus we have many well-off people who think of themselves as liberals because they take liberal positions on these noneconomic matters, and many not-so-well-off people who think of themselves as conservatives because that is the position they take on these issues.

Race and Ethnicity

If class has become a less clear-cut source of political cleavage, race has become more of one. Whites and blacks differ profoundly over whether children should be bused to achieve racially balanced schools and whether a person should be able to sell his or her home to anyone, even if it means refusing to sell it to a black. The differences extend to nonracial matters as well. Whites are more likely than blacks to support the death penalty for murder and to favor increased spending on national defense; they are less likely to endorse national health insurance. In the 1960s blacks were more opposed than whites to the war in Vietnam. An issue that divides blacks and whites in the 1990s is how to remedy the effects of past racial discrimination. As Seymour Martin Lipset has observed, "every national survey still shows that a sizable majority of whites is opposed to remedying the effects of past discrimination by giving special consideration to the less formally qualified with respect to hiring or school admissions."[24] For example, a 1991 Gallup poll asked, "Do you believe that because of past discrimination against black people, qualified blacks should receive preference over equally qualified whites in such matters as getting into college or getting jobs?" Only 19 percent of whites, compared to 48 percent of blacks, responded positively.[25] More generally, a 1996 report by the Center for New Black Leadership documented wide and persistent differences of opinion between blacks and whites on a number of important public policy issues. For example, blacks have long been more in favor of welfare expenditures and school prayer, and less in favor of the death penalty, than whites.[26]

There are, however, many issues on which the two races feel pretty much the same, such as allowing the police to search the homes of known drug dealers without a warrant, opposing a woman's right to abortion on demand, and opposing the legalization of marijuana. And despite broad differences over how to remedy the effects of past discrimination, majorities of both blacks and whites oppose policies requiring specific quotas and numerical goals for integration.[27] Finally, between 1974 and

TABLE 5.9 Changes in Race and Public Opinion

	Whites		Blacks	
	1974	1992	1974	1992
Government should help blacks	25%	19%	63%	42%
Unsure	26	26	25	24
Blacks should help themselves	50	54	12	33
	101%	100%	100%	100%

SOURCE: From Robert S. Erikson and Kent L. Tedin, *American Public Opinion*, 5th ed. Copyright © 1995 by Allyn and Bacon. Reprinted by permission.

1992 the gap between black and white views on the government's responsibility to help blacks narrowed somewhat (see Table 5.9).

Blacks have become the most consistently liberal group within the Democratic party.[28] Nevertheless, a majority of blacks believe they are as a group better off today than they were ten years ago and that their children's opportunities will be better yet.[29]

There appears to be less class cleavage among blacks than among whites—that is, the differences in opinion between poor and better-off blacks is less than it is between poor and better-off whites.[30] This means that at every income level blacks are more liberal than whites.* However, there is a significant gap between the leaders of black organizations and black people generally. A 1985 survey of over one hundred black leaders and six hundred black citizens found that the leaders were much more likely than the rank and file to favor abortions, school busing, affirmative action, and forcing U.S. corporations to pull out of South Africa. Most black leaders

* One problem in interpreting opinion polls on race issues is that responses will differ depending on whether the interviewee is being questioned by a person of the same or a different race. In 1986 a *New York Times*/CBS poll found that 56 percent of all blacks said that they approved of how Reagan was handling the presidency, but a *Washington Post*/ABC poll, asking the same question at about the same time, found that only 23 percent of all blacks said that they approved of Reagan as president. One major difference: the *Washington Post*/ABC poll used only black interviewers to question blacks, and they prefaced their questions by saying that they were doing a survey of blacks only, perhaps inducing respondents to "think black." There is no way to know which responses were the "right" ones.

TABLE 5.10   Party Identification and Political Attitudes of Ethnic Groups in California (1984)

	Anglo-White	Black	Latino	Asian-American
Party Identification				
Democrat	37%	78%	54%	35%
Republican	35	3	20	38
In between, other	28	18	26	27
Political attitude				
Favor increased military spending	32	18	28	38
Favor increased welfare spending	59	84	73	66
Favor prayer in public schools	50	62	53	46
Favor death penalty for murder	75	47	57	73
Favor abortion on demand	60	47	40	53
Favor bilingual education programs	41	63	69	51
Number	409	335	593	305

SOURCE: Bruce Cain and Roderick Kiewit, "California's Coming Minority Majority," *Public Opinion* (February–March 1986): 50–52. Reprinted with permission of American Enterprise Institute for Public Policy Research.

deny that blacks are making progress, while most black citizens think they are.[31] This cleavage between the black political elite and black voters should not surprise us; as we shall see, there are similar cleavages between white political elites and white voters.

Though there are an estimated 20 million Hispanics and 7 million Asian-Americans in this country, they tend to be concentrated in a few locations, and so not enough appear in the usual national opinion polls to permit us to say much about their views.

However, a survey of ethnic groups in California, a state where fully one-third of all recent immigrants to this country live, gives us some knowledge of how Latinos and Asian-Americans feel about political parties and issues. As you can see in Table 5.10, Latinos identify themselves as Democrats, but much less so than do blacks, and Asian-Americans are even more identified with the Republican party than Anglo-whites. On such issues as spending on the military and welfare programs, prayer in the public schools, and the imposition of the death penalty for murder, Asian-American views are much more like those of Anglo-whites than either blacks or Hispanics. Latinos are somewhat more liberal than Anglos or Asian-Americans, but much less lib-

eral than blacks, except with respect to bilingual education programs.[32]

These figures conceal important differences within these ethnic groups. For example, Japanese-Americans are among the more conservative of Asian-Americans, whereas Korean-Americans (perhaps because they are among the most recent immigrants) are more liberal. Similarly, Latinos, the fastest-growing ethnic group in the United States, are a diverse mix of Cuban-Americans, Mexican-Americans, Central Americans, and Puerto Ricans, each with distinct political views. A study of Latino voting in the 1988 presidential election found that Mexican-Americans were the most Democratic, Cuban-Americans were the most Republican, and Puerto Ricans were in between the other two groups.[33]

Region

It is widely believed that geographic region affects political attitudes and in particular that southerners and northerners disagree significantly on many policy questions. As we will see, southern members of Congress tend to vote differently—and more conservatively—than northern ones, and it should stand to reason that this is because their constituents, southern voters, expect them to vote differently. At one time white southerners were conspicuously less liberal than easterners, midwesterners, or westerners on such questions as aid to minorities, legalizing marijuana, school busing, and enlarging the rights of those accused of crimes. Although more conservative on these issues, they held views on economic issues similar to those of whites in other regions of the country. This helps to explain why the South was for so long a part of the Democratic party coalition: on national economic and social welfare policies, southerners expressed views not very different from northerners. That coalition was always threatened, however, by the divisiveness produced by issues of race and liberty.

Today the political views of white southerners are less distinct from those of whites living in other parts of the country. As Table 5.11 illustrates, the proportion of white Protestants in the South who gave liberal answers to questions regarding both civil liberties/civil rights issues and economic/welfare issues in 1992 was only somewhat different from that of white Protestants in other regions. (The

Recently, immigrants have been applying for American citizenship in record numbers.

TABLE 5.11   **Does the South Differ?**

Percentage giving "liberal" response among white Protestants living in different regions, 1992.

Issue	Northeast[a]	North Central[b]	South[c]	West[d]
Economic and welfare issues				
More government services	26.4	27.4	28.8	26.5
More government job guarantees	23.0	19.2	20.7	21.2
Increase social security	55.1	39.7	43.8	42.0
Cut defense spending	47.3	36.4	37.0	44.4
Civil rights and civil liberties issues				
Government aid to black citizens	10.4	13.8	12.0	21.7
Laws to protect homosexuals against job discrimination	61.1	45.8	50.3	56.8
Women's equality	72.5	66.8	72.1	75.8
Right to abortion	50.0	40.6	34.7	53.8
Average percentage liberal, all issues	43.2	36.2	37.4	42.8

[a] Northeast: Connecticut, Massachusetts, New Hampshire, New Jersey, New York, Pennsylvania
[b] North Central: Illinois, Indiana, Iowa, Kansas, Michigan, Minnesota, Missouri, Nebraska, Ohio, Wisconsin
[c] South: Alabama, Arkansas, Deleware, District of Columbia, Florida, Georgia, Louisiana, Maryland, North Carolina, Tennessee, Texas, Virginia, West Virginia
[d] West: Arizona, California, Colorado, Oregon, Washington, Wyoming
SOURCE: Compiled by Meenekshi Bose, using data from the ICPSR *1992 American National Election Survey,* University of Michigan.

WHO Governs? TO WHAT ENDS?

Public Opinion on Immigration

Just as it has been from the earliest days of the Republic, today America is a land —*the* land—of immigrants. About 1.1 million foreigners now come here to live each year, roughly seven hundred thousand as legal immigrants, one hundred thousand as refugees, and three hundred thousand without authorization. Compared to many other democracies, the United States has long had one of the most generous immigration policies in the world. (Just try immigrating to Japan!) In 1990, the number of immigrants in the United States climbed to 19.8 million, or roughly 7.9 percent of the total U.S. population—higher than in 1960, but still small by historic standards (see the accompanying pie charts). Earlier in the century, most foreign-born Americans came from Europe. Today, most foreign-born Americans come from non-European nations such as Mexico, the Philippines, Cuba, Vietnam, India, Guyana, and Iran.

Over the last decade, a debate has raged about restricting legal immigration below its present level and redoubling efforts to keep illegal aliens and their children out. This debate has given rise to lots of new federal laws, but the matter is far from settled.

Likewise, many states have acted on immigration. California, for example, is home to an estimated 40 percent of the nation's approximately 4 million illegal immigrants. In 1994, California voters approved Proposition 187, a ballot initiative to cut off most state and local benefits, including nonemergency medical services and public education, for unlawful immigrants. A federal judge has ruled that much of the law is unconstitutional.

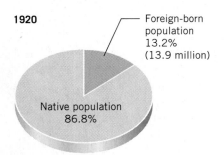

1920 Foreign-born population 13.2% (13.9 million)

Native population 86.8%

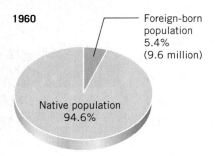

1960 Foreign-born population 5.4% (9.6 million)

Native population 94.6%

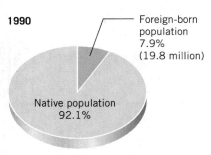

1990 Foreign-born population 7.9% (19.8 million)

Native population 92.1%

SOURCE: *The Public Perspective,* August/September 1995, p. 13.

Trying to figure out who governs on immigration and to what ends is no easy task. Contributors to immigration law and policy include the following:

Congress: In 1986 Congress passed a law barring the employment of illegal aliens. But then in 1990 it expanded legal immigration quotas to bring in more skilled workers. Between 1994 and 1996 members of Congress considered nearly a dozen proposals to overhaul U.S. policy on legal and illegal immigration, but they could agree on only a few major provisions.

The Courts: For decades the courts have shaped immigration policy. In 1948, for example, the U.S. Supreme Court struck down a California law denying commercial fishing rights to legal aliens who were ineligible to become naturalized citizens. In 1976 the Court ruled that Congress has the power to restrict federal health benefits to legal aliens. Today, California's Proposition 187 is facing various challenges in the courts.

The Bureaucracy: Congress's decisions on immigration are carried out by a much-criticized federal bureaucracy, the Immigration and Naturalization Service (INS). In addition to patrolling the border, the INS is responsible for enforcing an incredibly complicated array of laws and regulations governing the conditions under which foreigners may enter (or must leave) the country, determining the legal employability of various categories of immigrants, administering detention facilities for some nine thousand aliens, and much more.

Affected Groups: Business leaders, researchers, and spokespersons for various ethnic and religious groups also play a role. But here, too, there are differences of opinion and clashing interests. For instance, some business leaders want to import foreign workers with special high-tech job skills; others are more concerned about obtaining low-skill workers; and still others have no real stake in the issue. Spokespersons for diverse ethnic and religious groups occasionally speak with one voice on immigration (they did so during the 1996 debate in Congress, when they criticized proposed across-the-board cuts in family reunification visas and a possible cap on refugee admissions). But often they compete with one another to get their fellow nationals and believers in at the expense of individuals from other lands or of different religions (especially their historic ethnic or religious rivals).

Public Opinion: Since the mid-1980s, most polls have shown that a majority of Americans favor some cuts in legal immigration and strongly support measures to curtail illegal immigration and deport unlawful residents. In 1994, over 60 percent favored decreases in legal immigration, and nearly 60 percent favored having a law in their state similar to California's Proposition 187. Thus, as they debate whether and how to restrict immigration, lawmakers in most states must balance the general public sentiment in favor of cuts against concerted opposition from affected groups. Especially in high-immigration states such as California, politicians must contend with increasingly powerful currents of mass support for restricting the flow of foreigners, legal and illegal.

It is hard to know precisely how, if at all, public opinion on immigration would change if most people knew more about

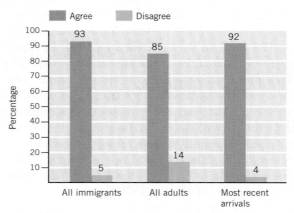

SOURCE: *The Public Perspective*, August/September 1995, p. 15.

QUESTION

[Do you agree or disagree that] people who work hard to better themselves can get ahead in this country?

it. For example, many people believe that today's immigrants are poor and poorly educated. In 1990, however, foreign-born Americans approximated native-born Americans in terms of education (20 percent of U.S.-born and foreign-born Americans held a bachelor's degree or higher), average annual household income (about $30,000 for native-born households, versus $28,000 for foreign-born ones), and careers (27 percent of native-born and 22 percent of foreign-born workers held managerial or professional jobs).

Likewise, many people have come to believe that today's immigrants resist learning English, are against "blending into" American culture, and don't believe in the American dream. But a 1995 survey found that for 69 percent of all immigrants, and 81 percent of those who arrived over two decades ago, English was the language used most often at home. As the graph above suggests, today's immigrants, including the most recent arrivals, remain dedicated to the "melting pot" ideal and the belief that America is the "land of opportunity." Moreover, despite the sometimes harsh rhetoric that has characterized the immigration debate, when asked whether they felt welcome in America, over 90 percent

of all immigrants, including the newest ones, said they felt welcome when they first arrived, and still do. Like most native-born Americans, their main complaints about America concern crime in the streets and an erosion in the moral values of society.

Where does public opinion on immigration fall in your home state? Does it differ by race, ethnic background, region, or religion? What, if any, changes in immigration policy have been made in your state since 1990, and how would you characterize these changes? Who has figured prominently in the debate? The governor? Members of Congress? Business leaders? And what have they advocated? Did they lead public opinion or follow it? Would you be inclined to support or oppose further restrictions on immigration, and why? If you were in charge of immigration policy in the United States, how would you govern, and to what ends?

SOURCES: Dick Kirschten, "Second Thoughts on Immigration," *National Journal*, January 21, 1995, pp. 150–155; Jeffrey Rosen, "The War on Immigrants," *The New Republic*, January 30, 1995, pp. 22–26; *The American Enterprise*, March/April 1995, p. 104; "The Immigration Story," *The Public Perspective*, August/ September 1995, pp. 13–17; Holly Idelson, "Economic Anxieties Bring Debate on Immigration to a Boil," *Congressional Quarterly Weekly*, March 16, 1996, pp. 697–701.

table is limited to white Protestants to eliminate the effect of the very different proportions of Catholics, Jews, blacks, and other ethnic groups living in various regions.)

The southern lifestyle is in fact different from that of other regions of the country. The South has, on the whole, been more accommodating to business enterprise and less so to organized labor than, for example, the Northeast; it gave greater support to the third-party candidacy of George Wallace in 1968, which was a protest against big government and the growth of national political power as well as against civil rights; and it was in the South that the greatest opposition arose to income-redistribution plans such as the Family Assistance Plan of 1969. Moreover, there is some evidence that white southerners became by the 1970s more conservative than they had been in the 1950s, at least when compared to white northerners.[34] Finally, white southerners have become less attached to the Democratic party: whereas over three-fourths described themselves as Democrats in 1952, only a third did by 1992 (see Figure 5.1).

These changes in the South can have great significance, as we shall see in the next three chapters when we consider how elections are fought. It is enough for now to remember that, without the votes of the southern states, no Democrat except Lyndon Johnson in 1964 would have been elected president from 1940 through 1976. (Without the South, Roosevelt would have lost in 1944, Truman in 1948, Kennedy in 1960, and Carter in 1976. And even though Carter carried the South, he did not win a majority of white southern votes.) Clinton won in 1992 and 1996 without carrying the South, but those were three-man races.

Political Ideology

Up to now the words **liberal** and **conservative** have been used here as if everyone agreed on what they meant and as if they accurately described general sets of political beliefs held by large segments of the population. Neither of these assumptions is correct. Like many useful words—*love, justice, happiness*—they are as vague as they are indispensable.

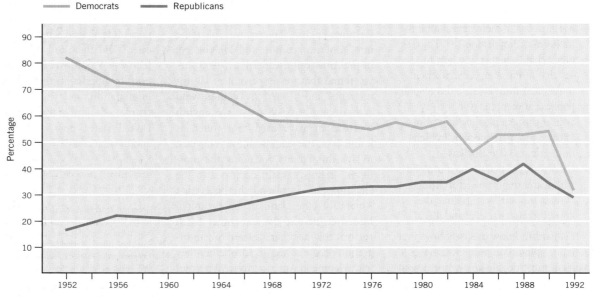

FIGURE 5.1   Whites in the South Leaving the Democrats

Percentage of southern white registered voters who identified with each party

SOURCE: ICPSR National Election Studies, Cumulative Data File, 1952–1990.

When we refer to people as liberals, conservatives, socialists, or radicals, we are implying that they have a patterned set of beliefs about how government and other important institutions in fact operate and how they ought to operate, and in particular about what kinds of policies government ought to pursue. They are said to display to some degree a **political ideology**—that is, a coherent and consistent set of beliefs about who ought to rule, what principles rulers ought to obey, and what policies rulers ought to pursue. Political scientists measure the extent to which people have a political ideology in two ways: first, by seeing how frequently people use broad political categories (such as "liberal," "conservative," "radical") to describe their own views or to justify their preferences for various candidates and policies, and second, by seeing to what extent the policy preferences of a citizen are consistent over time or are based at any one time on consistent principles.

This second method involves a simple mathematical procedure: measuring how accurately one can predict a person's view on a subject at one time based on his or her view on that subject at an earlier time, or measuring how accurately one can predict a person's view on one issue based on his or her view on a different issue. The higher the accuracy of such predictions (or correlations), the more we say a person's political opinions display "constraint," or ideology. Despite annual fluctuations, ideological self-identification surveys typically find that moderates are the largest group among American voters, conservatives the second-largest, and liberals the smallest (see Figure 5.2).

Except when asked by pollsters, most Americans do not actually employ the words *liberal* or *conservative* in explaining or justifying their preferences for candidates or policies, and not many more than half can give plausible definitions of these terms. Furthermore, there are relatively low correlations among the answers to similar questions asked by pollsters at different times and to comparable questions asked at the same time. From this, many scholars have concluded that the great majority of Americans do not think about politics in an ideological or even in a very coherent manner and that they make little use of such concepts, so dear to political commentators and professors alike, as "liberal" and "conservative."[35]

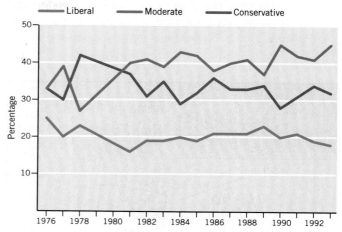

FIGURE 5.2 Ideological Self-Identification, 1976–1993

QUESTION

How would you describe your views on most political matters? Generally, do you think of yourself as a liberal, moderate, or conservative?

SOURCE: *The American Enterprise* (March/April 1993): 84, citing surveys by CBS/*New York Times*.

Consistent Attitudes

This does not settle the question entirely, however. Critics of the view that Americans are nonideological have argued that people can have general, and strongly felt, political predispositions even though they are not able to use such terms as *liberal* correctly. Moreover, public opinion polls must of necessity ask rather simple questions, and the apparent "inconsistency" in the answers people give at different times may mean only that the nature of the problem and the wording of the question have changed in ways not obvious to the people analyzing the surveys.[36]

People can have an ideology without using the words *liberal* or *conservative* and without having beliefs that line up neatly along the conventional liberal-versus-conservative dimension. We saw in Chapter 4 that most Americans share in a distinctive political culture—a belief in freedom, equality (of political condition and economic opportunity), and civic duty. They also attach a great deal of importance to "Americanism." Though these words may be vague, they are not trivial—at some level they are an ideology.

Scholars regularly discover that people have what some would consider "inconsistent" opinions. For example, a voter may want the government to spend more on education and the environment and at the same time favor a bigger military budget and a tough posture toward unfriendly nations. These

views are "inconsistent" only in the sense that they violate a political rule of thumb, common in the media and in national policy debates, that expects people who favor a bigger welfare state to favor a smaller military establishment as well. That is the conventional "liberal" view. Similarly, the rule of thumb in the media is that people who support a strong military posture are also going to favor prayer in the schools and oppose abortion on demand. That is the conventional "conservative" position. But of course many citizens violate these rules of thumb, picking and choosing their positions without regard to the conventional definitions of liberalism and conservatism.

What Do *Liberalism* and *Conservatism* Mean?

Just because most people are not consistent liberals or consistent conservatives does not prove that these terms are meaningless. As we shall see, they are very meaningful for political elites. And they even have meaning for ordinary citizens, but this meaning is a complicated one that requires careful analysis.

The definition of these words has changed since they first came into use in the early nineteenth century. At that time a liberal was a person who favored personal and economic liberty—that is, freedom from the controls and powers of the state. An economic liberal, for example, supported the free market and opposed government regulation of trade. A conservative was originally a person who opposed the excesses of the French Revolution and its emphasis on personal freedom and favored instead a restoration of the power of the state, the church, and the aristocracy.

Beginning around the time of Franklin Roosevelt and the New Deal, the meaning of these terms began to change. Roosevelt used the term *liberal* to refer to his political program—one that called for an active national government that would intervene in the economy, create social welfare programs, and help certain groups (such as organized labor) acquire greater bargaining power. In time the opponents of an activist national government began using the term *conservative* to describe themselves. (Barry Goldwater, in 1964, was the first major U.S.

Politically SPEAKING

Ideology: You Versus Your Enemies

A political ideology is a coherent set of political rules for explaining how the world works and prescribing how it ought to work.

Liberals describe

- *themselves* as "caring," "committed," "an activist," or "progressive";
- *their enemies* as "reactionary," "right-wing," and "extremist."

Conservatives describe

- *themselves* as "moderate," "responsible," "prudent," or "mainstream";
- *their enemies* as "crackpot," "knee-jerk," "left-wing," or "bleeding-heart."

An easy way to tell whether a politician, newspaper, or magazine is liberal or conservative is to see whether, in describing liberals or conservatives, it uses terms from the "nice" (themselves) list or the "hostile" (their enemies) list.

politician to proclaim himself a conservative.) In general a conservative favored a free market rather than a regulated one, states' rights over national supremacy, and greater reliance on individual choice in economic affairs.

Though the meaning of these terms changed, it did not in the process become more precise. Two persons may describe themselves as liberals even though the first favors both the welfare state and a strong national defense and the second favors the welfare state but wants a sharp reduction in military spending. Similarly, one conservative may favor enforcement of laws against drug abuse, and another may believe that the government should let people decide for themselves what drugs to take. Once, liberals favored laws guaranteeing equality of opportunity among the races; now some liberals favor "affirmative action" plans involving racial quotas or goals. Once, conservatives opposed American intervention abroad; today many conservatives believe the United States should play an active role in foreign affairs.

In view of this confusion one is tempted to throw up one's hands in disgust and consign words like *liberal* and *conservative* to the garbage can. While understandable, such a reaction would be a mistake, because in spite of their ambiguities, these words remain in general use, convey some significant meaning, and point to real differences between, for example, the liberal and conservative wings of the Democratic and Republican parties. Our task is to clarify these differences by showing the particular meanings these words have. One way to do this is by considering how self-described liberals and conservatives differ in their opinions on prominent issues, such as those listed in Table 5.12.

Various Categories

We can imagine certain broad categories of opinion to which different people subscribe. These categories are found by analyzing the answers people give to dozens of questions about political issues. Different analysts come up with slightly different categories,

TABLE 5.12 **How Liberals and Conservatives Differ**

Belief	Support Among Self-Declared Liberals	Support Among Self-Declared Conservatives
The government should provide "more services even if it means an increase in spending."	73%	32%
The government should guarantee "that every person has a job and a good standard of living."	55	21
Favor "government insurance plan which would cover all medical and hospital expenses for everyone."	82	27
The government "should make every effort to improve the social and economic position of blacks."	55	18
The U.S. "should spend less on defense."	85	65
"Aid to [Russia] should be increased."	36	32
"Women should have an equal role in running business, industry, and government."	96	81
The United States should always permit abortion "as a matter of personal choice."	72	36
"Homosexuals should be allowed to serve in U.S. Armed Forces."	70	45
"Oppose death penalty for persons convicted of murder."	35	15

SOURCE: Robert S. Erikson and Kent L. Tedin, *American Public Opinion*, 5th ed. (Boston: Allyn and Bacon, 1995), p. 69.

Thinking

Public Opinion on Homosexuality: Liberal, Conservative, or Neither?

When President Clinton announced his plan to end the U.S. military's ban on homosexuals, leaders on both sides of the issue claimed that the people were on their side. But numerous surveys indicate that public opinion is much more complicated than such assertions imply.

In sixteen national surveys conducted between 1973 and 1991, an average of about 70 percent of all Americans agreed with the statement "homosexual relations between adults are always wrong." But by 1996, the number had dropped to 61 percent, and Americans became more likely to agree that "homosexuality should be considered an acceptable lifestyle." Whether people agree that homosexuality is acceptable depends somewhat on their sex, age, party affiliation, and schooling. Men, older persons, Republicans, and those without a high school education are least tolerant; women, younger persons, Democrats, and people with a postgraduate education are most tolerant. But even with all of these differences, most people in every group think homosexuality is wrong.

Opinion on the issue of allowing homosexuals in the military is much more closely divided than is opinion on the morality of homosexuality. In 1992, half of Americans supported the ban, while 43 percent were in favor of lifting it. The strongest opposition came from within the military: 74 percent of enlisted personnel supported the ban; only 18 percent wanted it ended.

However, attitudes toward gays and lesbians in the military are not the same as feelings about them in other occupations. In 1992 large majorities felt that it was all right to hire homosexuals as salespersons, doctors, high school teachers, and members of the president's cabinet. In 1993 the public was evenly split as to whether "civil rights laws" should be extended to "include homosexuals."

Clearly, public opinion on this matter is complicated and changing. Labels such as *liberal* and *conservative* are not very precise.

SOURCES: *The American Enterprise* (March/April 1993): 82, 83; the National Opinion Research Center; the Gallup Organization; *The Gallup Poll Monthly* (April 1993): 33.

but on the whole there is a substantial amount of agreement. Three categories in particular have proved useful.

The first category involves questions about government policy with regard to the *economy*. We will describe as liberal those persons who favor government efforts to ensure that everyone has a job, to spend more money on medical and educational programs, and to increase rates of taxation for well-to-do persons.

The second involves questions about *civil rights* and race relations. We will describe as liberal those who favor strong federal action to desegregate schools, to increase hiring opportunities for minorities, to provide compensatory programs for minorities, and to enforce civil rights laws strictly.

The third involves questions about public and political *conduct*. We will describe as liberal those who are tolerant of protest demonstrations, who favor legalizing marijuana and in other ways wish to "decriminalize" so-called victimless crimes, who emphasize protecting the rights of the accused over punishing criminals, and who see the solution to crime in eliminating its causes rather than in getting tough with offenders.

Analyzing Consistency

Now, it is obvious that people can take a liberal position on one of these issues and a conservative position on another without feeling in the slightest degree "inconsistent." Several studies, such as those by Herbert McClosky and John Zaller and by Seymour Martin Lipset and Earl Raab, show that this is exactly what most people do.[37]

This fact does not mean that people are unideological but that we need more than two labels to describe their ideology. If we considered all possible combinations of the three sets of views described above, we would have nine categories of opinion; if people always stuck with whichever category they were in, we would need nine different ideological labels to describe those people.

To invent those labels and describe the people who have those views would take countless pages and bore the reader to tears. To avoid all that pain

and suffering, let's use just two sets of views—those on economic policy and those on personal conduct—and describe the kinds of people that have each of the four combinations (liberal or conservative on each set). The data are from a study by William S. Maddox and Stuart A. Lilie.

1. ***Pure liberals:***[38] These people are liberal on both economic policy and personal conduct. They want the government to reduce economic inequality, regulate business, tax the rich heavily, cure the (presumably) economic causes of crime, allow abortions, protect the rights of the accused, and guarantee the broadest possible freedoms of speech and press.

   Number: In 1994 about 17 percent of the population were pure liberals.

   Traits: Pure liberals are more likely than the average citizen to be young, college-educated, and either Jewish or nonreligious. They voted heavily against Ronald Reagan.

2. ***Pure conservatives:*** These people are conservative on both economic and conduct issues. They want the government to cut back on the welfare state, allow the market to allocate goods and services, keep taxes low, lock up criminals, and curb forms of conduct they regard as antisocial.

   Number: In 1994 about 28 percent of the population were pure conservatives.

   Traits: Pure conservatives are more likely than the average citizen to be older, to have higher incomes, to be white, and to live in the Midwest. They voted overwhelmingly for Ronald Reagan.

3. ***Libertarians:*** These people are conservative on economic matters and liberal on social ones. The common theme is that they want a small, weak government—one that has little control over either the economy or the personal lives of citizens.

   Number: In 1994 about 21 percent of the population were libertarians.

   Traits: Libertarians are more likely than the average citizen to be young, college-educated,

Thinking

CRITICAL

Public Opinion on Abortion: Liberal, Conservative, or Neither?

The media often depict abortion as a hotly divisive issue that pits pro-choice liberals against pro-life conservatives. But numerous surveys indicate that public opinion on abortion transcends conventional ideological definitions. The politics of abortion are complex because most people's ideas and feelings about abortion are complex. For example:

- Between 1975 and 1996 the majority of Americans believed that abortion should be legal "only under certain circumstances." There were no national majorities either for the position that abortion should be "legal under any circumstances" or for the position that it should be "illegal in all circumstances."[a]

- Between 1973 and 1989 most Americans *favored* a woman's right to obtain a legal abortion if her health was seriously endangered by the pregnancy, if she became pregnant as the result of rape, or if there was a strong chance of a serious defect in the baby.[b]

- Over the same years most Americans *opposed* a woman's right to obtain a legal abortion for any of the following reasons: she had a low income (or was unable to afford more children), she was unmarried and did not want to marry the child's father, or she was married but did not want to have any more children.[b]

- Democratic leaders and activists tend to be strongly pro-choice; their

Republican counterparts tend to be strongly pro-life. But rank-and-file members of the two parties hold strikingly similar views on the issue. In surveys taken from 1984 through 1988, of those who identified themselves as strongly committed Democrats, 34 percent said they favored abortion for any reason and 66 percent opposed abortion on demand. Among strong Republicans the distribution was identical—34 percent in favor, 66 percent opposed.[c]

- Jewish voters, women with postgraduate degrees, and persons with no religion are the most consistently pro-choice; born-again Christian vot-

ers, Asian-Americans, and persons who did not graduate from high school are the most strongly pro-life.[d] However, even among these groups there are many individual differences of opinion.

SOURCES: (a) *The American Enterprise* (May/June 1992), p. 99, citing surveys by the Gallup Organization. (b) *Public Opinion* (May/June 1989), p. 37, citing surveys by NORC (1975–1988) and the *Los Angeles Times* (1989). (c) Everett Carll Ladd, "The Partisan Consequences," *Public Opinion* (May/June 1989): 6, analyzing and citing data from NORC surveys (1984–1988). (d) *The American Enterprise* (January/February 1993): 103, citing 1992 surveys by the Voter Research & Surveys Consortium.

Activists tend to take political ideology more seriously than do most voters.

and white, to have higher incomes and no religion, and to live in the West. They voted for Ronald Reagan, but many also supported the third-party ticket of John Anderson.

4. ***Populists:*** These people are liberal on economic matters and conservative on social ones. They want a government that will reduce economic inequality and control business, but they also want it to regulate personal conduct, lock up criminals, and permit school prayer.

Number: In 1994 about 24 percent of the population were populists.

Traits: Populists are more likely than the average citizen to be older, poorly educated, low-income, religious, and female and to live in the South or Midwest. In 1980 they voted for Jimmy Carter, but in 1984 they voted for Reagan.[39]

   Obviously this classification is an oversimplification. There are many exceptions, and the number of people in each category changes from time to time. Moreover, this categorization leaves out about one-seventh of the population—their views do not fit any of these categories. Nonetheless, it is a useful way to explain how complex are the political ideologies in this country and why such terms as *liberal* and *conservative*, in their "pure" form, only describe the views of relatively few people.

Political Elites

There is one group that can be classified as liberals or conservatives in a pure sense, and it is made up of people who are in the **political elite**. By "elite" we do not mean people who are "better" than others. *Elite* is a technical term used by social scientists to refer to people who have a disproportionate amount of some valued resource—money, schooling, prestige, athletic ability, political power, or whatever. Every society, capitalist or communist, has an elite, because in every society government officials will have more power than ordinary folk, some persons will make more money than others, and some people will be more popular than others. (In the former Soviet Union they even had an official name for the political elite—the *nomenklatura*.)

In this country we often refer to the political elite as "activists"—people who hold office, run for office, work in campaigns or on newspapers, lead interest groups and social movements, and speak out on public issues. Being an activist is not an all-or-nothing proposition; people display differing degrees of activism, from full-time politicians to persons who occasionally get involved in a campaign (see Chapter 6). But the more a person is an activist, the more likely he or she will display ideological consistency on the conventional liberal-conservative spectrum.

The reasons for this greater consistency seem to be information and peers. First, information: in general, the better informed people are about politics and the more interest they take in politics, the more likely they are to have consistently liberal or conservative views.[40] This higher level of information and interest may lead them to find relationships among issues that others don't see and to learn from the media and elsewhere what are the "right" things to believe. This does not mean that there are no differences within liberal elites (or within conservative ones), only that the differences occur within a liberal (or conservative) consensus that is more well defined, more consistent, and more important to those who share it than would be the case among ordinary citizens.

Second, peers: politics does not make strange bedfellows. On the contrary, politics is a process of likes attracting likes. The more active you are in politics, the more you will associate with people who agree with you on some issues; and the more time you spend with those people, the more your other views will shift to match theirs.

The greater ideological consistency of political elites can be seen in Congress. As we shall note in Chapter 11, Democratic members of Congress tend to be consistently liberal, and Republican members of Congress tend to be consistently conservative—

far more consistently than Democratic voters and Republican voters. By the same token, we shall see in Chapter 7 that the delegates to presidential nominating conventions are far more ideological (liberal in the Democratic convention, conservative in the Republican one) than is true of voters who identify with the Democratic or Republican parties.

Is There a "New Class"?

Some writers have speculated that political elites now represent a "new class" in American politics. The old classes were those who owned the means of production (the capitalists) and those who were employed by those owners (the workers). The "new class" consists of people who possess certain advantages conferred not by the power, resources, and growth of business but by the power, resources, and growth of government.[41]

Politicians, bureaucrats, members of the media, interest-group leaders—these people and others like them have, it is claimed, a stake in the growth of government. Because of that, they often have liberal (that is, progovernment) views even though they also have high incomes. The emergence of the new class helps explain, in this theory, why affluent people are not as consistently conservative as they were in the 1940s and 1950s.

It is true, as we have already seen, that many well-off people are liberals. That these people benefit from big government may be one explanation for this fact. But there is another explanation: the spread of higher education.

High levels of schooling, especially at the postgraduate level, tend to make people more liberal. This was not always the case. For example, in the 1940s and 1950s a clear majority of Harvard students, and probably of most college students, preferred Republican candidates for president.[42] For whatever reason, things are different now. Some people with law degrees and Ph.D.'s may favor government because they get grants and jobs from it, but most people probably favor it because they have acquired an ideology that is consistent with a more activist government.

In any event, it is striking how strongly post-graduate education affects political preferences. John McAdams has analyzed the voting results for several presidential, gubernatorial, and senatorial elections and for various state referenda elections on issues such as the death penalty, school busing, nuclear energy, gun control, environmental protection, and the Equal Rights Amendment. In each and every case he discovered that those with a postgraduate education were much more likely to take a liberal position, even after holding constant age, race, and income.[43]

On the basis of his findings, McAdams suggests that the middle class in the United States has been split in two—one part he calls the "traditional middle class," and the other he calls the "new class" (though it might more appropriately be called the "liberal middle class").[44] The traditional middle class consists of people who often have gone to college but not graduate school and who live in the suburbs, go to church, are well disposed toward business, have conservative views on social issues, and usually vote Republican. The liberal middle class is more likely to consist of people who have a postgraduate education, live in or near big cities, are critical of business, have liberal views on social issues, and usually vote Democratic. The cleavage between the traditional and the liberal middle class has many of the same causes as the growing rift between orthodox and progressive ideologies discussed in Chapter 4.

As we shall see in Chapter 7, the strain within the middle class has been particularly felt by the Democratic party. That strain has made it harder to hold together the coalition (often called the New Deal coalition) that once made that party so strong, a coalition among blue-collar workers, southerners, blacks, and intellectuals. Increasingly the workers and white southerners have displayed conservatism on social issues, while members of the liberal middle class have displayed liberalism on these issues. Each side has a label for the other: the workers in the Democratic party call the members of the liberal middle class the "cheese and white wine set," while the people in the liberal middle class call the workers "Joe Six-Pack."

Political Elites, Public Opinion, and Public Policy

Though the elites and the public see politics in very different ways, and though there are often intense antagonisms between the two groups, the elites influence public opinion in at least two important ways.

First, elites, especially those in or having access to the media (see Chapter 10), raise and frame political issues. At one time environmentalism was not on the political agenda; at a later time not only was it on the agenda, it was up near the top of government concerns. At some times the country had little interest in what we should do in South Africa or Central America; at other times the government was preoccupied with these matters. Though world events help shape the political agenda, so also do political elites. A path-breaking study by John Zaller shows in fact that elite views shape mass views by influencing both what issues capture the public's attention and how those issues are debated and decided.[45]

Second, elites state the norms by which issues should be settled. (A **norm** is a standard of right or proper conduct.) By doing this, they help determine the range of acceptable and unacceptable policy options. For example, elites have for a long time emphasized that racism is wrong. Of late they have emphasized that sexism is wrong. Over a long period, the steady repetition of views condemning racism and sexism will at least intimidate, and perhaps convince, those of us who are racist and sexist.

A recent example of this process has been the public discussion of AIDS and its relationship to homosexuality. The initial public reaction to AIDS was one of fear and loathing. But efforts to quarantine people infected with AIDS were met with firm resistance from the medical community and from other policy elites. The elites even managed to persuade some legislatures to bar insurance companies from testing insurance applicants for the disease.

There are limits to how much influence elites can have on the public. For instance, elites do not define economic problems—people can see for themselves that there is or is not unemployment, that there is or is not raging inflation, that there are or are not high interest rates. Elite opinion may shape the policies, but it does not define the problem. Similarly, elite opinion has little influence on whether we think there is a crime or drug problem; it is, after all, *our* purses being snatched, cars being stolen, and children being drugged. On the other hand, elite opinion does define the problem as well as the policy options with respect to most aspects of foreign affairs; the public has little firsthand experience with which to judge what is going on in Panama or Iraq.

Because elites affect how we see some issues and determine how other issues get resolved, it is important to study the differences between elite and public opinion. But it is wrong to suppose that there is one elite, unified in its interests and opinions. Just as there are many publics, and hence many public opinions, there are many elites, and hence many different elite opinions. Whether there is enough variety of opinion and influence among elites to justify calling our politics "pluralist" is one of the central issues confronting any student of government.

SUMMARY

"Public opinion" is a slippery notion, partly because there are many publics, with many different opinions, and partly because opinion on all but relatively simple matters tends to be uninformed, unstable, and sensitive to different ways of asking poll questions.

The chief sources of political opinion are the family, religion, information, and schooling. Once, occupation (or income) was a central determinant of opinion, but with the spread of higher education, the connection between occupational status (or income) and opinion is no longer quite as close.

The chief source of cleavages in opinion are race and ethnicity, class (in which schooling is an important component), and region.

Americans are divided by their political ideologies but not along a single liberal-conservative dimension. There are several kinds of issues on which people may take "liberal" or "conservative" positions, and they often do not take the same position on all issues. Just using two kinds of issues—economic and social—it is possible to define four kinds of ideologies: pure liberal, pure conservative, libertarian, and populist.

Political elites are much more likely to display a consistently liberal or consistently conservative ideology. Elites are important because they have a disproportionate influence on public policy and even an influence on mass opinion (through the dissemination of information and the evocation of political norms).

KEY TERMS

John Q. Public   *p. 113*

middle America   *p. 113*

silent majority   *p. 113*

social status   *p. 117*

religious tradition   *p. 117*

gender gap   *p. 118*

poll   *p. 122*

random sample   *p. 122*

sampling error   *p. 123*

liberal   *p. 132*

conservative   *p. 132*

political ideology   *p. 131*

libertarians   *p. 135*

populists   *p. 137*

political elite   *p. 137*

norm   *p. 139*

SUGGESTED READINGS

Dionne, E. J. *Why Americans Hate Politics.* New York: Simon and Schuster, 1991. Misnamed, this book actually describes the emergence of various elite ideologies since the 1960s and why, in the author's view, none is relevant to actually solving problems.

Erikson, Robert S., and Kent L. Tedin. *American Public Opinion.* 5th ed. Boston: Allyn and Bacon, 1995. An excellent summary of how opinion is measured, what it shows, and how it affects politics.

Jennings, M. Kent, and Richard G. Niemi. *The Political Character of Adolescence: The Influence of Families and Schools.* Princeton, N.J.: Princeton University Press, 1974. A study of political attitudes among high school students.

——. *Generations and Politics.* Princeton, N.J.: Princeton University Press, 1981. A study of persistence and change in the political views of young adults and their parents.

Key, V. O., Jr. *The Responsible Electorate.* Cambridge, Mass.: Harvard University Press, 1966. An argument, with evidence, that American voters are not fools.

Lipset, Seymour Martin. *Political Man: The Social Bases of Politics.* Garden City, N.Y.: Doubleday, 1959. An exploration of the relationship between society, opinion, and democracy in America and abroad.

Nie, Norman H., Sidney Verba, and John R. Petrocik. *The Changing American Voter.* Cambridge, Mass.: Harvard University Press, 1976. Traces shifts in American voter attitudes since 1960.

Zaller, John. *The Nature and Origins of Mass Opinion.* Cambridge, England: Cambridge University Press, 1992. A pathbreaking study of how the public forms an opinion, illustrating the ways in which elite views help shape mass views.

6

Political Participation

★ The problem of nonvoting

★ The rise of the American electorate

★ Voter turnout

★ Who participates?

★ Different forms of participation

★ Causes of participation

A mericans are often embarrassed by their low rate of participation in national elections. Data such as those shown in Figure 6.1 on page 144 are frequently used to make the point: whereas well over 80 percent of the people vote in many European elections, only about half of the people vote in American presidential elections (and a much smaller percentage vote in congressional contests). Many observers blame this low turnout on voter apathy and urge the government and private groups to mount campaigns to get out the vote.

There are only three things wrong with this view. First, it is a misleading description of the problem; second, it is an incorrect explanation of the problem; and third, it proposes a remedy that won't work.

A Closer Look at Nonvoting

First, let's look at how best to describe the problem. The conventional data on voter turnout here and abroad are misleading, because they compute participation rates by two different measures. Figure 6.1 shows what proportion of the **registered voters** in various European nations went to the polls, but it shows what percentage of the **voting-age population** in the United States went to the polls. In this country only two-thirds of the voting-age population is registered to vote. To understand what this means, look at Table 6.1 on page 144. In column A are several countries ranked in terms of the percentage of the voting-age population that voted in the 1984 national election. As you can see, the United States, where 52.6 percent voted, ranked near the bottom; only Switzerland was lower. Now look at column B, where the same countries are ranked in terms of the percentage of registered voters who participated in the last national election. The United States, where almost 87 percent of registered voters turned out at the polls, is now up in the middle of the pack.[1]

Second, let's consider a better explanation for the problem. Apathy on election day is clearly not the source of the problem. Of those who are registered, the overwhelming majority vote. The real source of the participation problem in the United States is that a relatively low percentage of the adult population is registered to vote.

Third, let's look at how to cure the problem. Mounting a get-out-the-vote drive wouldn't make much difference. What would make a difference is a plan that would get more people to register to vote. But doing that does not necessarily involve overcoming the "apathy" of unregistered voters. Some people may not register because they don't care about politics or their duty as citizens. But there are other explanations for being unregistered. In this country the entire burden of registering to vote falls on the individual voters. They must learn how and when and where to register; they must take the time and trouble to go someplace and fill out a registration form; and they must reregister in a new county or state if they happen to move. In most European nations registration is done for you, automatically, by the government. Since it is costly to register in this country and costless to register in other countries, it should not be surprising that fewer people are registered here than abroad.

In 1993 Congress passed a law designed to make it easier to register to vote. Known as the **motor-voter bill**, the law requires states to allow people to register to vote when applying for driver's licenses and to provide registration through the mail and at some state offices that serve the disabled or provide public assistance (such as welfare checks). As we can see in Figure 6.2, some 49 million voting-age people who were not registered to vote had driver's licenses or state-issued identification cards. The motor-voter bill took effect in 1995. In just two months, 630,000 new voters signed up in twenty-seven states. It ap-

FIGURE 6.1 Average Voter Turnout from the 1950s to 1980s

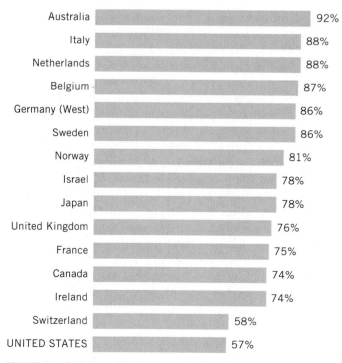

Australia	92%
Italy	88%
Netherlands	88%
Belgium	87%
Germany (West)	86%
Sweden	86%
Norway	81%
Israel	78%
Japan	78%
United Kingdom	76%
France	75%
Canada	74%
Ireland	74%
Switzerland	58%
UNITED STATES	57%

SOURCE: Russell J. Dalton and Martin P. Wattenberg, "The Not So Simple Act of Voting," in *Political Science: The State of the Discipline*, ed. Ada Finifter, 2nd ed. (Washington, D.C.: APSA, 1993), 210. Reprinted by permission of American Political Science Review.

TABLE 6.1 Two Ways of Calculating Voting Turnout

A Turnout as Percentage of Voting-Age Population		B Turnout as Percentage of Registered Voters	
Austria	89.3%	Belgium	94.6%
Belgium	88.7	Australia	94.5
Sweden	86.8	Austria	91.6
Netherlands	84.7	Sweden	90.7
Australia	83.1	New Zealand	89.0
Denmark	82.1	West Germany	88.6
Norway	81.8	Netherlands	87.0
West Germany	81.1	UNITED STATES	86.8
New Zealand	78.5	France	85.9
France	78.0	Denmark	83.2
United Kingdom	76.0	Norway	82.0
Japan	74.4	United Kingdom	76.3
Canada	67.4	Japan	74.5
Finland	63.0	Canada	69.3
UNITED STATES	52.6	Finland	64.3
Switzerland	39.4	Switzerland	48.3

SOURCE: Adapted from tables in David Glass, Peverill Squire, and Raymond Wolfinger, "Voter Turnout: An International Comparison," *Public Opinion* (December–January 1984); 50, 52. Reprinted with permission of American Enterprise Institute for Public Policy Research.

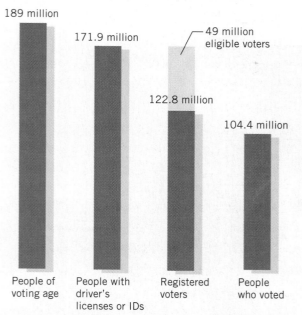

MOTOR VOTER
REGISTRATION INSTRUCTIONS

You must complete steps 1-3. Failure to provide this information may jeopardize your registration.

BOX 1　Print your name on the line in box # 1.

BOX 2　Please read the oath and then sign your name in the grey shaded area next to the RED X. This signature attests that you meet the qualifications of the oath.

BOX 3　Enter your daytime phone number, and date of birth.

BOX 4　If you are changing your address, or name, or have been registered to vote before, please write the name and address at which you were previously registered in box 4.

BOX 5　Do you want to be registered at the address on your current license or I.D. card?
- If Yes, skip box #5.
- If No, please write the address where you live in box #5. (You may not use a work address as your residence address.)

BOX 6　If your mailing address is different from the address where you live please write your mailing address in box #6. (You may not use a work address for mailing purposes.)

BOX 7　Please sign your name next to the RED X on the lower half of the form.

BOX 8　Please print your name.

OATH

"I declare that the facts relating to my qualifications as a voter recorded on this voter registration form are true. I am a citizen of the United States, I am not presently denied my civil rights as a result of being convicted of an infamous crime, I will have lived in this state, county, and precinct for thirty days immediately preceding the next election at which I offer to vote, and I will be at least eighteen years of age at the time of voting."

When you apply for a driver's license in the state of Washington, you are given this form so that you can register to vote at the same time. This "motor-voter" idea became the basis of a federal law passed in 1993.

pears that the measure has increased voter registration throughout the country. In many states, the party breakdown among motor-voters has been about even. But some analysts stress that record numbers of new voters have been registering in the South, with the gains concentrated in fast-growing Republican suburbs. Only future elections will tell, but if the motor-voter law does end up helping Republicans more than Democrats, it will be a testimony to our national lawmakers' limited powers of political prognostication: in 1993 the bill was opposed by nearly 90 percent of all congressional Republicans and supported by over 95 percent of all congressional Democrats.

A final point: voting is only one way of participating in politics. It is important (we could hardly be considered a democracy if nobody voted), but it is not all-important. Joining civic associations, supporting social movements, writing to legislators, fighting city hall—all these and other activities are ways of participating in politics. It is possible that,

FIGURE 6.2　The Motor-Voter Bill, 1992

- 189 million — People of voting age
- 171.9 million — People with driver's licenses or IDs
- 49 million eligible voters
- 122.8 million — Registered voters
- 104.4 million — People who voted

NOTE: The voting-age figure includes 11 million illegal aliens and 600,000 convicted felons who are not eligible to vote. It does not include about 600,000 Americans overseas who are eligible to vote.
SOURCE: Richard Sammon, "Senate Filibuster Kills Threat, Clears 'Motor-Voter' Bill," *Congressional Quarterly* (May 15, 1993): 1221.

by these measures, Americans participate in politics *more* than most Europeans—or anybody else, for that matter. Moreover, it is possible that low rates of registration indicate that people are reasonably well satisfied with how the country is governed. If 100 percent of all adult Americans registered and voted (especially under a system that makes registering relatively difficult), it could mean that people are deeply upset about how things are run. In short, it is not at all clear whether low voter turnout is a symptom of political disease or a sign of political good health.

The important question about participation is not how much participation there is but how different kinds of participation affect the kind of government we get. This question cannot be answered just by looking at voter turnout, the subject of this chapter; it also requires us to look at the composition and activities of political parties, interest groups, and the media (the subjects of later chapters).

Nonetheless, voting is important. To understand why participation in American elections takes the form that it does, we must first understand how laws have determined who shall vote and under what circumstances.

The Rise of the American Electorate

It is ironic that relatively few citizens vote in American elections, since it was in this country that the mass of people first became eligible to vote. At the time the Constitution was ratified, the vote was limited to property owners or taxpayers, but by the administration of Andrew Jackson it had been broadened to include virtually all white male adults. Only in a few states did property restrictions persist: they were not abolished in New Jersey until 1844 or in North Carolina until 1856. And, of course, black males could not vote in many states, in the North as well as the South, even if they were not slaves. Women could not vote in most states until the twentieth century; Chinese-Americans were widely denied the vote; and being in prison is grounds for losing the franchise even today. Aliens, on the other hand, were often allowed to vote if they had at least begun the process of becoming a citizen. By 1880 only an estimated 14 percent of all adult males in the United States could not vote; in England in the same period about 40 percent of adult males were disfranchised.[2]

In the first years of the republic, voting was frequently restricted to male property owners.

From State to Federal Control

Initially it was left entirely to the states to decide who could vote and for what offices. The Constitution gave to Congress only the right to pick the day on which presidential electors would gather and to alter state regulations regarding congressional elections. The only provision of the Constitution requiring a popular election was the clause in Article I stating that members of the House of Representatives be chosen by the "people of the several states."

Because of this permissiveness, early federal elections varied greatly. Several states picked their members of the House at large (that is, statewide) rather than by district; others used districts but elected more than one representative from each. Still others had their elections in odd-numbered years, and some even required that a congressional candidate win a majority, rather than simply a plurality, of votes to be elected (when that requirement was in effect, runoff elections—in one case as many as twelve—were necessary). Furthermore, presidential electors were at first picked by state legislatures rather than by the voters directly.

Congress, by law and constitutional amendment, has steadily reduced state prerogatives in these matters. In 1842 a federal law required that all members of the House be elected by districts; other laws over the years required that all federal elections be held in even-numbered years on the Tuesday following the first Monday in November.

The most important changes in elections have been those that extended the suffrage to women, blacks, and eighteen-year-olds and made mandatory the direct popular election of United States senators. The Fifteenth Amendment, adopted in 1870, said that the "right of citizens of the United States to vote shall not be denied or abridged by the United States or by any state on account of race, color, or previous condition of servitude." Reading those words today,

When Reconstruction ended in 1876, black voting shrank under the attack of white supremacists.

After the Civil War, while Union forces were still in control, blacks began to vote in the South, as here in Richmond, Virginia, in 1871.

TABLE 6.2   **Voter Registration in the South**

		Ala.	Ark.	Fla.	Ga.	La.	Miss.	N.C.	S.C.	Tenn.	Tex.	Va.	Total
		Percentage of Voting-Age Population That Is Registered											
1960	White	63.6	60.9	69.3	56.8	76.9	63.9	92.1	57.1	73.0	42.5	46.1	61.1
	Black*	13.7	38.0	39.4	29.3	31.1	5.2	39.1	13.7	59.1	35.5	23.1	29.1
1970	White	85.0	74.1	65.5	71.7	77.0	82.1	68.1	62.3	78.5	62.0	64.5	62.9
	Black	66.0	82.3	55.3	57.2	57.4	71.0	51.3	56.1	71.6	72.6	57.0	62.0
1986	White	77.5	67.2	66.9	62.3	67.8	91.6	67.4	53.4	70.0	79.0	60.3	69.9
	Black	68.9	57.9	58.2	52.8	60.6	70.8	58.4	52.5	65.3	68.0	56.2	60.8

* Includes other minority races.

SOURCE: Voter Education Project, Inc., of Atlanta, Georgia, as reported in *Statistical Abstract of the United States, 1990*, 264.

one would assume that they gave blacks the right to vote. That is not what the Supreme Court during the 1870s thought that they meant. By a series of decisions, it held that the Fifteenth Amendment did not necessarily confer the right to vote on anybody; it merely asserted that if someone was denied that right, the denial could not be explicitly on the grounds of race. And the burden of proving that it was race that led to the denial fell on the black who was turned away at the polls.[3]

This interpretation opened the door to all manner of state stratagems to keep blacks from voting. One was a **literacy test** (a large proportion of former slaves were illiterate); another was a requirement that a **poll tax** be paid (most former slaves were poor); a third was the practice of keeping blacks from voting in primary elections (in the one-party South the only meaningful election was the Democratic primary). To allow whites who were illiterate or poor to vote, a **grandfather clause** was added to the law, saying that you could vote, even though you did not meet the legal requirements, if you or your ancestors voted before 1867 (blacks, of course, could not vote before 1867). When all else failed, blacks were intimidated, threatened, or harassed if they showed up at the polls.

There began a long, slow legal process of challenging in court each of these restrictions in turn. One by one, the Supreme Court set most of them aside. The grandfather clause was declared unconstitutional in 1915,[4] and the **white primary** finally fell in 1944.[5] Some of the more blatantly discriminatory literacy tests were also overturned.[6] The practical result of these rulings was slight: only a small proportion of voting-age blacks were able to register and vote in the South, and they were found mostly in the larger cities. A dramatic change did not begin until 1965, with the passage of the Voting Rights Act. This act suspended the use of literacy tests and authorized the appointment of federal examiners who could order the registration of blacks in states and counties (mostly in the South) where fewer than 50 percent of the voting-age population were registered or had voted in the last presidential election. It also provided criminal penalties for interfering with the right to vote.

Though implementation in some places was slow, the number of blacks voting rose sharply throughout the South. For example, in Mississippi the proportion of voting-age blacks who registered rose from 5 percent to over 70 percent in just ten years (see Table 6.2). These changes had a profound effect on the behavior of many white southern politicians: Governor George Wallace stopped making prosegregation speeches and began courting the black vote.

Women were kept from the polls by law more than by intimidation, and when the laws changed, women almost immediately began to vote in large numbers. By 1915 several states, mostly in the West, had begun to permit women to vote. But it was not until the Nineteenth Amendment to the Constitution was ratified in 1920, after a struggle lasting many decades, that women generally were allowed to vote. At one stroke the size of the eligible voting population almost doubled. Contrary to the hopes of some and the fears of others, no dramatic changes occurred in the conduct of elections, the identity of the winners, or the substance of public policy. Initially, at least, women voted more or less in the same manner as men, though not quite as frequently.

The political impact of the youth vote was also less than expected. The Voting Rights Act of 1970 gave eighteen-year-olds the right to vote in federal elections, beginning January 1, 1971. It also contained a provision lowering the voting age to eighteen in state elections, but the Supreme Court declared this unconstitutional. As a result a constitutional amendment, the Twenty-sixth, was proposed by Congress and ratified by the states in 1971. The 1972 elections became the first in which all people between the ages of eighteen and twenty-one could cast ballots (before then, four states had allowed those under twenty-one to vote). About 25 million people suddenly became eligible to participate in elections, but their turnout was lower than for the population as a whole, and they did not flock to any particular party or candidate. George McGovern, the Democratic candidate for president in 1972, counted heavily on attracting the youth vote but did not succeed. Most young voters supported Nixon (though college students favored McGovern).[7]

National standards now govern almost every aspect of voter eligibility. All persons eighteen years of age and older may vote; there may be no literacy test or poll tax; states may not require residency of more than thirty days in that state before a person may vote; areas with significant numbers of citizens not speaking English must give those people ballots written in their own language; and federal voter registrars and poll watchers may be sent into areas where less than 50 percent of the voting-age population participates in a presidential election. Before 1961 residents of the District of Columbia could not vote in presidential elections; the Twenty-third Amendment to the Constitution gave them this right.

The campaign to win the vote for women nationwide succeeded with the adoption of the Nineteenth Amendment in 1920.

Voting Turnout

Given all these legal safeguards, one might expect that participation in elections would have risen sharply. In fact the proportion of the voting-age population that has gone to the polls in presidential elections has remained about the same—between 50 percent and 60 percent of those eligible—at least since 1932 and appears today to be much smaller than it was in the latter part of the nineteenth century (see Figure 6.3, page 150). In every presidential election between 1860 and 1900, at least 70 percent of the eligible population apparently went to the polls, and in some years (1860 and 1876) over 80 percent seem to have voted. Since 1900 not a single presidential election turnout has reached 70 percent, and on two occasions (1920 and 1924) it did not even reach 50 percent.[8] Even outside the South (where efforts to disfranchise blacks make data on voting turnout especially hard to interpret) turnout seems to have declined: over 84 percent of the voting-age population participated in presidential elections in nonsouthern states between 1884 and 1900, but only 68 percent participated between 1936 and 1960, and even fewer have done so since 1960.[9]

Scholars have vigorously debated the meaning of these figures. One view is that this decline in turn-

FIGURE 6.3 Voter Participation in Presidential Elections, 1860–1996

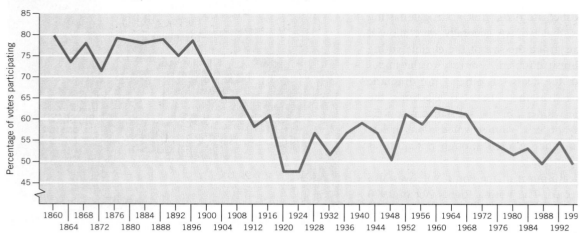

NOTE: Several southern states did not participate in the 1864 and 1868 elections.
SOURCES: For 1860–1928: Bureau of the Census, *Historical Statistics of the United States, Colonial Times to 1970*, Pt. 2, 1071; 1932–1992: *Statistical Abstract of the United States, 1992*, 517.

out, even allowing for the shaky data on which the estimates are based, has been real and is the result of a decline of popular interest in elections and a weakening of the competitiveness of the two major parties. During the nineteenth century, according to this theory, the parties fought hard, worked strenuously to get as many voters as possible to the polls, afforded the mass of voters a chance to participate in party politics through caucuses and conventions, kept the legal barriers to participation (such as complex registration procedures) low, and looked forward to close, exciting elections. After 1896, by which time the South had become a one-party Democratic region and the North heavily Republican, both parties became more conservative, national elections usually resulted in lopsided victories for the Republicans, and citizens began to lose interest in politics because it no longer seemed relevant to their needs. The parties ceased functioning as organizations to mobilize the mass of voters and fell under the control of leaders, mostly conservative, who resisted mass participation.[10]

There is another view, however. It argues that the decline in voter turnout has been more apparent than real. Though elections were certainly more of a popular sport in the nineteenth century than they are today, the parties were no more democratic then than now, and voters then may have been more easily manipulated. Until around the beginning of the twentieth century, voting fraud was commonplace because it was easy to pull off. The political parties, not the government, printed the ballots; they were often cast in public, not private, voting booths; there were few serious efforts to decide who was eligible to vote, and the rules that did operate were easily evaded.

Under these circumstances it was easy for a person to vote more than once, and the party machines made heavy use of these "floaters," or repeaters. "Vote early and often" was not a joke but a fact. "Big Tim" Sullivan, a boss in New York's old Tammany Hall, once had his party's ballots soaked in perfume so that he could use scent as well as sight to ensure that his voters put the right ballot in the right box.[11] The parties often controlled the counting of votes, padding the totals whenever they feared losing. As a result of these machinations, the number of votes counted was often larger than the number cast, and the number cast was in turn often larger than the number of individuals eligible to vote. For example, in 1888 West Virginia officially claimed that there were 147,408 persons in the state eligible to vote, but mysteriously 159,440 votes were cast in the

CRITICAL Thinking

Voter Turnout: Some Myths and Realities

MYTH	REALITY
Turnout is declining because the poor are dropping out of politics.	Turnout is declining because *all* groups—the poor, the middle class, and the rich—have become less likely to vote.
Today's voters see no differences between Democrats and Republicans.	More voters see more important differences between the parties today than they did in the 1960s.
Nonvoters don't vote because the policies they prefer haven't been debated or adopted.	Voters and nonvoters differ very little in their policy preferences.
Many elections are decided by levels of voter turnout.	Levels of turnout do not, as a rule, make much of a difference in election outcomes.
Registration reform (for example, the "motor-voter" bill, Figure 6.2 on page 145) would definitely help the Democrats and hurt the Republicans.	Nobody really knows, but surveys suggest that the political leanings of voters and nonvoters do not differ enough for the addition of even millions of nonvoters to make much of a partisan impact.

SOURCE: Adapted from Ruy A. Teixeira, "Voter Turnout in America," *The Brookings Review* (Fall 1992): 28–31. Reprinted with permission of the Brookings Institution.

presidential election, for a "voter turnout" of 108 percent![12]

Around 1890 the states began adopting the **Australian ballot.** This was a government-printed ballot of uniform size and shape that was cast in secret, created to replace the old party-printed ballots cast in public. By 1910 only three states were without the Australian ballot. Its use cut back on (but certainly did not eliminate) vote buying and fraudulent vote counts.

In short, if votes had been legally cast and honestly counted in the nineteenth century, the statistics on election turnout might well be much lower than the inflated figures we now have.[13] To the extent that this is true, we may not have had a decline in voter participation as great as some have suggested. Nevertheless, most scholars believe that turnout probably did actually decline somewhat after the 1890s. One reason was that voter-registration regulations became more burdensome: there were longer residency requirements; aliens who had begun but not completed the process of becoming citizens could no longer vote in most states; it became harder for

blacks to vote; educational qualifications for voting were adopted by several states; and voters had to register long in advance of the elections. These changes, designed to purify the electoral process, were aspects of the Progressive reform impulse (described in Chapter 7) and served to cut back on the number of persons who could participate in elections.

Strict voter-registration procedures tended, like most reforms in American politics, to have unintended as well as intended consequences. These changes not only reduced fraudulent voting but also reduced voting generally, because they made it more difficult for certain groups of perfectly honest voters—those with little education, for example, or those who had recently moved—to register and vote. This was not the first time, and it will not be the last, that a reform designed to cure one problem created another.

Even after all the legal changes are taken into account, there has still been a decline in citizen participation in elections. Between 1960 and 1980 the proportion of voting-age people casting a ballot in presidential elections fell by about 10 percentage points, a drop that cannot be explained by how ballots were printed or how registration rules were rewritten. By the same token, these factors cannot explain the 5 percent increase in turnout from the 1988 to the 1992 presidential election (from 50 to 55 percent).

Who Participates in Politics?

To understand better why voting turnout declined and what, if anything, that decline may mean, we must first look at who participates in politics.

Forms of Participation

Voting is by far the most common form of political participation, while giving money to a candidate and being a member of a political organization are the least common. Many Americans exaggerate how frequently they vote or how active they are in politics. In a study by Sidney Verba and Norman Nie, 72 percent of those interviewed said that they vote "regularly" in presidential elections. Yet we know that since 1960, on average only 56 percent of the

voting-age population has actually cast presidential ballots. Careful studies of this discrepancy suggest that 8 to 10 percent of Americans interviewed misreport their voting habits: they claim to have voted when in fact they have not. Young, low-income, less-educated, and nonwhite people are most likely to misreport than others.[14] If people misreport their voting behavior, it is likely that they also misreport—that is, exaggerate—the extent to which they participate in other ways.

Indeed, most research shows that "politics is not at the heart of the day-to-day life of the American people."[15] Work, family, church, and other voluntary activities come first, both in terms of how Americans spend their time and in terms of the money they donate. For example, a recent study by Verba and others found that a higher proportion of citizens take part in nonpolitical than political activities: "More citizens reported giving time to church-related or charitable activities than indicated contacting a government official or working informally on a community problem, two of the most frequent forms of political participation beyond the vote"[16] (see Figure 6.4).

In an earlier study, Verba and Nie analyzed the ways in which people participate in politics and came up with six forms of participation that are characteristic of six different kinds of U.S. citizens. About one-fifth (22 percent) of the population is completely inactive: they rarely vote, they do not get involved in organizations, and they probably do not even talk about politics very much. These inactives typically have little education and low incomes and are relatively young. Many of them are black. At the opposite extreme are the complete **activists,** constituting about one-ninth of the population (11 percent). These people are highly educated, have high incomes, and tend to be middle-aged rather than young or old. They tend to participate in all forms of politics.

Between these extremes are four categories of limited forms of participation. The voting specialists are people who vote but do little else; they tend not to have much schooling or income and to be substantially older than the average person. Campaigners not only vote but also like to get involved in campaign activities. They are better educated than the average voter, but what seems to distinguish

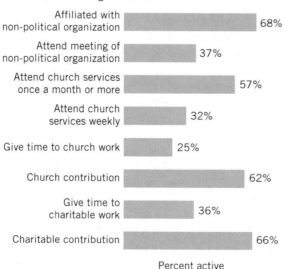

FIGURE 6.4   Nonpolitical Voluntary Activity Among Citizens

	Percent active
Affiliated with non-political organization	68%
Attend meeting of non-political organization	37%
Attend church services once a month or more	57%
Attend church services weekly	32%
Give time to church work	25%
Church contribution	62%
Give time to charitable work	36%
Charitable contribution	66%

FIGURE 6.5 Voter Turnout in Presidential Elections, by Age, Schooling, and Race, 1964–1992

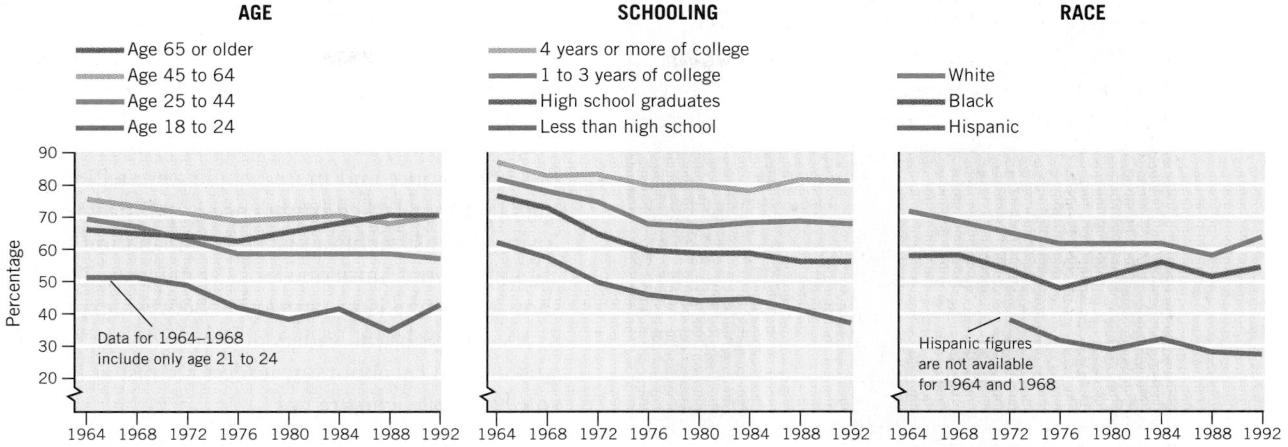

SOURCE: Gary R. Orren, "The Linkage of Policy to Participation," in *Presidential Selection,* ed. Alexander Heard and Michael Nelson (Durham, N.C.: Duke University Press, 1987) and tabulated by Daron Shaw; data for 1992 are from *Statistical Abstract of the United States, 1993,* 283.

them most is their interest in the conflicts, passions, and struggle of politics, their clear identification with a political party, and their willingness to take strong positions. Communalists are much like campaigners in social background but have a very different temperament: they do not like the conflict and tension of partisan campaigns. They tend to reserve their energies for community activities of a more nonpartisan nature—forming and joining organizations to deal with local problems and contacting local officials about these problems. Finally, there are some parochial participants who do not vote and stay out of election campaigns and civic associations but are willing to contact local officials about specific, often personal, problems.[17]

The Causes of Participation

Whether participation takes the form of voting or being a complete activist, it is higher among persons who have gone to college than among persons who have not and higher among persons who are over thirty-five years of age than among persons who are under thirty-five. (The differences in voting rates for these groups are shown in Figure 6.5.) Even after controlling for differences in income and occupation, the more schooling one has, the more likely

one is to vote. Of course it may not be schooling itself that causes participation but something that is strongly correlated with schooling, such as high levels of political information.[18]

In fact the differences in participation that are associated with schooling (or its correlates) are probably even greater than reported in this figure, since we have already seen that less-educated persons exaggerate how frequently they vote. An excellent study of turnout concludes that people are more likely to vote when they have those personal qualities that "make learning about politics easier and more gratifying."[19]

Religious involvement also increases political participation. If you are a regular churchgoer who takes your faith seriously, the chances are that you will be more likely to vote and otherwise take part in politics than if you are a person of the same age, sex, income, and educational level who does not go to church. Church involvement leads to social connectedness, teaches organizational skills, increases one's awareness of larger issues, and puts one in contact with like-minded people.[20]

Men and women vote at about the same rate, but blacks and whites do not. Although at one time that difference was largely the result of discrimination, today it can be explained mostly by differences

"HURRAH FOR OLD TIPPECANOE."

HARD CIDER
AND
LOG CABIN
ALMANAC
18 FOR 41
HARRISON AND TYLER.

NEW YORK:
TURNER & FISHER, 52 CHATHAM STREET,
AND No. 11 NORTH SIXTH STREET, PHILADELPHIA.
Of whom may be had all the Principal Almanacs now Published.

In the 1840 presidential campaign, political parties strove to increase political participation with slogans ("Tippecanoe and Tyler Too!") and less subtle appeals (free hard cider).

in social class—blacks are poorer and have less schooling, on average, than whites. However, among people of the same socioeconomic status—that is, having roughly the same level of income and schooling—blacks tend to participate *more* than whites.[21]

Because the population has become younger (due to the baby boom of the 1960s and 1970s) and because blacks have increased in numbers faster than whites, one might suppose that these demographic changes would explain why the turnout in presidential elections has gone down a bit since the early 1960s. And they do—up to a point. But there is another factor that ought to make turnout go *up*—schooling. Since college graduates are much more

likely to vote than those with less educational experience, and since the college-graduate proportion of the population has gone up sharply, turnout should have risen. But it has not. What is going on here?

Perhaps turnout has declined despite the higher levels of schooling due to the rising level of distrust of government. We saw in Chapter 4 that, well into the 1990s, more and more people were telling pollsters that they lacked confidence in political leaders. Rising distrust seems a plausible explanation for declining turnout, until one looks at the facts. The data show that there is *no correlation* between expressing distrust of political leaders and not voting.[22] People who are cynical about our leaders are just as likely to vote as people who are not.

As we have seen, turnout is powerfully affected by the number of people who have registered to vote; perhaps in recent years it has become harder to register. But in fact exactly the opposite is true. Since 1970 federal law has prohibited residency requirements longer than thirty days for presidential elections, and a Supreme Court decision in 1972 held that requirements much in excess of this were invalid for state and local elections.[23] By 1982 twenty-one states and the District of Columbia, containing about half the nation's population, had adopted laws permitting voters to register by mail. In four states—Maine, Minnesota, Oregon, and Wisconsin—voters can register and vote on the same day, all at once.

What is left? Several small things. First, the greater youthfulness of the population, together with the presence of growing numbers of blacks and other minorities, has pushed down the percentage of voters who are registered and vote.

Second, political parties today are no longer as effective as they once were in mobilizing voters, ensuring that they are registered, and getting them to the polls. As we shall see in Chapter 7, the parties once were grassroots organizations with which many people strongly identified. Today the parties are somewhat distant, national bureaucracies with which most of us do not identify very strongly.

Third, the remaining impediments to registration exert some influence. One study estimated that if every state had registration requirements as easy as the most permissive states, turnout in a presidential election would be about 9 percent higher.[24] The experience of the four states where you can register and vote on the same day is consistent with this: in 1976, when same-day registration first went into effect, three of the four states that had it saw their turnout go up by 3 or 4 percent, while those states that did not have it saw their turnout go down.[25] If an even bolder plan were adopted, such as the Canadian system of universal enrollment, whereby the government automatically puts on the voter list every eligible citizen, there would probably be some additional gain in turnout.[26]

Fourth, if *not* voting is costless, then there will be more nonvoting. Several nations with higher turnouts than ours make voting compulsory. For example, in Italy a person who does not vote has his or her government identification papers stamped *"DID NOT VOTE."*[27] In Australia and other countries fines can be levied on nonvoters. As a practical matter such fines are rarely imposed, but just the threat of them probably induces more people to register and vote.

Finally, voting (and before that, registering) will go down if people do not feel that elections matter much. There has been a decline in the proportion of people who feel that elections matter a lot, corresponding to the decrease in those who do participate in elections.

In short there are a number of reasons why we register and vote less frequently here than do citizens of other countries. Two careful studies of all these factors found that almost all of the differences in turnout among twenty-four democratic nations, including the United States, could be explained by party strength, automatic registration, and compulsory voting laws.[28]

The presence of these reasons does not necessarily mean that somebody ought to do something about them. We could make registration automatic—but that might open the way to voter fraud, since here people move around and change names often enough to enable some of them, if they wanted to, to vote more than once. We could make voting compulsory, but Americans have an aversion to government compulsion in any form and probably would object strenuously to any plan for making citizens carry identification papers that the government would stamp.

Democrats and Republicans fight over various measures designed to increase registration and voting because one party (usually the Democrats)

Registering to vote will become easier now that the "motor-voter" law has been passed.

thinks that higher turnout will help them and the other (usually the Republicans) fears that higher turnout will hurt them. In fact no one really knows whether either party would be helped or hurt by higher voter turnout.

Nonvoters are more likely than voters to be poor, black or Hispanic, or uneducated. However, the proportion of nonvoters with some college education rose from 7 percent in 1960 to 18 percent in 1980. In addition, the percentage of nonvoters who held white-collar jobs rose from 33 percent to 50 percent in the same period. Many of these better-off nonvoters might well have voted Republican had they gone to the polls. And even if the turnout rates only of blacks and Hispanics had increased, there would not have been enough votes added to the Democratic column to affect the outcome of the 1984 or 1988 presidential elections.[29]

Latino Americans tend to participate less frequently in elections than other groups. This billboard tries to change that: "Don't leave yourself out. Arm yourself. Register to vote."

Both political parties try to get a larger turnout among voters likely to be sympathetic to them, but it is hard to be sure that these efforts will produce real gains. If one party works hard to get its nonvoters to the polls, the other party will work just as hard to get its people there. For example, when Jesse Jackson ran for the presidency in 1984, registration of southern blacks increased, but registration of southern whites increased even more.

The Meaning of Participation Rates

Americans may be voting less, but there is evidence that they are participating more. As Table 6.3 shows, between 1967 and 1987 the percentage of Americans who voted regularly in presidential and local elections dropped, but the percentage who participated increased for ten out of twelve other political activities, steeply in some cases. Thus, although Americans are going to the polls less, they are campaigning, contacting government officials, and working on community issues more. And while the proportion of the population that votes is lower in the United States than in many other democracies, the percentage of Americans who engage in one or more political activities beyond voting is higher (see Table 6.4).

Public demonstrations such as sit-ins and protest marches have become much more common in recent decades than they once were. By one count there were only 6 demonstrations per year between 1950 and 1959 but over 140 per year between 1960 and 1967. Though the demonstrations of the 1960s began with civil rights and antiwar activists, public protests were later employed by farmers demanding government aid, truckers denouncing the national speed limit, disabled persons seeking to dramatize their needs, parents objecting to busing to achieve racial balance in the schools, conservationists hoping to block nuclear power plants, and construction workers urging that nuclear power *not* be blocked.[30]

Although we vote at lower rates here than people do abroad, the meaning of our voting is different. For one thing, we elect far more public officials than do the citizens of any other nation. One scholar has estimated that there are 521,000 elective offices in the United States and that almost every week of the year there is an election going on somewhere in this country.[31]

A citizen of Massachusetts, for example, votes not only for the U.S. president but also for two senators, the state governor, the member of the House of Representatives for his or her district, a state representative, a state senator, the state attorney general, the state auditor, the state treasurer, the secretary of state, a county commissioner, a sheriff, and clerks of various courts, as well as (in the cities) for the mayor, the city councillor, and school committee members and (in towns) for selectmen, town-meeting members, a town moderator, library trustees, health board members, assessors, water commissioners, the town clerk, housing authority members, the tree warden, and the commissioner of the public burial ground. (There are probably others that we have forgotten.)

In many European nations, by contrast, the voters get to make just one choice once every four or five years: they can vote for or against a member of parliament. When there is only one election for one office every several years, that election is bound to assume more importance to the voter than many elections for scores of offices. But one election for one office probably has less effect on how the nation is governed than many elections for thousands of offices. Americans may not vote at high rates, but

TABLE 6.3   **How Citizens Participate**

Specific Activity	Percentage Engaging in Fourteen Acts of Participation, 1967 and 1987		
	1967	1987	Absolute Change
VOTING			
Regularly vote in presidential elections	66%	58%	−8%
Always vote in local elections	47	35	−12
CAMPAIGNING			
Persuade others how to vote	28	32	+4
Actively work for party or candidate	26	27	+1
Attend political meetings or rallies	19	19	0
Contribute money to a party or candidate	13	23	+10
Participate in a political club	8	4	−4
CONTACTING GOVERNMENT			
Contact local officials: issue-based	14	24	+10
Contact state or national officials: issue-based	11	22	+11
Contact local officials: particularized	7	10	+3
Contact state or national officials: particularized	6	7	+1
TAKING ACTION IN THE COMMUNITY			
Work with others on a local problem	30	34	+4
Actively participate in community problem-solving organization	31	34	+3
Form group to help solve local problem	14	17	+3

SOURCE: Reprinted by permission of the publisher from *Voice and Equality: Civic Voluntarism in American Politics* by Sidney Verba, Kay Lehman Scholzman and Henry A. Brady, Cambridge, Mass.: Harvard University Press, Copyright © 1995 by the Presidents and Fellows of Harvard College. Data from p. 72.

TABLE 6.4   **Participation Beyond Voting in Fourteen Democracies**

Percentage of adult population who engaged in some form of political participation beyond voting in 1990

Britain	77%	Italy	56
Sweden	74	Iceland	55
Norway	68	Netherlands	54
UNITED STATES	66	Belgium	51
Denmark	59	Ireland	46
France	57	Finland	38
West Germany	57	Spain	32

SOURCES: U.S. percentage calculated from Sidney Verba et al., *Voice and Equality: Civic Voluntarism in American Politics* (Cambridge, Mass.: Harvard University Press, 1995), 83; other percentages calculated from Max Kaase and Kenneth Newton, *Beliefs in Government*, vol. 5 (New York: Oxford University Press, 1995), 51.

FIGURE 6.6 Voter Turnout in National Elections in Three Countries, by Occupation

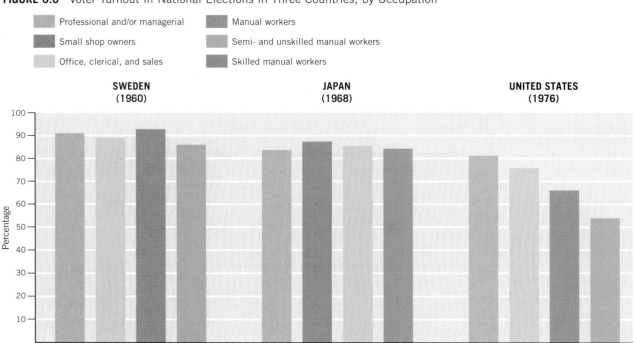

SOURCES: For Japan: The Society for Promotion of Clean Elections, Survey of 34th General Election, 1976. Reprinted from an unpublished paper by Gary Orren, "Political Participation and Public Policy: The Case for Institutional Reform" (Cambridge, Mass., November 1985), 16A. Data on U.S. and Sweden from *No Easy Choice* by Samuel P. Huntington and Joan M. Nelson (Cambridge, Mass.: Harvard University Press, 1976), 88.

voting affects a far greater part of the political system than abroad.

The kinds of people who vote here are also different from those who vote abroad. Since almost everybody votes in many other democracies, the votes cast there mirror almost exactly the social composition of those nations. Since only slightly over half of the voting-age population turns out even for presidential elections here, the votes cast in the United States may not truly reflect the country.

That is in fact the case. Figure 6.6 shows the proportion of each major occupational group that usually votes in Japan, Sweden, and the United States. Each occupational group—or, if you prefer, social class—votes at about the same rate in Japan and Sweden. But in the United States the turnout is heavily skewed toward higher-status persons: those in professional, managerial, and other white-collar occupations are overrepresented among the voters.

Although nonwhites and Latinos are the fastest-growing segment of the population, they tend to be the most underrepresented groups among American voters. Little is known about the relationship between political participation and such variables as command of the language and involvement in nonpolitical institutions that provide information or impart skills relevant to politics (such as workplaces and voluntary associations). However, such factors could be quite important in explaining differences in political participation rates among poor and minority citizens. As we can see in Figure 6.7, although less involved than whites, blacks participate in voting and political activities at higher rates than do Latino citizens. One excellent study suggests that these differences are due in part to the fact that blacks are more likely than Latinos to be members of churches that stimulate political interest, activity, and mobilization.[32] Language barriers also make it harder for many Latinos to get in touch with a public official, serve on local governing boards, and engage in other forms of political participation in which command of English is an asset. The lower participation rates of minority citizens are likely compounded by their being disproportionately of